Silicon Valley Cinema

This one's for you, Carys. Love you, from Dad.

Silicon Valley Cinema

Joe Street

Edinburgh University Press is one of the leading university presses in the UK. We publish academic books and journals in our selected subject areas across the humanities and social sciences, combining cutting-edge scholarship with high editorial and production values to produce academic works of lasting importance. For more information visit our website: edinburghuniversitypress.com

© Joe Street, 2023, 2024

Edinburgh University Press Ltd
13 Infirmary Street, Edinburgh, EH1 1LT

First published in hardback by Edinburgh University Press 2023

Typeset in 11/13 Adobe Sabon by
IDSUK (DataConnection) Ltd

A CIP record for this book is available from the British Library

ISBN 978 1 3995 0582 6 (hardback)
ISBN 978 1 3995 0583 3 (paperback)
ISBN 978 1 3995 0584 0 (webready PDF)
ISBN 978 1 3995 0585 7 (epub)

The right of Joe Street to be identified as author of this work has been asserted in accordance with the Copyright, Designs and Patents Act 1988 and the Copyright and Related Rights Regulations 2003 (SI No. 2498).

Contents

Figures   vi
Acknowledgements   vii

Introduction   1

Part 1: Precursors

1. Technology and Surveillance in Millennial Hollywood   21
2. Critiquing Twenty-First-Century Capitalism   33
3. Hollywood's Bay Area   42

Part 2: Real Genius

4. The Silicon Valley Biopic   61
5. Constructing the Silicon Valley Icon   78

Part 3: Silicon Valley's Dystopian Utopia

6. Technology Solutionism and the World of Work   99
7. Dystopian Diversity   118

Part 4: Silicon Valley's Evil Geniuses

8. Posthumanity and Masculinity   137
9. The Turbo-capitalist Tech Bro   156

Conclusion: *Why Him?* and the Dialectics of Silicon
Valley Cinema   173

Bibliography   183
Index   202

Figures

1.1	*The Lawnmower Man*'s virtual Jobe, crucifying science in cyberspace	25
2.1	*Margin Call*'s Chief Executive Officer enjoys a meal, a fine bottle of red and the crossword	37
3.1	'The Rock' reunites the American family, after the Pacific Ocean destroys much of San Francisco	50
3.2	We watch Caul and his colleague leer over two unwitting victims of their surveillance	56
4.1	Marylin heads back towards humanity while Zuckerberg ponders his reflection in Facebook	70
5.1	The off-kilter Apple board vote to oust Jobs in *Steve Jobs*	82
5.2	Lisa and Jobs connect over the Mac's 'save' icon	84
5.3	'What are we doing here?' Jobs and Woz head in a different direction to the countercultural hordes	91
6.1	Mae Holland's workspace, complete with instant surveillance from her followers	108
6.2	*The Internship*'s interns reflect on a bacchanalian night out in San Francisco	113
8.1	Darren Cross experiences alienation as Yellowjacket while threatening the very existence of Scott Lang's Ant-Man	146
8.2	The vulnerable humanity of Eddie Brock encounters the 'ugliest looking thing' he has 'ever seen'	149
9.1	Will Rodman cedes his presentation about his new wonder drug to profit/loss projections	159
9.2	*Rise of the Planet of the Apes*' Caesar pondering a posthuman future	162
10.1	American capitalism and the new American family enjoy Christmas together	175

Acknowledgements

This book emerged from a series of conversations that I had with Martin Eve and Russ Hunter. Suffice it to say that, without Martin and Russ, you would not be reading these words. I want to thank them both for their generosity in freely giving their time to help push me towards writing something about Silicon Valley and film, and Russ especially for his enthusiasm and wise counsel. I also want to send my thanks to the many other people who contributed to this book. Mike Brown, Mike Collins and Zara Dinnen offered excellent suggestions early on; Mike B was particularly helpful in commenting on an early draft that later became Chapters 8 and 9. Thank you to my fabulous colleagues at Northumbria University, especially Charlotte Alston, for her perceptive ideas, good sense and equanimity; the king of Simpsons memes Paddy Andelic; David Gleeson (whose observations really helped clarify some of the ideas in Chapters 7 and 8); James McConnel; Laura O'Brien (who went far beyond the call of duty in voluntarily watching *The Internship*); Linsey Robb; and the great Brian Ward (a tower of strength who offered his usual sage advice at key moments). While I would love to blame these fine people for the book's faults, sadly those faults are mine alone.

Elsewhere, I want to thank my UCU comrades who, alongside my colleagues in Humanities, prove daily how important solidarity and community are to any workplace (and special thanks to Adam Hansen for his immense support during some particularly trying months). My BAAS partners-in-crime Zalfa Feghali, Martin Halliwell, Michelle Houston, Gavan Lennon and George Lewis, provided friendship, good humour and great company. Gillian Leslie and Sam Johnson at EUP were, quite simply, magnificent. Thank you both: I could not wish for better people to help shepherd this book into print. Thank you also to my friends Matt, Pete, John, Jacko, Mark and Dave for their sparkling wit and repartee, which has kept me sane over the last goodness-knows-how-many years; Albion Twitter, especially Vampire Townsend; and everybody connected with the mighty Heaton Stannington FC.

Finally, and most important, to my family for letting me into their lives, especially Ruth and Carys, who bring more joy to me than I could ever wish for. I love you both even more than Billy and Nick love Google. To find out what that means, read on . . .

Introduction

In 2015, Google's co-founder Larry Page saw the Disney science-fiction film *Tomorrowland* (Brad Bird, 2015). According to the *New York Times*, 'he didn't like it', feeling that its vision of a future led by genius inventors and the technological wonders they develop was, if anything, 'too utopian'. The *Times*'s reporter went on to conclude that Page 'hit on a central problem with attempts to imagine the future in the sunny way that many in Silicon Valley see it: a perfect future makes for a boring story'.[1] Page's comments reveal some central assumptions of what might be termed a Silicon Valley perspective: that its corporations hope to develop a perfect future for humanity; that these corporations' founders have opinions that matter; and that old Hollywood cannot fully capture or represent the future these seers envisage. In a similar vein, two Hollywood films about Silicon Valley corporations have key characters opining on their role in forging our human future. Both are fictional, but one bases itself on real-life events and the other traces events that are far from inconceivable. The fictional Google intern Billy McMahon gasps in *The Internship* (Shawn Levy, 2013), 'I've seen the future and it's beautiful . . . Google. The place is amazing', while *Steve Jobs* (Danny Boyle, 2015) has its titular character protesting to a group of bureaucrats, 'I sat in a fucking garage with [Steve] Wozniak and invented the future!'[2]

These films are but two in a 2010s trend in Hollywood cinema which sees various filmmakers question Silicon Valley's role in late twentieth- and early twenty-first-century culture, revealing Hollywood's proprietorial investment in curating the popular understanding of Silicon Valley and its visions of the human future. At first glance, they might appear to have little in common beyond their shared use of real locations in the San Francisco Bay Area. *Steve Jobs* is a prestige biopic directed by a major filmmaker, while *The Internship* is a light-hearted comedy. They are joined by yet another chapter in Arnold Schwarzenegger's killer robot franchise, *Terminator: Genisys* (Alan Taylor, 2015), and *The Circle* (James Ponsoldt, 2017), a dystopian thriller, while other Silicon Valley-related films range from biopics to superhero action blockbusters. All locate the source of the decade's major cultural anxieties firmly within the geographical boundaries of the Bay Area and the modus operandi of Silicon Valley corporations, culture and ideology. Sometimes these anxieties lie at the core of the film's plot, such as *The Circle*'s apprehensions about social media corporations' ability to surveil every aspect of our lives. Other times, the anxieties are embedded more deeply, such as in *Rise of the Planet of the Apes* (Rupert Wyatt, 2011), which suggests that the destruction of humanity could be traced to Silicon Valley's refusal to acknowledge the dangers of scientific experimentation.

As Slavoj Žižek observed, 'to discover ideology at its purest' we ought to interrogate Hollywood 'at its most innocent'.[3] He might have been introducing a typically idiosyncratic Lacanian-Marxist evaluation of the cartoon *Kung Fu Panda* (John Stevenson and Mark Osborne, 2008), but his wider point is vital: ideology is always present in Hollywood film. Approaching Hollywood film with an eye to such underlying assumptions necessitates engagement with what Frederic Jameson terms the political unconsciousness of a text: the subtexts that even the text's authors might not acknowledge, understand or even accept.[4] So, while *The Internship* might ostensibly be, as Larry Page suggested, another marketing opportunity for Google, a close reading suggests that the film deconstructs Google's idealised image of itself and the world it hopes to create.[5] As this suggests, we should approach these Silicon Valley films with a view towards considering Hollywood's representation of the negative implications of believing that technology – and metonymically, Silicon Valley – can solve the world's ills. In this, the films are best viewed with one eye focused on their engagement with what the technology critic Evgeny Morozov terms 'technology solutionism'.[6] Silicon Valley, Morozov argues, is stuffed with individuals and corporations who share, 'an unhealthy preoccupation with sexy, monumental, and narrow-minded solutions – the kind of stuff that wows audiences at TED Conferences – to problems that are extremely complex, fluid, and contentious'.[7] Technology solutionism is insidious and problematic. It rests on the presumptions that any complex situation is a problem to be solved and that an objectively correct solution (often reduced to a yes–no binary) will come via the application of some technological miracle such as a complicated algorithm. That tech evangelists dismiss the notion that this 'solution' itself creates further problems – and often 'solves' a problem that recent technology has actually created – is, for Morozov, exceedingly problematic. For example, the 'quantified self' fad of the 2010s spurred an interest in sleep quantification, facilitated by powerful sleep tracking devices that claimed to offer a supposedly objective analysis of the amount and quality of sleep the wearer has each night. Yet such devices cannot comprehend, let alone interpret, the myriad factors that might influence an individual's sleep, and their judgement on that individual's sleep fitness could just as well lead to anxiety about said sleep, which is itself likely to lead to sleep problems.[8] Elsewhere, Robin Sloan's novel, *Mr Penumbra's 24-Hour Bookstore* (2013) lauds Google's genius for logging and cataloguing all human knowledge while hinting at Google's lack of respect for book publishers and authors' intellectual copyright.[9] Its suggestion that print-on-demand could solve the crisis enveloping the publishing industry highlights precisely the problem of solutionism: in attempting to solve a problem created by themselves, Silicon Valley solutionists fail to question their own problematic influence.

But what is 'Silicon Valley'? Broadly defined, it is a region in California to the south of the San Francisco Bay. Encompassing the cities of Cupertino, Menlo Park, Mountain View, Palo Alto, Redwood City, San Jose, Santa Clara and Sunnyvale, it currently houses the headquarters of many of the largest technology companies in the world, including Apple, Facebook (since 2021 a subdivision of Meta), Google (now part of the Alphabet corporation), Hewlett-Packard, Oracle, Cisco, PayPal, Adobe, Intel and Yahoo. In 2019 *Fortune* ranked Apple as the third largest company in the world in revenue terms; Alphabet the fourth and Facebook fifth in terms of market value; and Intel and Cisco also in the top twenty according to market value. As the most popular social media platform in the world, Facebook bestrode the 2010s like a colossus, engaging with over two billion users each month by 2019. Alphabet's Android was the most widely used operating system for mobile telephones, and its search engine became ubiquitous enough that it is now a verb.[10] Apple, meanwhile, so dominated the cultural consciousness that the death of its co-founder Steve Jobs prompted grief-stricken memorials worldwide, and even its CEO's annual report is international news.[11] As a group, these corporations spent millions of dollars each month lobbying the US Congress and the European Parliament to protect their interests and prevent the passage of antagonistic legislation.[12] It is no great stretch of the imagination to suggest that Silicon Valley technology companies exerted a defining influence over the early twenty-first century, economically, culturally and politically.

'Silicon Valley' is not merely this geographic location and the companies within it though; the term is also a synecdoche for a particular manifestation of American capitalism. While Silicon Valley's voters tend to lean towards Democrat and be in favour of racial diversity, the area's philosophical tendencies are towards a libertarian faith in the free market, influenced by Frederick Hayek and Milton Friedman. Above these influencers lies the novelist and would-be philosopher Ayn Rand, whose Silicon Valley acolytes include Travis Kalanick, Uber's driving force; Peter Thiel, one of Silicon Valley's most influential investors; and Jimmy Wales, founder of Wikipedia.[13] More broadly, as the former Silicon Valley programmer Antonio García Martínez notes, Randian selfishness and individualism drive Silicon Valley's culture.[14] Rand sketched out a philosophy in a number of novels, most notably (and lengthily) *The Fountainhead* (1943) and *Atlas Shrugged* (1957). In essence, 'objectivism', as she called it, relies on the self-interest of the individual for the most efficient running of society. The rich and powerful exist because of their own genius, rather than any structural advantages that came to them courtesy of birth (such as inherited wealth, gender or race) or the networks they inhabit (such as through family ties or education). Government, meanwhile, steals taxes from these geniuses to redistribute goods and services inefficiently to the workshy poor. Her two signature heroes – *The Fountainhead*'s Howard Roark and *Atlas Shrugged*'s John Galt – are individualists par excellence, classically masculine characters with white skin, lantern jaws and immovable principles. Considering themselves highly rational and thus intelligent, they despair of lesser humans' emotional feelings towards other human beings. Galt even turns his back on society, compelling other business leaders to follow suit, with the aim of replacing collective endeavour with individualism, a strategy echoed in *Tomorrowland*'s secret trans-dimensional enclave for 'the smartest, most creative people in the world . . . free[d] from politics, from bureaucracy . . . where they could build whatever they were crazy enough to imagine'.[15] Rand's lauding of individual genius is highly seductive for the often self-absorbed, socially awkward, and highly individualist tech evangelists in Silicon Valley, many of whom aspire to the level of greatness Rand affords Roark and Galt.[16]

As this might suggest, Silicon Valley's leaders such as Zuckerberg, Jobs and Elon Musk present themselves as messianic and their products as epochal and world-changing, while hoarding cash reserves and aggressively pursuing or even crushing rivals in Randian fashion.[17] Such tendencies were spoofed throughout six seasons of the

HBO satire *Silicon Valley* (2014–2020), largely in the persona of the avaricious, megalomaniacal capitalist Gavin Belson, who offers a sharp, ironic commentary on tech leaders, one that encourages us to puncture their self-centredness and messianism. The CEO of Hooli, a gargantuan tech corporation modelled on Google, Belson is wont to make absurdly grandiose claims for Hooli's products. 'If we can make your audio and video files smaller,' he said early on, 'we can make cancer smaller. And hunger. And [pause] AIDS.'[18] Similarly, reflecting on a trip he took during a sabbatical from Hooli (in reality, he was fired; his insistence that this was a 'sabbatical' an example of tech leaders' reality distortion fields), he tells how he

> toured the wonders of the world, seeking inspiration from mankind's greatest achievements. The Parthenon, Angkor Wat, the Great Pyramid of Giza. But it wasn't until my flight home that I had my epiphany. Yes, those wonders are visited by thousands of people every year, but 2.4 million people visit HooliSearch every minute ... And then it occurred to me. What I have built is a far greater achievement, than any of the ancient world. And the ideal version of myself, was the man I already was.[19]

Belson's notion that his company's search engine outstripped the greatest of humankind's achievements, coupled with his self-aggrandising insistence that he and not Hooli's engineers created it, not to mention his belief that he has achieved perfection as a human, encapsulates the self-absorption that prevails among many (fictional, if not actual) Silicon Valley entrepreneurs.

While less overtly malevolent than Belson, many Silicon Valley CEOs are also young white men who possess a peculiar, almost otherworldly charisma that cannot be divorced from their immersion in computer programming. They sit on top of a remarkably homogenous group of employees. In 2014, Google released data on its staff profile, confirming that only 2% of its employees were Black, 3% Latinx and 30% female. Thanks to an equality drive, the numbers of women increased by a staggering 1% in the following four years.[20] Facebook is little different in gender terms, being only 31% female in 2014, although its diversity drive boosted that percentage to 36% in 2018, whereas Black employees in Facebook's American offices increased from 2% in 2014 to 3.5% in 2018; Asian employees meanwhile increased from 34% to 41%.[21] Apple was similarly male dominated (34% women in 2018, up 4% in four years) but 9% of its employees were Black and 27% Asian.[22] Likewise, 92%

of partners in the venture capital companies that bankroll many Silicon Valley enterprises are men (nearly 40% of the nation's venture capital investment is located in the Bay Area, in part because of the search for the next Facebook).[23]

Studies suggest that Silicon Valley's unbalanced employment profile is only partially explained by the gender and racial distribution in the pool of college and university graduates from which it selects.[24] As such, Silicon Valley hiring practices and staff culture demand interrogation. In the 2010s, some startup companies promoted vacancies with adverts featuring scantily clad women, called for programmers who like to 'crush' code as if it were a beer can, and convened so-called 'gangbang' job interviews dominated by large groups of men.[25] While the most egregious examples came from small startups rather than larger corporations that had their own Human Resources departments, they feed into what has become termed a masculine, homosocial 'tech bro' culture that is even more pernicious than the gender disparity among the workforce would suggest. When working at Google, for example, a pregnant Sheryl Sandberg – already a major Silicon Valley player – was called a 'whale' to her face and later held conference calls while pumping breast milk or breast-feeding her first baby because she was so worried that a period of maternity leave would lead to her losing her job. Google co-founders Sergei Brin and Larry Page's largesse extended to offering her a combined gift of two full hours of babysitting, which she did not even utilise. Such was Google's culture that she felt compelled to leave a jacket on the back of her chair when she left work, to give the impression that she might still be in the building.[26] Even worse, women across Silicon Valley have reported condescension, discriminatory pay and hiring practices, predatory attitudes towards sex, jokes about sexual assault, male colleagues openly watching pornography at work, and an 'asshole culture' permeating their working lives.[27] *The Guardian* newspaper reported in March 2017 that, 'startups and tech corporations skirt employment laws and reject HR practices while sometimes fostering a party culture where young male executives encourage socialising and drinking'.[28] Uber, for example, provided kegs of beer in the office, promoting a culture that often included men forcefully making unwelcome propositions to women staff. Surveys suggest that most women who work in the tech industry have experienced sexual harassment, and a number of female whistle-blowers faced further harassment online after going public, a damning indictment of tech-bro culture.[29]

The reception for *The Circle* (2013), Dave Eggers's novel about a fictional Silicon Valley corporation, on which the film is based, is hugely instructive here. Not long after its publication, Katherine Losse identified numerous similarities between its opening pages and her memoir of life at Facebook, *The Boy Kings* (2012). Eggers's response, claiming that he had not even heard of Losse and her book, reflected the dismissive attitude of many Silicon Valley men towards women.[30] As important, Eggers – a famous, rich, and powerful male author – received major plaudits across the international press. Losse, meanwhile, protested that her personal experience was not received 'with the same gravitas as this guy who is basically retelling the story'.[31] Losse originally outlined her objections in a blog post that she has since deleted, which might be interpreted as another example of the silencing of women's voices in Silicon Valley. Yet her memoir is essential for an understanding of gender politics in Silicon Valley, one that anticipates, if it does not directly inform, all later accounts of employment in the Valley.[32]

Losse arrived during Facebook's earliest days in Palo Alto. Her new colleagues, she says, 'seemed startled, if not displeased to see a strange new woman in the office'.[33] They saw no problem coating the walls of their office with juvenile graffiti featuring large-breasted women. Describing this office as the 'nerdiest fraternity house in Silicon Valley', Losse initially found the nerds' lack of respect for women wryly amusing and an indication of social awkwardness. Increasingly, however, she became angered by her colleagues' chronic misogynist trolling and assumptions that women were little more than sexual playthings.[34] Her educational background lay in the humanities. By contrast, men in the tech industry tend to be engineers. As the tech journalist John Battelle commented, 'We aren't humanists or philosophers. We are engineers. To Google and Facebook, people are algorithms': essentially, they are problems to be solved through a sequence of logical steps.[35] Mark Zuckerberg is a key example: a man who, the journalists Sheera Frenken and Cecilia King state, believes that an algorithm could be written that would neutrally decide what content is suitable for uploading to Facebook, who cannot comprehend why people might not want to share personal data, who essentially thinks in zeros and ones.[36] As such, it is little surprise that such men cannot comprehend why objectifying women is problematic and that they place such faith in technology's potential to solve human problems.

This fraternity culture is alluded to more than once in the Zuckerberg biopic *The Social Network* (David Fincher, 2010): as its screenwriter Aaron Sorkin recalled, 'I was writing about a very angry and deeply misogynistic group of people.'[37] Women are notably absent from the working culture at *The Social Network*'s Facebook, only appearing at coding sessions to encourage a party atmosphere. Back in the real world, once Facebook became successful and its people rich, the boys became the kings of Losse's book title, developing obscure rituals designed to remind all around them of their power. Zuckerberg became wont to conclude staff meetings with the shouted exhortation, 'Domination!' and even extended this interest in power to his haircut. According to the tech journalist Max Chafkin, as Facebook grew, he adopted a hairstyle based on the vain, slippery, autocratic imperialist Roman Emperor Augustus; a man, lest we forget, who considered himself the son of a god.[38] More problematically, the boy kings used their power to humiliate women who did not meet their aesthetic standards and to insist that women be one – and only one – of two things: pretty or smart. Even when Sheryl Sandberg joined Facebook, such attitudes continued to rule. Zuckerberg told his staff that 'everyone should have a crush on Sheryl', in part because she possesses 'really good skin'.[39]

These problematic cultures did not impact on Facebook's profitability during the 2010s. By the decade's end, it was raking in over $85 billion each year. While it and Google gobbled up advertising revenues, old media outlets found one of their most important revenue streams drying up, while others such as consumer sales also faltered.[40] Meanwhile, Hollywood found itself threatened by upstarts from northern California. In 2014 the Silicon Valley-based streaming platform Netflix announced its intention to branch out into producing original feature films. Netflix's direct-to-consumers distribution method offered a major challenge to traditional lines of cultural communication through the medium of film. By 2018 it was spending $8 billion per annum on feature films, with other tech companies following it into the production game, and by the end of the decade, Netflix even muscled in on Hollywood talent: major filmmakers such as Martin Scorsese (*The Irishman*, 2019), the Cohen brothers (*The Ballad of Buster Scruggs*, 2018), Spike Lee (*Da 5 Bloods*, 2020), and David Fincher (*Mank*, 2020) released films on its platform rather than the usual distribution channels.[41] Perhaps as important, subscribers to services such as Netflix have access to every single film in the studio's portfolio from their home and even on mobile devices, freeing them from the need to travel to the cinema, purchase a separate ticket for each film they wish to see, sit through ads and trailers, suffer the exclamations of less respectful cinemagoers, and then return home. Consequently, subscribers weigh up cinema attendance against the convenience of streaming services, adding another reason to be more selective about the films they watch at the cinema. Conversely, subscription systems free producers from obsessing over the profits generated by films, with subscriber numbers instead dictating their margins; meanwhile data-scraping of user preferences enables such corporations to target future production at key audience sets.[42]

Higher ticket prices and DVD revenues kept Hollywood profits buoyant during the early years of the twenty-first century, although audience numbers began dropping while producers cast nervous glances at the digital technology that was transforming both the production and consumption of cinema. Significantly, by the end of the 2010s, almost all cinemas across the globe projected digital rather than analogue images onto their screens, a development that was not unrelated to one of Hollywood's attempts to remind viewers that home-viewing was distinctly second-rate: the 3D blockbuster.[43] In typical self-congratulatory mode, industry executives presented the release of the 3D film *Avatar* (James Cameron, 2009) as a transformative event for cinema. *Avatar* certainly aided News Corp's profitability in 2010, but not all the studios shared in this bonanza.[44] The novelty of 3D soon wore off, while other technological innovations such as shooting and screening films at 48 frames per second also struggled to win audiences.[45] Other responses from Hollywood producers were more successful. One was the near logarithmic expansion of the Marvel Cinematic Universe into a multi-stranded spectacle. Its multitudinous episodes increasingly required an almost forensic level of dedication and concentration on the viewer's part to follow its plots and subplots while being bombarded with increasingly complex CGI battles and posterior-numbing running times, but each entry in the series was wildly successful.[46] Disney offered a similar response, pumping out expansions to the *Star Wars* franchise in cinemas and latterly on its own subscription service. Such spectacles were, their promotion campaigns suggested, best experienced on as large a screen as possible, in the company of fellow fans who would create an atmosphere impossible to create at home, no matter how large your lounge, how wide your television screen, or how loud your soundbar. These developments present the 2010s as a conjunctural moment for American cinema, where two major distribution methods, financial systems, and perhaps even cultures collided, with consumer spending shifting from the cinema to home entertainment, driven in part by technological improvements to televisions and DVD players, not to mention increased broadband speeds that enabled consumers to stream high-quality film in the home.[47]

Sitting alongside the bombast of metastasising superhero extravaganzas and *Star Wars* spin-offs lies a more considered and important response to the challenge from Silicon Valley, one that reveals the deeper fears among Hollywood studios. These fears revolve not merely around declining profits and Silicon Valley's challenge in the marketplace but reflect broader concerns about Silicon Valley's increasingly central role in our shared and private lives. The film historian Douglas Kellner observes that, 'when there is dissatisfaction in a society with a political regime, Hollywood is quick to exploit it with films transcoding the disaffection or anger with the ruling group, whatever its politics'.[48] As this suggests, Hollywood transcodes disaffection with Silicon Valley corporations through its own cultural products, attempting to harness wider concerns about Silicon Valley, in part to maintain its own position both as cultural arbiter and as profit-making enterprise. Yet these films also point to a continued fascination with Silicon Valley as a cultural entity in itself, as revealed by the films' revelry in the technological wonders offered by Silicon Valley corporations that runs alongside a critique of the impact that these wonders might have on humanity. As such, ambivalence is perhaps their driving emotion.

In 2018, Martin Eve and I identified a strain of recent literature (including Eggers's *The Circle*) that we dubbed the 'Silicon Valley novel'.[49] Concerned with both the economic and cultural ecosystem of Silicon Valley corporations and the periodising moment of the 2010s, these novels offer a dystopian vision of twenty-first-century work and life in Silicon Valley, where individuals find their working and private lives dominated by major Silicon Valley corporations. This book applies a similar lens to Hollywood, arguing that a sequence of films set in or near Silicon Valley from several different genres constitutes a distinct trend in Hollywood cinema that I call 'Silicon Valley cinema'. These films trace Silicon Valley's history from the 1970s to the present, offer critiques of its impact on society and those who work within its corporations, and project fears about the potential for Silicon Valley corporations not only to dominate our lives but also to dictate the future of humanity itself. Silicon Valley cinema negotiates between the technology solutionism of Silicon Valley boosters and critiques of what the digital technology scholar Nick Srnicek calls 'platform capitalism'. Srnicek argues that giants like Facebook, Google and Uber have transformed the ways in which major capitalist firms operate. For him, platform capitalism is undermining the very foundations of the late twentieth-century economy. He states that, 'The platform has emerged as a new business model, capable of extracting and controlling immense amounts of data, and with this shift we have seen the rise of large monopolistic firms.'[50] As any competent student of capitalism is aware, one of capitalism's fundamental rules is that firms constantly search for new markets, new products to sell and new ways to extract profit, even if this means further exploiting their staff, customers and the natural resources of the Earth. The platform's reification of the user as income-generation node both feeds off our willingness to share our individual data, such as through our Facebook updates, Tweets or Google searches – thus reinforcing our postmodern status – and also packages us with others who share similar interests, ideals, dreams, fears and purchase histories, thus simultaneously depriving us of our treasured individualism while profiting from selling data associated with our online identity. This convergence of user and income source drives the famous adage that defines much platform capitalism, which according to legend originated on a Metafilter discussion board: 'if you are not paying for it, you're not the customer; you're the product being sold'.[51]

Collectively, these films' shared setting in the San Francisco Bay Area encourages an analysis that brings this location's specific history to bear on their representation of Silicon Valley. The events in the films might be fictional but they exist in dialogue with the factual historical, present, and potentially future reality of the Bay Area. The third film in the long-running *X-Men* franchise offers a useful example to demonstrate how the Bay Area acts as an important agent within a diegetic world (one that obliquely references Silicon Valley itself). *X-Men: The Last Stand* (Brett Ratner, 2006) continues the series' metaphoric interrogation of the role of genetic mutations in human life. The mutated genes of Warren Worthington III serve as a thinly veiled commentary on homosexuality, the battles of adolescents with their emerging sexuality, and their parents' attitudes towards teenage sexuality and independence. His mutation takes the form of wings that sprout from his back. Early scenes see him attempting to cut them back to prevent his anti-mutant father seeing them. He cannot deny his reality, however: his wings will grow irrespective of his attempt to conceal them. Meanwhile, his father's corporation has developed a drug that promises to 'cure' such mutations, and which will, at his father's insistence, be administered to him. Worried about the consequences, he resists and takes flight, literally and metaphorically, breaking out of his closet and entering a new, liberated phase in his life.[52] That Worthington lives in San Francisco, the unofficial capital of gay America, reinforces and renders more transparent the audience's understanding of the metaphor.

When the two are considered in parallel, the humans' quest for a medical cure for genetic mutations echoes the bigoted insistence that homosexuality is a disease that can and should be cured. While the central metaphor here would work perfectly well in any location, the shift of the film's action from the Eastern seaboard (which dominates the first two entries in the series) to San Francisco encourages us to consider the film within the 'real' history of the city, thus heightening the metaphor's significance. The film's fiction, then, engages in a dialogue with the city's fact, a process that deepens its political subtext.[53]

Like *The Last Stand*, Silicon Valley cinema inhabits a hybrid real and imagined San Francisco Bay Area, created by both real and fictional corporations. Crucially, the films' shared concerns about the power of Silicon Valley cut across genre boundaries, further reinforcing the importance of their critique of the region's tech industry. Sometimes this critique is deeply encoded beneath the film's surtext, such as in *The Internship*, which sees two Generation X slackers inducted into Google's utopian world of work. Other films tackle the tech giants head-on, such as *The Social Network* (David Fincher, 2010), which suggests that Facebook reflects the human shortcomings of its founder. Yet more films create fictional tech giants through which they might explore the influence of Silicon Valley without having to consult teams of lawyers. *The Circle*'s titular company, for example, operates much like a Facebook-Twitter-Google-PayPal-Amazon hybrid. For science-fiction films like *Rise of the Planet of the Apes* and *Terminator: Genisys*, fictional corporations threaten humanity's very existence. Even the Marvel Cinematic Universe and one of its related franchises gets in on the act, with *Ant-Man* (Peyton Reed, 2015) and *Venom* (Ruben Fleischer, 2018) musing about various tech bros' amoral designs on world domination through their control of influential Bay Area-headquartered tech corporations.

Silicon Valley cinema most obviously points to a dystopian future, but every film analysed here engages somewhat in a debate over utopianism versus dystopianism.[54] All offer viewers the opportunity to envisage a better future than the present we currently have, sometimes implicitly, as in the gleaming Apple future envisaged in *Steve Jobs*. Of course, Jobs's notion of a utopian future involves only thinking the impossible about the design, marketing and contents of consumer products, rather than dreaming of a new political economy or a world free from oppression. At other times, the films' utopian premises are challenged by their own dystopian elements, as in *The Internship*'s subtle indictment of Google's creation of a dystopian employment landscape for millennials exiting the nation's universities amid its surtextual celebration of Google's whimsical world of work. Google might consider itself a utopia but *The Internship*'s dystopian elements position it far closer to *The Circle*'s damning presentation of employment in Silicon Valley than Google's higher echelons would care to admit. In some respects, then, in thinking the impossible about Silicon Valley, these films peek under Silicon Valley corporations' gleaming hoods to examine the ugly motors that propel them and us into the future.

Following the introductory section, 'Precursors' (Part 1), the core of *Silicon Valley Cinema* is then split into three parts (Parts 2 to 4). Part 2 analyses a sequence of Steve Jobs biopics and the Mark Zuckerberg/Facebook biopic *The Social Network*. Its title, 'Real Genius', references the suggestion in each of the films that their subject possesses a rare genius that both helps to explain the wonders of their corporations' products and offers insight into their shortcomings. By setting the films against each other and analysing them within the biopic tradition, the book argues that only *The Social Network* offers a thorough critique of these idols, while noting that the entire biopic enterprise by definition individualises and thus blunts this critique, even as *The Social Network* wrestles with and pushes to breaking point some of the genre's conventions. Chapter 4 discusses the significance of each film's framing devices and casting choices before considering their interpretation of a key biopic trope: the psychological motivations that drive their subjects to their goals. This first chapter also lays important foundations for Chapter 5's shift from genre to the films' exploration of the 'liminal space between fiction and actuality', which prompts further analysis of how the films burnish their subjects' legends.[55]

Part 3 uses *The Internship* and *The Circle* to interrogate Silicon Valley's culture of work. While the two films could not be much more different in style and genre, they share a fascination with the working life at tech companies real and fictional, and as such are inextricably linked. Chapter 6 focuses on the films' presentation of work in these corporations, with Chapter 7 shifting to their depiction of Silicon Valley's idiosyncratic approach to diversity. This chapter focuses intently on the way in which women are treated at these companies, and particularly how women are singled out for punishment, in an echo of the misogynist culture endemic across Silicon Valley.

Part 4 projects Silicon Valley into the future, analysing a sequence of science-fiction thrillers that present Silicon Valley at the heart of transformations that threaten humanity's very existence. While

Venom, *Ant-Man* and *Terminator: Genisys* suggest that *übermenschen* superheroes might come to our rescue, *Rise of the Planet of the Apes* ends on the depressing conclusion that we humans cannot – and perhaps should not – be saved from ourselves. Chapter 8 discusses the films' warnings of a posthuman future and their critique of Silicon Valley masculinity, before Chapter 9 interrogates the films' critique of Silicon Valley capitalism more deeply, capping one of the book's central themes. It leads to the book's coda, which muses on the dialectical qualities of *Why Him?* (John Hamburg, 2016), in which James Franco and Bryan Cranston play the yin and yang of American capitalism in a comedic battle over Cranston's daughter's heart. This film's attempt to develop synthesis between Silicon Valley and traditional American industries begs consideration of the relationship between Silicon Valley cinema and other 2010s critiques of Silicon Valley, such as Shoshana Zuboff's monumental *The Age of Surveillance Capitalism*.

Before these analyses, however, *Silicon Valley Cinema* must historicise these films (Part 1: Precursors). While they emerged in response to – and, crucially, helped to shape – a particular historical moment, they also draw on three lineages in American cinema history. The first is a series of late 1990s thrillers that express concerns about the growth of computing power, the nascent internet and the ability of those who can manipulate computers to control the lives of others. A second set of films made in the early twenty-first century seeks to interrogate and undercut the messianic assumptions of neoliberal capitalism. The third set of precursors presents San Francisco as a location for contests over the decline of society, from key films noir to thrillers, sometimes resulting in the destruction of the city itself. And while two 1980s blockbusters suggest that humanity (not to mention the local tech industry) might be saved by the intervention of superspies or time-travelling space explorers, a sequence of other films highlights the baleful impact of the tech companies on the social fabric of the Bay Area, and consequently the world beyond northern California. The section ends with a reconsideration of a film that draws many of these themes together. *The Conversation* (Francis Ford Coppola, 1974) unites the surveillance theme that underpins the tech thrillers with a critique of corporate capitalism, while presenting the Bay Area as the location for a major struggle defined in part by the local tech industry. In anticipating the suggestion that technology will ultimately destroy us, *The Conversation* proves highly prescient, further cementing its status as an enduring classic of Hollywood cinema. But first, we must head to the late 1990s and contemplate Hollywood's ruminations on the looming millennium.

Notes

1. Farhad Manjoo, 'In Jobs Film, Love for Mac, Not the Man', *New York Times*, October 10, 2015, A1.
2. *The Internship*, 12m; *Steve Jobs*, 1h05m.
3. Žižek, *Living in the End Times*, 66.
4. Burnham, *Fredric Jameson and* The Wolf of Wall Street, 18–19.
5. Kelly, 'Why Google Loves *The Internship*'.
6. Morozov, *To Save Everything, Click Here*, xiii–xv.
7. Morozov, 'The Will to Improve', 12.
8. Morozov, *To Save Everything*, 230–3; Hannah Devlin, 'Sleep Apps Backfire by Causing Anxiety and Insomnia, says Expert', *The Guardian*, June 7, 2019, <https://www.theguardian.com/lifeandstyle/2019/jun/07/sleep-apps-backfire-by-causing-anxiety-and-insomnia-says-expert> (consulted June 28, 2022).
9. Sloan, *Mr Penumbra's 24-Hour Bookstore*; Foroohar, *Don't Be Evil*, 98–9.
10. *Fortune 500*; Zuboff, *The Age of Surveillance Capitalism*, 162; Srnicek, *Platform Capitalism*, 104.
11. Meghan O' Rourke, 'Mourning Steve Jobs: The Purpose of Public Grief', *New Yorker*, October 6, 2011, <https://www.newyorker.com/news/news-desk/mourning-steve-jobs-the-purpose-of-public-grief> (consulted June 28, 2022); Gurman, 'Cook Says Apple is "Rolling the Dice" on Future Products'.
12. Davis, 'Lobbying on the Up as Silicon Valley Feels the Regulatory Squeeze'; Cooper and Hirst, 'Silicon Valley Tech Lobbyists Swarm Brussels'.
13. Ferenstein, 'A Deeper Look at Silicon Valley's Long-Term Politics'; Carr, 'Travis Shrugged: The Creepy, Dangerous Ideology Behind Silicon Valley's Cult of Disruption'; Nick Bilton, 'Silicon Valley's Most Disturbing Obsession', *Vanity Fair*, October 5, 2016, <https://www.vanityfair.com/news/2016/10/silicon-valley-ayn-rand-obsession> (consulted June 28, 2022); Cohen, *Know-It-Alls*, 142, 158, 170–1, 176; 'Q&A with Jimmy Wales'.
14. Martínez, *Chaos Monkeys*, 232.
15. *Tomorrowland*, 40m.
16. Wolfe, *Valley of the Gods*, 30–1; Losse, *The Boy Kings*, 55, 134; Foroohar, *Don't Be Evil*, xvii, 41, 48–9; Cohen, *The Know-It-Alls*, 166–7, 179, 191, 196; Thiel with Masters, *Zero to One*, 123, 127–8.
17. Cohen, *Know-It-Alls*, 157; Hunter, Balakrishnan, 'Apple's Cash Pile Hits $285.1 Billion, A Record'; 'Mark Zuckerberg Says These 5 Technologies Will Completely Change How We Live'; Julia Carrie

Wong, Olivia Solon, 'Uber Accused of "Calculated Theft" of Google's Self-Driving Car Technology', *The Guardian*, February 24, 2017, <https://www.theguardian.com/technology/2017/feb/23/alphabet-sues-uber-self-driving-cars-technology-waymo-otto> (consulted June 28, 2022); Solon and Farivar, 'Mark Zuckerberg Leveraged Facebook User Data to Fight Rivals and Help Friends, Leaked Documents Show'; Shimal, 'Mark Zuckerberg Couldn't Buy Snapchat Years Ago, and Now He's Close to Destroying the Company'.
18. 'Articles of Incorporation', *Silicon Valley* series 1 episode 3 (HBO, 2014).
19. 'Grow Fast or Die Slow', *Silicon Valley* series 5 episode 1 (HBO, 2018).
20. Claire Cain Miller, 'Is Blind Hiring the Best Hiring', *New York Times*, February 25, 2016, <https://www.nytimes.com/2016/02/28/magazine/is-blind-hiring-the-best-hiring.html> (consulted June 28, 2022); 'Getting to work on Diversity at Google'; Chang, *Brotopia*, 85.
21. 'Distribution of Facebook Employees Worldwide from 2014 to 2020, by Gender'; 'Distribution of Facebook Employees in the United States from 2014–2020, by Ethnicity'; Williams, 'Driving Diversity at Facebook'.
22. Peterson, 'Apple Hiring Data Shows Increasingly Diverse Workforce'.
23. Chang, *Brotopia*, 7, 43–4; Walker, *Pictures of a Gone City*, 21.
24. Julia Carrie Wong, 'Segregated Valley: The Ugly Truth About Google and Diversity in Tech', *The Guardian*, August 7, 2017, <https://www.theguardian.com/technology/2017/aug/07/silicon-valley-google-diversity-black-women-workers> (consulted June 28, 2022).
25. Tasneem Raja, '"Gangbang Interviews" and "Bikini Shots": Silicon Valley's Brogrammer Problem', *Mother Jones*, April 26, 2012, <https://www.motherjones.com/media/2012/04/silicon-valley-brogrammer-culture-sexist-sxsw> (consulted June 28, 2022).
26. Sandberg, *Lean In*, 3, 98, 127–9; Chang, *Brotopia*, 209, 217.
27. Ehrenkrantz, 'Leaked Apple Emails Reveal Employees' Complaints About Sexist, Toxic Work Environment'; Baron, 'Oracle Paid White Men More Than Women, Blacks, Asians: Labor Department Lawsuit'; Sam Levin, 'Uber's Sexual Harassment Case Shines Light on Startup's Culture of Defiance', *The Guardian*, February 21, 2017, <https://www.theguardian.com/technology/2017/feb/21/uber-sexual-harassment-discrimination-scandal> (consulted June 28, 2022); Fowler, 'Reflecting on One Very, Very Strange Year at Uber'; Julia Carrie Wong, 'Uber's "Hustle-Oriented" Culture Becomes a Black Mark on Employees' Resumes', *The Guardian*, March 7, 2017, <https://www.theguardian.com/technology/2017/mar/07/uber-work-culture-travis-kalanick-susan-fowler-controversy> (consulted June 28, 2022). See also Lyons, *Disrupted*, 5, 114, 135–6; Chang, *Brotopia*, 11–12, 58–9, 116–20; Wiener, *Uncanny Valley*, 114, 116, 121–2, 138–9.
28. Sam Levin, 'Startup Workers See Sexual Harassment on "Breathtaking" Scale in Silicon Valley', *The Guardian*, March 1, 2017, <https://

www.theguardian.com/world/2017/mar/01/silicon-valley-sexual-harassment-startups?CMP=Share_AndroidApp_Inbox> (consulted June 28, 2022).
29. Levin, 'Startup Workers'; Lyons, *Disrupted*, 155–6, 158; Chang, *Brotopia*, 58–9; Wiener, *Uncanny Valley*, 148, 176.
30. Baker, 'Is Dave Eggers' New Novel a Ripoff of a Female Writer's Work'.
31. Losse quoted in Tiku, '*Circle* Jerks: Why Do Editors Love Dave Eggers?'; Dinnen, *Digital Banal*, 115.
32. 'Welcome to the Facebook'.
33. Losse, *Boy Kings*, 4.
34. Losse, *Boy Kings*, 5, 6 (quote), 24–6, 30, 33, 43, 45, 171, 186.
35. Foroohar, *Don't Be Evil*, xvii.
36. Frenkel and Kang, *An Ugly Truth*, 65–6, 79, 207–8.
37. Quoted in Paskin, 'Aaron Sorkin Would Like to go Door-to-Door Apologizing for *The Social Network*'s Woman Problem'.
38. Evan Osnos, 'Can Mark Zuckerberg Fix Facebook Before It Breaks Democracy?' *New Yorker*, September 10, 2018, <https://www.newyorker.com/magazine/2018/09/17/can-mark-zuckerberg-fix-facebook-before-it-breaks-democracy> (consulted June 28, 2022); Chafkin, *The Contrarian*, 76; Beard, *SPQR*, 340, 354, 357, 363–4, 370–3.
39. Losse, *Boy Kings*, 34, 134, 168 (both quotes), 170–1.
40. Frenkel and Kang, *An Ugly Truth*, 4; Foroohar, *Don't Be Evil*, xii; Walker, *Pictures of a Gone City*, 30.
41. Lawler, 'Netflix's Exclusive Content Push Continues with a Foray into Film'; Perez, 'Netflix Moves into Original Feature Films, Starting this October'; Wayne, *Marxism Goes to the Movies*, 89.
42. Hadida et al., 'Hollywood Studio Filmmaking', 222–4; Bingham, 'Introduction', in Bingham (ed.), *American Cinema in the 2010s*, 24–5.
43. Timothy Corrigan, 'Introduction', in Corrigan (ed.), *American Cinema in the 2000s*, 8–10; Hadida et al., 'Hollywood Studio Filmmaking in the Age of Netflix', 231; Bingham, 'Introduction', in Bingham (ed.), *American Cinema in the 2010s*, 22–3; Dana Polan, '2009: Movies, a Nation, and New Identities', in Corrigan (ed.), *American Cinema in the 2000s*, 231–2, 234–6.
44. Carl DiOrio, 'If Exhibs Voted on Oscars. . .' *Hollywood Reporter*, March 16, 2010, 3; Georg Szalai, 'Which Movie Studio Is Most Profitable?' *Hollywood Reporter*, March 13, 2011, <https://www.hollywoodreporter.com/movies/movie-news/movie-studio-is-profitable-166988/#!> (consulted June 28, 2022).
45. Phil Hoad, 'Hasta La Vista: Why Not Even James Cameron Can Save 3D Movies', *The Guardian*, August 23, 2017, <https://www.theguardian.com/film/filmblog/2017/aug/23/hasta-la-vista-why-not-even-james-cameron-can-save-3d-film-terminator-2-judgment-day-rerelease> (consulted June 28, 2022); Ben Child, 'Peter Jackson Admits to "Softening"

HD Version of *The Desolation of Smaug*', *The Guardian*, December 13, 2013, <https://www.theguardian.com/film/2013/dec/13/peter-jackson-48fps-tone-down-hobbit-desolation-smaug-hd> (consulted June 28, 2022).
46. Clark, 'All 28 Marvel Cinematic Universe Movies Ranked'.
47. Hadida et al., 'Hollywood Studio Filmmaking', 213–14.
48. Kellner, *Cinema Wars*, 35.
49. Eve and Street, 'The Silicon Valley Novel', 81–97.
50. Srnicek, *Platform Capitalism*, 6.
51. 'blue_beetle' post at 'User-driven discontent' forum.
52. *X-Men: The Last Stand*, 31m.
53. *Her* (Spike Jonze, 2013) offers an instructive counterpoint. While its plot echoes the San Francisco-set *Electric Dreams* (Steve Barron, 1984) in musing on the potential for love between human and computer, *Her*'s setting in a near-future Los Angeles positions the film within viewers' understanding of that city. Thus, they are drawn towards thinking about its vision of Los Angeles and specifically of the city's architecture, the public spaces through which its central character strolls, and its relationship with other cinematic representations of the city. The film scholar Lawrence Webb suggests that its vision of a near-utopian Los Angeles stands in sharp contrast to the dystopian city of *Blade Runner* (Ridley Scott, 1982). As such, this does not preclude analysis of the film's presentation of the role of the tech industry in creating the world experienced by Theodore Twombly and his operating system – or indeed of the dystopian elements of a computer operating system that is so seductive that humans might engage in a romantic relationship with it – but the geographical separation between the film's location and Silicon Valley renders this approach less urgent. Lawrence Webb, 'When Harry Met Siri: Digital Romcom and the Global City in Spike Jonze's *Her*', in Andersson and Webb (eds), *Global Cinematic Cities*, 96–8, 100, 106.
54. Burnham, *Frederic Jameson and* The Wolf of Wall Street, 87–8.
55. Bingham, *Whose Lives Are They Anyway*, 7.

Part 1
Precursors

Chapter 1

Technology and Surveillance in Millennial Hollywood

The 1990s saw a sequence of films, informed in part by nebulous cultural concerns about the impending millennium, present computer processing power and the internet as both enabling for the few who understand it and destructive for those at the mercy of the powerful few. These films draw on the paranoid thriller cycle of the early 1970s to present computer technology facilitating both a lawless space akin to the nineteenth-century western frontier, where individuals are free to redefine themselves as they see fit, and a sinister space where shadowy corporations or even malevolent government departments decide the fate of society. At an individual level, the films debate the anarchic and subversive potential of hackers, the threat of cybernetics to the inviolability of the human body, and the potential for the government to monitor citizens' lives through surveillance technology. As such, they anticipate many of the concerns embedded in Silicon Valley cinema.

Strange Days (Kathryn Bigelow, 1995) expresses anxieties about the potential for technology to record an individual's sensory experience that others might exploit, while *The Lawnmower Man* (Brett Leonard, 1992) considers the potential of virtual reality to control our minds. *Johnny Mnemonic* (Robert Longo, 1995), *eXistenZ* (David Cronenberg, 1999) and *Hackers* (Iain Softley, 1995) present these virtual worlds (in essence, the internet) as a battleground between corporations and ordinary individuals. *Enemy of the State* (Tony Scott, 1994) and *The Net* (Irwin Winkler, 1995) muse further on the potential for the internet to surveil, control and even destroy the individual. The first sees the machinery of the National Security Administration move against a lawyer to destroy not only his personal life but also his finances and professional reputation, while *The Net* has an agoraphobic hacker fight to reclaim her identity from a corporation in league with cyberterrorists. These films, all thrillers, share certain anxieties. The first surrounds the seductiveness of new technology, and particularly the sensory overload that immersion in such technology might prompt. The second revolves around the relationship between the individual, government and private corporations in the control of technology. Most germane to *The Net* and *Enemy of the State*, the third concern builds on the other two to consider the potential for tech to surveil and potentially devastate the individual's life.

Seduction

Strange Days presents virtual reality as a fantasy life, where an individual might try on different identities, from bank robber to murderer, or even relive particularly treasured moments from their own past for thirty-minute intervals. The film depicts this as a distraction from real life akin to hard drugs, a means to extend the surveillance state into individual lives, and as an evidence-gathering medium through which citizens might police the police. This technology, known as SQUID, was originally designed by the government but its outlawing forced it underground, where an illegal market emerged for the production, distribution and consumption of its fantasy experiences. The government's role in creating *Strange Days*' SQUID technology prompts viewers to consider the relationship between the Arpanet (the US government-funded computer network technology that underpins the internet) and the world wide web. The commodification of SQUID footage meanwhile prefigures the similar commodification of our shared memories by Facebook, albeit on a less industrial scale. Indeed, the film's central character, Lenny, seems much like a minor drug dealer in delivering thrills to his clients and employing underlings to create more product for him to distribute. He meanwhile uses his own recordings to escape from the crushing reality of the present, endlessly replaying his first sexual encounter with a woman whom he idealises. This masturbatory potential is highlighted by the slang for engaging with this material: like the characters in William Gibson's cyberpunk classic, *Neuromancer* (1984), you 'jack' into the footage.[1] Lenny says that, when jacked in, 'you're doing it, you're seeing it, you're hearing it, you're feeling it . . . [It's] almost as good as the real thing [but] a lot safer', he concludes, referencing then contemporary fears about inner city violence and the AIDS crisis.[2] The thrill of being jacked in also anticipates the heady rush of our first online experiences, and *Strange Days*' linkage of this experience to drug addiction offers a foretaste of internet addiction. Furthermore, as Lenny's creation of new product suggests, SQUID tech enables us to 'be' another person when we are immersed in it, rendering it somewhat akin to the way in which we construct different online personae for ourselves. Yet SQUID's limitations as a retrospective retreat prevent Lenny from truly experiencing his present and moving into his future, as his confidante, Mace, tells him: 'This is your *life*! Right here! right now!... These [recordings] are used emotions ... Memories were meant to fade Lenny. They're designed that way for a reason.'[3] While Lenny seeks salve in the promise that the potential futures embedded in this computerised past represent to him, Mace convinces him that the promise of the real future is more meaningful. She compels him to let his memories fade and look to the future with optimism, symbolised by them sharing a passionate kiss as the twentieth century turns to the twenty-first.

While the film revels in the revolutionary potential of this new technology for the individual user's experience of media, it rolls back from the tech's potential for social and political revolution, exemplified in Mace's decision not to publicise the recording of police murdering an African American rapper and political activist, and instead entrust it to the honest and upstanding police deputy commissioner. Order is thus restored, and traditional power structures remain intact. Yet viewers cannot also escape the anxieties that the film expresses about tech's role not in preventing crime (as per its original design) but in enabling vicarious pleasure at others committing crime and – even more disturbingly – creating and facilitating even newer crimes, such as forcing victims to experience their own violations from their violator's perspective as well as their own (thus intensifying their horror) or becoming addicted to or even overdosing on the cerebral stimulus provided by SQUID: an example of technology solutionism at its most malevolent. Furthermore, as Mace argues, the most pertinent anxiety surrounds the potential for this SQUID experience to be more vivid than real life, because it is essentially edited highlights, selected by the person who films the footage, akin perhaps to the curated presentation of somebody's online presence. The film thus worries about the potential for the real and the virtual to collapse into each other, and for humanity to become consumed by the ontological question: what is reality? Once we are jacked in and permanently online, would we ever leave? While the film's conventional ending comforts us with the thought that social reality trumps virtual reality and that humanity rather than technology will guide us through the uncertain future, viewers might remain puzzled by the simple fact that the film's most visceral and memorable moments come courtesy of its mimicking of the SQUID sensations. So, while it might suggest that we are most alive when we are in the present moment, the film is most alive in the virtual reality of the past.

Meanwhile, *The Lawnmower Man* predicts that virtual reality will be in 'widespread' use by the year 2000 and that some people 'fear it as a new form of mind control', while warning us that immersion in this virtual world might destroy us.[4] Exploring the frontier of technology, the film suggests, disconnects users from society and even family. A scientist chooses to experiment on the titular character, Jobe, in an attempt to improve his intelligence. Naturally, the scientist's willingness to take risks with various drugs and virtual reality has disastrous consequences. Beginning the film with learning disabilities, Jobe develops the power to read minds, control inanimate objects (including the memorably ludicrous telepathic manipulation of a lawnmower to terrorise and kill an abusive neighbour) and eventually warp reality itself. Yet the ability to control the social world is not enough for this augmented Lawnmower Man, who decides to become virtual and wrest control of the entire electronic network. As this suggests, his relationship with social reality breaks and finally collapses. The scientist's faith remains undimmed, however, as he concludes: 'If we can somehow embrace our wisdom instead of ignorance, this technology will free the mind of man, not enslave it', before closing down his machine to begin a new life freed from his Promethean urges.[5] The question, then, becomes whether we are in thrall to tech or it to us.

This potential for enslavement becomes the *deus ex machina* in *Johnny Mnemonic*. Here, corporations rule 2010s America, including one that specifically protects the cure for the film's 'Nerve Attenuation Syndrome' that afflicts large swathes of the population, an illness, one of the film's characters rages, caused by 'Information overload!' 'All the electronics around you, poisoning the airwaves! Technological fucking civilization! But we still have all this shit, cos we can't live without it.'[6] This corporation – suggestively called Pharmakom, after the philosophical notion that poison and remedy are one and the same – hoards both technology and profits after exploiting the population's technology-solutionist desire for bodily implants, which themselves cause as many problems for the nervous system as they do benefits.

Both films worry about the implications of human–machine integration while expressing concerns about religious dogma. A priest in *The Lawnmower Man* declares that such experiments 'feed . . . the devil' into the subject's head.[7] He might suggest that reckless scientific experimentalism debases God's plan and God's work, but his mental

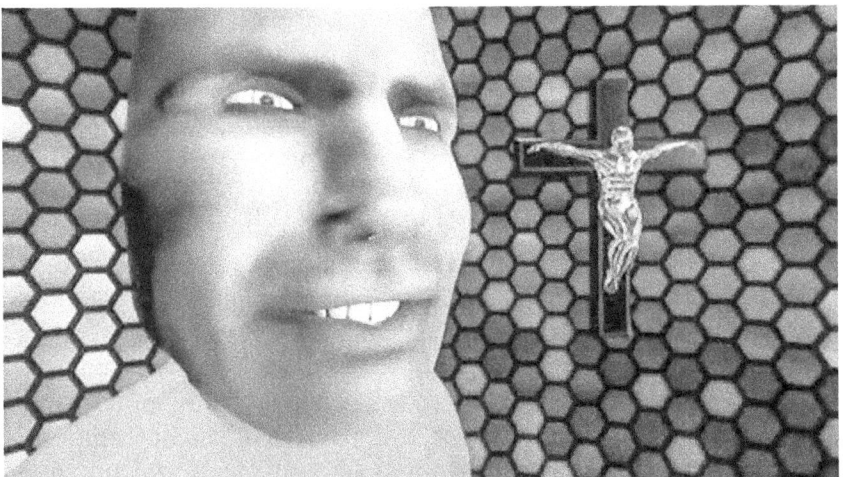

Figure 1.1 *The Lawnmower Man*'s virtual Jobe, crucifying science in cyberspace. (Cropped screenshot, 1h31m).

and physical abuses of Jobe indicate that Christianity is as problematic. 'Judgment Day is here,' announces Jobe in retaliation, before condemning the priest to hell by making his body spontaneously combust.[8] Jobe later declares himself the God of the machine and pins the avatar of the scientist who 'created' him to a virtual cross.

Johnny Mnemonic has an Isaiah-quoting Street Preacher attempting to prevent the titular character succeeding in his mission to enable low-cost healthcare for all. Played by Dolph Lundgren – familiar to viewers from his role as the pharmacologically enhanced Soviet boxer Ivan Drago in *Rocky IV* (Sylvester Stallone, 1985) and the genetically altered *Universal Soldier* (Roland Emmerich, 1992) – this posthuman preacher is reliant on constant updates to his bodily implants to ensure that he continues to function, leading another character to state that he has the relationship between God and technology 'ass-backwards'.[9] He might consider himself a vessel of God's wrath but in fighting against the loose agglomeration of hackers and critics of technology he rejects humanity, eventually sacrificing himself to the God of tech in cruciform pose.[10] Religion, then, might be wielded by technology in service of its solutionist goals, the films warn: we must be sceptical of both the God in the church and the God in the machine.

Like *Johnny Mnemonic* and *The Lawnmower Man*, *eXistenZ* touches on the relationship between tech and religion, locating scenes where game players enter and leave the game inside a church, as if to suggest that they worship at the altar of the virtual-reality game designers. The notion that technology is 'an extension of the human body' is one of its writer and director David Cronenberg's enduring fascinations.[11] *eXistenZ* takes the suspicion that tech might overwhelm the human to its unnatural conclusion, where bodily implants facilitate a virtual-reality experience so powerful that it is nearly impossible to differentiate it from the social reality outside the titular video game. To reinforce this point, the film eschews computer-generated images, instead depicting the game's various layers of virtual reality naturalistically, deliberately making each, in Cronenberg's words, 'look like an alternative now'.[12] As such, the film collapses the barriers between the virtual and the real. Typically for a Cronenberg film, it moves much further politically than its contemporaries in its suggestion that virtual reality's unboundaried and unpoliced world might enable a revolutionary reconstruction of social reality: hence the existence of armed militias determined to destroy the titular game and its potentialities, and the film's final, unanswered and highly ontological question: 'are we still in the game?'[13]

Control

The future, according to *Johnny Mnemonic* and *eXistenZ*, will be defined by battles between major corporations and a multigenerational and multiracial association of countercultural hackers. *Hackers* brought this future crashing into the present, opening with the conviction of its central character Dade Murphy for crashing Wall Street's trading systems back when he was merely eleven years old. Where his descendants in *Johnny Mnemonic* live off grid in grungy hovels, Murphy, and the titular group he joins, live in 1990s New York City, and organise alongside each other to defend the environment against corporate-facilitated destruction. While they might be on the social margins, they succeed at school while taking advantage of others' ignorance of how computers work to enter and manipulate corporate and governmental systems, usually for fun. Like hackers such as Mark Zuckerberg, they live in a world that the rest of us do not understand, one that is exciting and edgy, as signified in the film's hacking sequences where fast cuts and then-cutting-edge techno (such as The Prodigy's 'Voodoo People') heighten the viewer's sense that these young people are not merely tapping on a keyboard but speeding towards the future. The film represents their embrace of future-facing technology not only through their interaction with computers but also in their relationship with the city: they outwit the car-driving Secret Service agents through hacking the New York City traffic system to create traffic jams, and then outrunning their discombobulated pursuers on rollerblades: another technology that their ageing pursuers do not comprehend and a signifier of their nimble manipulation of this new world. Meanwhile, like *The Lawnmower Man*, the computer visuals reference *Tron* (Steven Lisberger, 1982), prompting viewers to wonder at the technological marvels conducted by these young revolutionaries, again intensifying the sense that the hackers balance on the leading edge of science, culture and technology.

These 'terrorists' represent a 'grave threat to the national security', according to the Secret Service. Its agents pursue the hackers while expressing confusion over the meaning of a Hacker Manifesto they uncover. Here, the film's diegetic world intersects with real life. Published as 'The Conscience of a Hacker' in 1986, the Manifesto juxtaposed the criminalisation of hackers' desire to explore computer systems with warmongering, bomb-building, and state-sponsored murder. Confirming that they exist in an entirely separate world to the hackers, the film's government agents consider the hackers terrorists, and their rejection of the status quo as 'commie bullshit', offended at its appeal to a youthful generation of outcasts more comfortable exploring computer systems than deferring to their elders, and entirely ignorant of the hackers' own indifference towards Marxist ideology.[14] As such, generational tension and misunderstanding lie at the core of the hackers' relationship with order and stability.

Yet beneath this, *Hackers* accepts that hacking might be employed for personal gain, as the computer security officer of the Ellingson Mineral Company proves in his attempt to steal $25 million through causing an environmental catastrophe. Having hoodwinked both his bosses and the Secret Service, this 'bad actor' is only thwarted by the actions of multicultural groups of ethically minded hackers (including African Americans, LatinXs, Asian Americans and a smattering of global citizens male and female) who temporarily unite to protect the environment from him. Nevertheless – and here the film's conservatism bubbles to the surface – their victory ultimately exposes only the individual villain, while allowing the corporation to continue its extraction of oil for profit. The hackers' celebration at overcoming evil, then, overlooks the fact that their work has failed to overthrow the system that they so often rail against; they might have brought down the bad actor, but the theatre remains. Thus, *Hackers* suggests that we should not fear that which we do not understand and that hackers could develop into a preventative cadre of activists. Ultimately, however, while these hackers possess an environmentalist streak, they remain uninterested in condemning the deeper problematics at play in postmodern capitalism. *Hackers* consequently anticipates a critique that re-emerged in the Silicon Valley films of the 2010s. Its hackers do not create worlds in which we might become lost, as per *Strange Days*, but instead only seek to uncover criminality when it threatens to destabilise the prevailing economic system. So, whereas *Strange Days* might muse on the loss of control represented by SQUID tech, *Hackers* presents the human individual – or, rather, a particular kind of human individual – in control of aspects of the tech-enabled future. These talented but slightly odd kids are the ancestors of Zuckerberg and co.

Surveillance

The technology that plays such a central role in these films also facilitates surveillance. As the film historian Catherine Zimmer argues, certain action films from the 1990s and 2000s 'incorporate surveillance into their continuity devices as a narrative technology'.[15] These films' plots and *mises en scène* revolve around the tracking of an individual, usually on closed-circuit television or other such devices. Building on the paranoid thrillers of the 1970s, they present surveillance both as a form of contemporary politics and as 'structurally necessary to the functioning' of the world system in which we, as subjects, move.[16] Surveillance thus begets the totality of a world system and enables its controllers to manipulate or even destroy the lives of people who live on the ground.[17]

Enemy of the State is a touchstone for late twentieth-century surveillance cinema. Its lead character, Dean, unwittingly receives a computer disc containing footage of a congressman's murder, plunging him into a personal nightmare. Thanks to its control of the data trail he leaves in his daily life, the National Security Agency (NSA) decodes his entire adult past from his finances to his telephone records, before having him fired, deprived of access to his bank accounts and separated from his family. It even puts his life in danger until he unites with a paranoid former NSA analyst. In a citation of the most famous American surveillance film of the post-World War Two period, *The Conversation* (Francis Ford Coppola, 1974), this undercover surveillance expert is played by Gene Hackman. He helps Dean wield the tools of surveillance against the evildoers, turning their technology against them in order to prove Dean's innocence. In presenting Dean as Everyman, *Enemy* suggests that we are all subject to the power of the state to control our fortunes. Again, however, the conspiracy at the heart of the film is led by a sole corrupt politician. The system itself is most definitely not guilty, even if its technology facilitated the hounding of an innocent and the deaths of others.

Uniting surveillance cinema with hacker cinema, *The Net* has Angela Bennett (played by America's sweetheart Sandra Bullock) sucked into a Hitchcockian nightmare when her digital identity is stolen and she finds that she is now 'Ruth Marx'. She is no revolutionary, however, and uses her hacking skills (honed by her freelance work scrubbing viruses for corporate clients) to recombine her social and digital identities. In contrast to *Hackers*, the world of the computer nerd first appears less bleeding edge than mundane, homely even. Her online friends might cite Tod Browning's *Freaks* (1932) in declaring her 'one of us', but Bennett demonstrates how straightforward it is to order a takeaway pizza online (which would have been at the forefront of online tech that year, thanks to the Netscape web browser first enabling relatively secure online financial transactions), while enlivening her hermetic life with a digital fire broadcasting from her hearth. As this suggests, she sees no gulf between business and pleasure in her online world.[18]

In contrast to *Hackers*, *The Net* offers no visual fireworks or aural excitement when hacking occurs, reinforcing the normalisation of online interaction to the extent that it might appear boring. Even Bennett sees this, cheerfully revealing that 'You just go into people's systems, find their faults, and fix it, that's all.'[19] Nevertheless, once Bennett's online bubble has been punctured, the film presents immersion in online life as problematic: as soon as her digital identity is changed, she finds that her neighbours do not recognise her because she has so rarely interacted with them. The architect of this ploy was previously one of her online friends, she discovers. Indeed, in an even more shocking violation, the film's villain manipulates his way into her bed thanks to the breadcrumb trail of personal information she left online: she has been catfished. Her cyberstalker and his cyberterrorist employers know everything about her, leading her to lament leaving her whole life on the computer but articulating this as a general warning: 'Our whole lives are on the computer and they knew!'[20] Later, she tells her lawyer, 'our whole world is sitting there on a computer . . . begging for somebody to screw with [it] . . . Imagine what they could do with this power! Anything!'[21] Indeed, viewers see Bennett's online identity literally being rewritten in real time, learning how easily bad actors might subvert their online identity. This identity crisis seeps from Bennett's digital to her social identity, leading her to question her own identity, recalling Arnold Schwarzenegger's 'if I'm not me, who the hell am I?' identity crisis in the Philip K. Dick adaptation *Total Recall* (Paul Verhoeven, 1990).[22]

'They', of course, have also outwitted the government and the FBI. The tech-savvy corporate capitalists of the San Francisco-based Gregg Microsystems convince the federal government to entrust its whole digital world to them, using its friendly public face to conceal its nefarious plans. Thus, while *Hackers* might present hacking as youthful idealism and exuberance, *The Net* explores its more malevolent side, where airports shut down or Wall Street itself grinds to a halt. 'Information', declares a government spokesman, 'is sacred, information is power. Society must protect that from these terrorists', unaware that his government has entrusted this information and power to these very terrorists.[23] *The Net* thus rejects *Hackers'* notion that a generational divide lies at the heart of the relationship between the online and offline worlds, while revealing who the real terrorists are: not a gaggle of rollerblading outcasts but truly malevolent characters whose ability to conceal their true intentions can hoodwink almost anybody. Indeed, *The Net*'s government is so inattentive that it doesn't even realise the nature of the threat until Bennett has destroyed Gregg Microsystems' programming. Again, order is restored when the government belatedly acts, and Bennett logs off in another symbolic moment. 'It seems like summer is finally here,' opines a weather forecaster as the cyberterrorists' symbol briefly appears onscreen, to remind us of the importance of vigilance in this new online world.[24]

As a whole, these films present computer technology as a pervasive feature of present society, but crucially one that is 'up for grabs', as government, corporations and individuals compete for control of both the tech and its impact on wider society. In each, government seems to lag behind individuals and corporate raiders in its ability to manipulate the new electronic world. That even the director of the NSA in *Enemy* is unaware of the activities of his subordinate (who coordinates the campaign against Dean) is significant in revealing to us the extent to which these wars occur under our noses even if our eyes do not register them.

As the references to God or the superhuman skills of the hacker suggest, those who control the technological frontier control the future of humanity. In this, even the Hackers' success is destabilising: they are young, preternaturally talented, converse in occasionally unintelligible argot, and confidently outwit everybody around them.

Similarly and more discomfortingly, the films suggest that any victories are temporary. Johnny Mnemonic and his comrades might defeat Pharmakom, but society remains impoverished and unprotected by the remains of the government. Gregg Microsystems' boss might be in jail, but corporate America retains a stranglehold over American capitalism. The symbolic return of Angela Bennett to social life and of *The Lawnmower Man*'s scientist to his family offer only individualised successes. Indeed, as *Enemy of the State* observes at its conclusion, the surveillance society is undamaged, with satellites still impassively observing our every movement in ultra-high definition: we cannot permanently remove ourselves from the machine.

At roughly the same time as these tech films were circulating, the academics Richard Barbrook and Andy Cameron outlined their critique of what they termed the 'California Ideology', which specifically linked Silicon Valley corporations and boosters such as *Wired* magazine to a hyper-individualist neoliberal ideology. They foresaw a digital future that would be a 'hybrid of state intervention, capitalist entrepreneurship and DIY culture'.[25] *Hackers* most explicitly engages with this digital future, noting that this hybrid would be riven with competing visions and ideals, and that it would be by no means settled but instead exist in a permanent state of tension. Yet considering this issue some twenty-five years later suggests that this tension has abated somewhat. The state has rolled back to allow the entrepreneurs to dictate the terms under which many users engage with the web. Building on state surveillance, Google Maps and Google Street View offer a panoptic vision of our neighbourhoods. We record our every activity from the mundane to the momentous on Facebook. We don't even need SQUID technology to access real-time footage of human beings and other animals conducting any number of activities: Facebook Live, YouTube and Twitch do that for us. Tethered to our mobile phones, our whole lives are vulnerable to spyware without us knowing that our devices have been compromised.[26] We scoff that Johnny Mnemonic's brain is nearly overloaded by a mere 520 gigabytes of data: we have memory sticks smaller than a credit card that hold as much. Hackers now no longer merely munch pizza while messaging their online friends about IRL meetings but operate at a near-industrial level, even becoming part of international espionage networks. They steal our credit card details, empty our bank accounts, hold our data to hostage and hobble our employers' networks to prevent us conducting business. At times, these two worlds intersect, when hackers infiltrate our computers to launch DDoS attacks on other websites or even entire governments.

As this suggests, the *Hackers* have metastasised into real saboteurs while governments themselves wield this formerly DIY culture at an industrial level. Meanwhile, from positions of almost unassailable power Silicon Valley corporations act with even more impunity than Gregg Microsystems or Pharmakom. Perhaps the most important link between these techno-thrillers and our present is the sense that our triumphs are only fleeting and individual. It will take more than revelations about their mendacity, information hoarding and profiteering, let alone a gaggle of social misfits or even Sandra Bullock herself, to bring our tech overlords down.

Notes

1. Mark Berrettini, 'Can "We All" Get Along?', 161.
2. *Strange Days*, 20m, 30m.
3. *Strange Days*, 1h38.
4. *The Lawnmower Man*, 0m.
5. *Lawnmower Man*, 1h37.
6. *Johnny Mnemonic* 50m.
7. *Lawnmower Man*, 31m.
8. *Lawnmower Man*, 1h05m
9. *Johnny Mnemonic*, 56m.
10. *Johnny Mnemonic*, 1h36.
11. Bowler, '*eXistenZ* and the Spectre of Gender', 104.
12. Cronenberg quoted in von Busack, 'Pod Man Out'.
13. Bowler, '*eXistenZ* and the Spectre of Gender', 108; *eXistenZ* 1h35.
14. *Hackers*, 32m, 36m (quote); the Mentor, 'The Conscience of a Hacker'.
15. Zimmer, *Surveillance Cinema*, 9.
16. Zimmer, *Surveillance*, 117.
17. Zimmer, *Surveillance*, 123
18. O'Hara, *The Code*, 306; *The Net*, 7m, 20m, 40m.
19. *The Net*, 25m.
20. *The Net*, 52m.
21. *The Net*, 1h19m.
22. *The Net*, 44m, 51m; *Total Recall*, 27m.
23. *The Net*, 1h28m.
24. *The Net*, 1h48m
25. Barbrook and Cameron, 'The Californian Ideology'.
26. Craig Timberg, Reed Albergotti and Elodie Guéguen, 'Despite the Hype, iPhone Security No Match for NSO Spyware', *Washington Post*, July 19, 2021, <https://www.washingtonpost.com/technology/2021/07/19/apple-iphone-nso/?utm_source=pocket-newtab-global-en-GB> (consulted June 28, 2022).

Chapter 2

Critiquing Twenty-First-Century Capitalism

The second set of precursors to Silicon Valley cinema follow in the footsteps of *Wall Street* (Oliver Stone, 1987), critiquing American capitalism by depicting groups of financial traders dictating the rise and decline of American firms and thus by extension the entire economy. As such, like the technology thrillers, they highlight fears of shadowy cabals manipulating our world for their own benefit. Each film engages with the fallout from the economic collapse of 2007–2008. Their venal and corrupt capitalists see no ethical problem in using illegally obtained information to manipulate stock values and boost their personal finances.[1] As important, their critique of the influence of toxic masculinity and the traders' devotion only to their own wealth accumulation develops a deeper philosophical connection with Silicon Valley cinema, one surrounding Ayn Rand's valorising of the self-interest of the self-appointed great men of our times.

Based on its anti-hero's memoir, *The Wolf of Wall Street* (Martin Scorsese, 2013) recounts Jordan Belfort's rise to Wall Street notoriety courtesy of his preternatural sales skills and his willingness to flout both convention and the law when selling stocks. Obsessed with money and the attendant opportunities for sex- and drug-fuelled bad behaviour, Belfort finds his company under investigation by the FBI and the American Securities and Exchange Commission, with his conviction and jailing following soon afterwards. This downfall presages a shift into a different grift: motivational speaking, where he dispenses the supposed secret to financial success to conference rooms full of suckers desperate to make a fast buck in sales. *Margin Call* (J. C. Chandor, 2011) reveals how analysts at a fictional investment bank discover in 2008 that the company is on the verge of bankruptcy thanks to it underestimating the risks attached to mortgage-backed securities. The firm's heads, operating according to capitalist exigencies, decide to sell as many of these assets as they can before the price drops so low that it will endanger the firm. This throws the rest of the securities market to the wolves, with the film ending on the verge of another Wall Street Crash. The mysteries of these mortgage-backed securities are unravelled in the documentary *Inside Job* (Charles Ferguson, 2010), which details the close relationship between bankers, regulators and academics in the decades before the 2007–2008 financial crash, indicting all three for greed, laziness and corruption. While ostensibly more light-hearted, the lightly fictionalised *The Big Short* (Adam McKay, 2015) follows the depressing story of various financial specialists who discover, and in some cases, exploit for financial gain, the increasing instability of the financial system of the 2000s thanks to the problematic nature of mortgage-backed securities.[2]

Collectively, these films reveal the gulf between the worlds of investment bankers, stockbrokers and their likes, and the world inhabited by those who live with the consequences of decisions made by these masters of the universe, as Tom Wolfe would call them. As this suggests, the bankers appear akin to Greek Gods, indifferently launching the occasional financial lightning bolt at the mortals beneath their feet. More broadly, this set of precursors reinforces the suggestion in the tech films that the people who manipulate our (digital) world are very different from the rest of us. They also offer further insights into two key elements of Silicon Valley cinema, namely the baleful influence of masculine codes on the worlds these men create and the Randian insulation of the protagonists from the world around them.

Insularity

As if to highlight the insularity of the bankers' world, neither *The Wolf of Wall Street* nor *Margin Call* examine the fallout of the stockbrokers' and investment bankers' failures. This is crucial: sheltered by their wealth and their foresight from the consequences of their actions, they are free to act with impunity in order to feather their nests even more lavishly. Like Eric Packer in *Cosmopolis* (David Cronenberg, 2012), whose luxury car literally insulates him from the streets, they are untouchable – although unlike Packer few deign to set foot outside this bubble, lest the masses take revenge. This separation reinforces the films' suggestion that capitalism has been subverted by an amoral elite who care not for decency, fair play, equality of opportunity and other such social niceties. For example, Jordan Belfort's mentor at the L. F. Rothschild merchant bank, Mark Hanna, admits on Belfort's first day that no broker knows what will happen to stock prices; the broker merely must ensure that the client reinvests their money in new stock. 'All we care about is getting fucking rich,' he announces, before pointing out to Belfort that the entire world of finance is nothing but a world of smoke and mirrors designed only to enrich the brokers.[3] Their invention of the(ir) future involves merely the creation of an immaterial, incorporeal wealth. One of *Margin Call*'s junior staff observes that all he does is 'push numbers around a computer screen' while 'a bunch of glorified crack addicts . . . bet it against some other jock halfway around the world'. 'At the end of the day, one guy wins, one guy loses,' he shrugs, reducing the world of financialised capitalism to two men fighting it out in a zero sum game.[4] Later, the firm's CEO echoes the writer of the book on which *The Big Short* was based, Michael Lewis, in admitting that the whole industry relies on guesswork rather than anything even vaguely scientific.[5] They quite happily sell garbage investments to anybody who is buying, irrespective of the deal's value to the customer. Little wonder that they can do their jobs perfectly well while high, drunk or both. Such chemical enhancements narcotise and anaesthetise them against any moral thoughts they might have about financialised capitalism and instead enable them to focus on sales volume in order to maintain their social status. These traders might follow Belfort in focusing their energies on selling to the already rich, but they are merely attempting to join the ranks of the 1%, not redistribute the wealth hoarded by these robber barons.

The films, then, argue that the vast majority of bankers and traders had a vested interest in not questioning what they did and why: they simply allowed the money to roll in. Even *The Big Short*'s tiny number of 'outsiders and weirdos' who worked out that mortgage-backed securities were a timebomb primed to destroy the entire economy were no Robin Hoods: they use their superior analysis of the situation to profit from the calamity they foresee rather than prevent it happening.[6] The system will endure. As one of their collaborators acidly comments:

> You just bet against the American economy . . . [I]f we're right . . . people lose homes, people lose jobs, people lose retirement savings, people lose pensions. You know what I hate about fucking banking? It reduces people to numbers. Here's a number: every point unemployment goes up, 40 thousand people die.[7]

As this suggests, of the fictional films, only *The Big Short* considers the impact of financial fraud on the wider world. Two analysts visit a housing development where renters will soon be evicted because their landlords have defaulted on their mortgages. Some of their former neighbours have simply abandoned their homes to the local wildlife. Reinforcing this message, montages that depict the lives of the ordinary Americans who were soon to find their livelihoods destroyed by the venality of the bankers occasionally interrupt the narrative. One major character, Mark Baum, immerses himself in therapy and work to distract himself from trauma in his personal life. He is frequently depicted walking the streets of New York City, dodging pedestrians and battling for taxicabs, implicitly separating him from the insulated bankers whom he despises so much. One of *The Big Short*'s ironies is that Baum's method of distracting his attention from his personal trauma helps to cause the mass trauma following the banking crash: like a character in an Adam Curtis documentary, he is ineffably postmodern, believing that the entire capitalist system is a lie and a fraud, while being fully enmeshed in that very same system. The postmodern condition also envelops *Margin Call*'s conflicted senior manager Sam Rogers and the firm's head of risk management Eric Dale. While both become aware of the fraud at the heart of their company and the system that it represents, neither can fully escape its clutches. Rogers attempts to resign on principled grounds but is bought off; the heavily mortgaged Dale, meanwhile, receives a large cash boost in return for a silence that will preserve the company's finances. His house stands as a metaphoric representation of neoliberal financialised capitalism: bought by Dale with leveraged cash, only he and his family benefit from its security, and his silence ensures that the criminality in which he is enmeshed remains undisclosed.

Meanwhile, in a subversive demystification of the world of financialised capital, *The Big Short* offers a series of fourth-wall breaking cameos from celebrities who explain the neologism-, abbreviation- and acronym-rich language used by the traders for those unversed in banker-speak. The message of these interludes is simple: the complex financial instruments created by the bankers and traders are designed purely to enrich them and nobody else. Yet the film's conclusion shows the huge profits made by its weirdos, all of whom made tens of millions of dollars out of the destruction of millions of ordinary people's livelihoods, thus stepping back from Uwe Boll's gonzo *Assault on Wall Street* (2013), in which a wronged working-class man extracts violent revenge after the banks ruin his finances and his life.

Chillingly, in *Margin Call*'s final scene, the firm's owner muses exultantly that 'there's going to be a lot of money to be made coming out of this mess': a mess that his fire sale has created. Literally elevated

Figure 2.1   *Margin Call*'s Chief Executive Officer enjoys a meal, a fine bottle of red and the crossword while New York City discovers the wreckage his firm has made of the financial system. (Cropped screenshot, 1h30m).

from the street-level New Yorkers as he dines in the firm's executive dining room high up in its skyscraper, he is insulated by his wealth and skulduggery from the chaos wrought on the markets and hence the lives of those below. From this visual and metaphoric vantage point, the little people at ground level are too inconsequential to deserve his attention, which focuses instead on a newspaper puzzle. Symbolically freed from any shackles binding him to their insignificant lives, he is the Randian hero made flesh. His cynical awareness that 'there have always been and always will be the same percentage of winners and losers, happy fucks and sad sacks, fat cats and starving dogs in this world' finally confirms capital's dedication only to the perpetuation of the 1%'s financial hegemony.[8]

Toxic Masculinity

Reflecting the macho world of finance capitalism, all these films are resolutely masculine and homosocial. Here, the films hint at an often-overlooked relationship between Wall Street and Silicon Valley. The wave of tech bros who headed to Silicon Valley in the early 2010s are the kind of men – and they are almost all men – who used to go to Wall Street to make their fortunes as investment bankers, who share their forebears' disregard for the common weal.[9] Women in the films, meanwhile, are almost completely marginalised, thus presenting Wall Street as a male sphere, and toxic masculinity and hubristic stupidity at the core of capitalism's failures. This, naturally, reflects the real Wall Street, as *Inside Job* confirms. Despite predicting the financial crash, for example, *Margin Call*'s chief risk management officer and only female member of staff is sacrificed to enable the company to deny that its entire modus operandi is at fault. No female employees in Jordan Belfort's firm possess enough power to challenge their male colleagues' rampant sexism and exploitation of women. Meredith Whitney, arguably the pivotal figure in Michael Lewis's book, was written out of McKay's *The Big Short*. In October 2007 Whitney argued that Citigroup, one of the major American banking conglomerates, was in danger of bankruptcy. 'From that moment,' Lewis writes, 'when she spoke, people listened.'[10] Throughout the following year, Whitney argued consistently that Wall Street's bankers – like *Margin Call*'s firm – were failing to acknowledge their mismanagement of their businesses, particularly when it came to subprime mortgages. Her mentor had been Steve Eisman, another analyst who treated Wall Street boosters with extreme scepticism and who was betting against the Collateralized Debt Obligations that played a central role in the banking collapse (and that are alluded to as problematic and potentially illegal by Jordan Belfort). Eisman became one of Lewis's key sources and was written into *The Big Short* film as Mark Baum. As Whitney's erasure suggests, *The Big Short* also relegates women to low statuses: Mark Baum's wife appears twice, both times to express her concern for his mental health; Michael Burry's wife was deleted from the final cut; other women include strippers, an indolent US Securities and Exchange Commission analyst who craves a Wall Street job, and a myopic ratings agency analyst who admits that she 'can't see a damn thing' before confessing that the agencies do not perform due diligence on the financial packages they are paid to assess.[11] The only other women are the actors Margot Robbie and Selena Gomez, appearing as themselves to offer to-camera explanations of complex financial instruments (here the film fleetingly satirises the notion that beautiful women might lack brains).

As important, throughout *The Wolf of Wall Street*, Belfort juxtaposes the good life represented by trading with the life of poverty that is an ever-present threat to the unsuccessful trader:

> There is no nobility in poverty . . . If anyone here thinks I'm superficial, or materialistic, go get a job at fuckin' McDonalds, cause that's where

you fuckin' belong. But before you depart this room full of winners, I want you to take a good look at the person next to you, go on. Because sometime in the not-so-distant future, you're going to be pulling up to a red light in your beat-up old fuckin' Pinto, and that person's going to be pulling up right alongside you, in their brand-new Porsche, with their beautiful wife by their side, who's got big voluptuous tits, and who are you gonna be sitting next to? Some disgusting wildebeest with three days of razor stubble, in a sleeveless muumuu, crammed in next to you an' a carload full of groceries from the fuckin' Price Club.[12]

Only stock trading prevents postmodern capitalism reducing Belfort and company to poverty (metaphorically represented by cheap cars and hairy, overweight wives). The choice they face is clear: sell junk stocks to dupes, or be reduced to ugliness. Only wealth leads to beauty (an equation reversed by Apple in producing beautiful products that attract premium prices that make their designers – but not the people who actually make these machines – extremely wealthy).

The bankers' amorality is most obviously articulated in their predilection for prostitutes and strip bars, where the self-interest, hedonism, casual misogyny and immorality of financialised capitalism is at its most untethered, which *Inside Job* again indicates is based on real life. While *The Wolf of Wall Street* shows Belfort and his gang revelling in debauchery, its detached gaze encourages audiences to consider the grubby vacuity of such a lifestyle, to agree with Scorsese that 'finance capital itself is a form of high-level gangsterism', and thus that Belfort's sidemen are not dissimilar to the mobsters of *Goodfellas* (Martin Scorsese, 1990) or *Casino* (Martin Scorsese, 1995). As important, it suggests that no thin blue line exists between the legal and the illegal: it is, as *Inside Job* alleges, an industry that, thanks to toxic masculinity, is out of control.[13]

Together, the films present a capitalist elite unaffected by the economic crisis of the late 2000s and 2010s because of their connivance in creating financial instruments that work only to benefit the ultra-rich, which now includes them. Money, their characters collectively insist, 'makes you a better person'.[14] Notably, Belfort's company lifts his original co-workers out of the working class, relocating them in the world of the mega-rich, as signified by holiday homes in the Hamptons, bespoke suits, flashy cars and trophy brides. They might be ugly men, but they project wealth and power by surrounding themselves with beauty. In short, this is affluence, underpinned by their willingness to operate outside the law, according only to their own rules. Scorsese's Belfort might be cartoonishly over-the-top, but nothing in the other films suggests that his venality is unique. He might initially have suffered in the 1987 stock market crash but the lessons he learned from Hanna ('fuck the clients . . . Move the money from your client's pocket into your pocket') enable him to bounce back higher than before.[15] And while *The Wolf of Wall Street* takes place in the years between 1987 and 2007, the film's post-2008 release encourages audiences to wonder whether anything changed in the world of financial trading during the intervening years. More troublingly, the film's epilogue, in which the post-prison Belfort mesmerises an audience of neophyte salespeople with his sales tactics, suggests that people simply want to partake in his world, rather than reject him and all he stands for.

These films stand in sharp contrast to other cultural interrogations of neoliberalism, most notably television's *The Wire* (HBO, 2002–2008), which meticulously examines the destruction of the working class amid the wholesale gutting of the American city by neoliberalism and its acolytes. In reducing financialised capitalism to a battle between good actors such as Mark Baum and bad actors such as Belfort, these films sit firmly within the long tradition of Hollywood films that valorise a more humane form of capitalism while offering stern critiques of the corrupt individuals that operate within this system. As Alberto Toscano and Jeff Kinkle argue, this tendency to 'personify' a systemic crisis reflects cinema's inability to react to current events, and anticipates elements of Hollywood's critique of Silicon Valley.[16] In personalising the problems of finance capitalism, these Hollywood films stop short of offering a thorough, consistent critique of neoliberal capitalism. Influenced in part by the immersion of their production companies in that very system and the formal need to present digestible, entertaining product with a(n ideally photogenic) human face, these films instead focus on the bad actors who have manipulated stock trading and investment banking for their own benefit. Thus, to borrow Fredric Jameson's suggestion that all Hollywood films include utopian tendencies, the utopia presented by post-2008 financial films is merely a return to a kinder, gentler capitalism, one perhaps represented by Hollywood itself.

Notes

1. These films are not alone in probing American capitalism in the wake of 2008. The film scholar Suzanne Ferriss positions *The Great Gatsby* (Baz Luhrmann, 2013) and *American Hustle* (David Russell, 2013)

alongside *Wolf* as critiques of the relationship between con artistry and American capitalism. Ferriss, 'Refashioning the Modern American Dream: *The Great Gatsby*, *The Wolf of Wall Street*, and *American Hustle*'.
2. Grobar, '*The Big Short* scribe Charles Randolph'.
3. *The Wolf of Wall Street*, 7m.
4. *Margin Call*, 23m.
5. *Margin Call*, 48m; Lewis, *Big Short*, xvii.
6. *The Big Short*, 3m.
7. *The Big Short*, 1h18m.
8. *Margin Call*, 1h34m
9. Lyons, *Disrupted*, 157; Wiener, *Uncanny Valley*, 84–5.
10. Lewis, *Big Short*, xvi.
11. Lewis, *Big Short*, xvii–xviii; *The Big Short*, 1h02m.
12. *Wolf of Wall Street*, 1h23m.
13. Burnham, *Fredric Jameson and* The Wolf of Wall Street, 99–100, 118 (quote).
14. Jordan Belfort in *Wolf of Wall Street*, 4m
15. *Wolf of Wall Street*, 9m.
16. Toscano and Kinkle, *Cartographies of the Absolute*, 120.

Chapter 3

Hollywood's Bay Area

The writer Nathaniel Rich opens his *San Francisco Noir* (2005) by wrestling with the apparent paradox at the heart of cinematic representations of San Francisco: how can 'one of the happiest, most beautiful, and romantic cities in the world' also be 'so sinister and dark' onscreen?[1] Obviously, Rich's genre focus defines this paradox: after all, as the film scholar Edward Dimendberg notes, the film noir metropolis 'seldom appears . . . [as] a space of genuinely enhanced freedom'.[2] But Rich's curiosity at the disjuncture between what might be termed image and reality raises important questions for students of the relationship between cinema and the cities it depicts, not least because Rich hints here that two 'San Franciscos' exist: the physical one, in which young folks gambol in sunlight-dappled parks, and the cinematic one, where evil forces, enshrouded in fog, lurk at the corner of every building. Of course, this is an oversimplification, both of the 'real' and the 'cinematic' city: there is no single, unified cinematic (or indeed, real) San Francisco – as Rebecca Solnit suggests in her book of the same name, it is an *Infinite City*. Instead, we must consider the ways in which San Francisco-set films metaphorically create the city and inscribe it with values, ideas and emotions that deepen their plot, *mises en scène*, atmosphere, post-production and perhaps even distribution.[3] Thus, the Hollywood reimagining of the city encourages the active cinema viewer to interrogate the 'real' and the 'cinematic' city in order to develop a richer understanding of both. As such, the two partake in a dialogic relationship: the real informs the cinematic, while at the same time the cinematic informs and helps shape our understanding of the real.

The variety of cinematic representations of San Francisco runs from the sunny modernist city, full of wide boulevards, chic residencies and lavish hotels of *What's Up Doc?* (Peter Bogdanovich, 1972), to the ruined post-apocalyptic wasteland of *The Book of Eli* (Allen Hughes and Albert Hughes, 2010). Most germane to Silicon Valley cinema are films that present San Francisco as a location for struggles over the future of society, or even over the potential end of the world. This runs from the celebrated films noir of the 1940s that often wield San Francisco's built environment metaphorically, to more recent special effects blockbusters that see the city levelled in service of spectacle. Significantly, two 1980s blockbusters, *A View to a Kill* (John Glen, 1985) and *Star Trek IV: The Voyage Home* (Leonard Nimoy, 1986), present the Bay Area as a battleground over technology and the very future of humanity. Most of these films, however, ignore the Bay Area beyond San Francisco, an elision that relates to the whiteness of their characters. A selection of recent films exploring the twenty-first-century African American experience of the Bay Area offers further insights into the insularity of Silicon Valley and the impact of its vast wealth and influence on the neighbourhoods and people around it. While not precursors as such, they offer a useful counterpoint to the whiteness of Silicon Valley cinema. Finally, the film that perhaps unites all the themes of this section – technology, capitalism and the locality – presents the Bay Area in transition between modernity and postmodernity. As important, *The Conversation* (Francis Ford Coppola, 1974) presents surveillance technology as an uncanny power that can determine quotidian life at both a private and public level.

Crime

Just as San Francisco looms large over Silicon Valley cinema, film noir looms large over the cinematic image of the American city, and while Los Angeles will always be the archetypal noir location, a small but important corpus of noir films prominently feature San Francisco. Noir presents modernity itself as a highly ambiguous, threatening and alienating miasmic force. Among the most influential noirs, *The Maltese Falcon* (John Huston, 1941) uses San Francisco's topography to render the city itself an active agent, arguably more so than any other single film. Despite not being filmed in San Francisco, it traces the private investigator Sam Spade's movements around the city in an almost uncannily accurate representation of the city's actual geography.[4] Tight shots depict buildings looming over the film's characters. That viewers rarely see the sky above these buildings adds to the foreboding atmosphere and the sense that the natural world has been overwhelmed by modernity and its attendant vices.

Elsewhere, surveillance plays a key theme in San Francisco's noir tradition, laying important foundations for the surveillance narratives that inform aspects of Silicon Valley cinema. The perfunctory anticommunist encomium to the FBI, *Walk A Crooked Mile* (Gordon Douglas, 1948), sees its dedicated agents tracing a communist cell working across California. The nominatively-determinist Agent Hunter helps establish 24-hour monitoring of the activities of suspected communists in San Francisco through wiretaps, telescope surveillance and a fake domestic services van (suggestively titled 'American cleaners') that houses a movie camera.[5] Anticipating the affectless pod people of *Invasion of the Body Snatchers* (Don Siegel, 1956; Philip Kaufman, 1978) and perhaps even Mark Zuckerberg's famed awkwardness when interacting with humans, the communists in the almost maniacal *The Woman on Pier 13* aka *I Married a Communist* (Robert Stevenson, 1949) lose all emotion when they talk political theory. Hellbent on destroying American democracy, they ruthlessly attempt to exploit San Francisco's growing reputation for nonconformity. The viewer here becomes a surveillance cadre, watching the Communist Party fight for control of San Francisco's waterfront and presumably cheering once the subversives are rooted out.

Jules Dassin's *Thieves' Highway* (1949) turns this notion of San Francisco housing a subversive element on its head through a family of European immigrants who suffer at the front line of American capitalism. After returning from the Second World War, Nick Garcos discovers that a San Francisco fruit dealer's rapaciousness has physically and financially crippled his farmer father. The dealer's cronies rip off Garcos, while his partner dies at Altamont transporting apples to San Francisco, an event that prompts a final confrontation between the dealer and Garcos in the small town that later housed another disaster. Justice is served, far away from American capitalism's seedy core in the metropolis. This notion that the city might ostensibly welcome outsiders but is far from a city of sanctuary informs three of the most celebrated San Francisco noirs. *D.O.A.* (Rudolph Maté, 1950) sees the small-town accountant Frank Bigelow visit the city for a brief break from his stultifying home and job. He unwittingly ingests a slow-acting poison and spends the rest of the film hunting his poisoner. While Los Angeles houses the conspirators who kill him, San Francisco emerges as a mysterious, impassive metropolis whose carefree reputation masks a sleazy, malevolent core. In *Out of the Past* (Jacques Tourneur, 1947), a private investigator moves to a dingy office in San Francisco to escape from organised crime. Naturally, this proves an elusive goal: even though he physically escapes the city, he cannot free himself from the forces that chase him to his grave. Like him, Michael O'Hara in *The Lady from Shanghai*

(Orson Welles, 1947) cannot escape San Francisco's underbelly. In similar fashion to *D.O.A.* and *Out of the Past*, *Shanghai* juxtaposes wholesome small-town life with the big city's corrupt decadence, warning viewers that San Francisco might not be the playground it at first appears. 'Stay away!' these films seem to howl.

The Lineup (Don Siegel, 1958) also suggests that something fishy is taking place in San Francisco. Siegel's take on the Steinhart Aquarium might be less impressionist than *The Lady from Shanghai*'s famous scene, but his film equally presents the harbour as a crime-ridden location, the landing point for heroin smuggling. *The Lineup* also deserves to be remembered for its concluding car chase. Partly shot on the incomplete Embarcadero Freeway, the chase presents the urbanising city as a striking location for the restoration of order, courtesy of the police who chase Eli Wallach's increasingly frantic criminal as the freeway's concrete gradually but inexorably boxes him in. Like many other San Francisco noir characters, he finds himself trapped by modernity's transformation of the city. Crucially, in interrogating the relationship between modernity and crime *The Lineup* anticipates *Bullitt* (Peter Yates, 1968) and lays the foundations for the latter's celebrated car chase in showing cars soaring into the air as they crest some of the city's hilly roads, revealing the ability of the city's changing geography to facilitate the spectacular.

Bullitt itself highlights the malignant influence of organised crime on the city. Its titular hero must protect the brother of a Chicago Mafia boss before he testifies at a Senate hearing. Over the course of a weekend, he discovers that he is being set up by the mob, and triumphs only after going rogue. The film thus emphasises the city's fragility and its reliance on the upstanding morality of (native) individuals ranged against the power of organised crime, the self-interest of politicians and the indolence of the San Francisco Police Department. *Dirty Harry* (Don Siegel, 1971), meanwhile, is rich enough a source to merit its own book-length analysis. Here, the individualist cop becomes a one-man vigilante unit, preventing the depravity of the 1960s counterculture spilling from the city's underbelly while outwitting the city's criminals, its complacent liberal political establishment, and its technocratic but ineffective police department. Such was his popularity with audiences that Harry Callahan returned in four sequels, all set in the Bay Area, all presenting him as the defender of the system against radicals from all sides of the political spectrum.[6] Echoes of *Bullitt* also feature in the romantic screwball comedy *What's Up Doc?* courtesy of another extended chase scene through San Francisco's built environment. Here, however, the agents of chaos are not so much murderers, political extremists or other miscreants but the wayward daughter of a local judge, some small-time crooks searching for a bag of jewels and two bumbling chumps who fight over a bag of top-secret papers.

These late-1960s and 1970s films suggest, then, that chaos is never far from the city's surface. Sometimes this chaos is merely good-natured anarchy, as represented by *What's Up Doc?*'s ditzy heroine Judy Maxwell; other times this chaos is led by criminals such as *Dirty Harry*'s many antagonists, all of whom seek to upend traditional structures of authority. Significantly, most San Franciscans continue their daily lives blissfully unaware of the various threats to their city. The films thus hint that even more pernicious crimes might be taking place that even they cannot identify, a theme that Silicon Valley cinema references in its suggestion that the future is being made by tech overlords who insulate themselves from wider society. Moreover, while order is always restored, in presenting the city under constant threat, these films also hint at another long-term threat: environmental disaster.

Disaster

As the film scholar Stephen Keane notes, *San Francisco* (Woody Van Dyke, 1936) is something of an ur-text for the disaster movie genre.[7] Although ostensibly a romance between Clark Gable's saloon owner, Blackie, and Jeannette McDonald's singer, Mary, audiences were primed to expect the climactic destruction of the city courtesy of the film's temporal setting in early 1906, just before April's major earthquake. The film offers a sublimated moral condemnation of the licentiousness of the Barbary Coast, as the earthquake hits soon after a rowdy crowd joins Mary in a lusty rendition of the film's theme tune 'San Francisco'. In case this was too subtle, the film's moral core, Father Mullin, tells Mary, 'you're in probably the wickedest, most corrupt city, most Godless city in America. Sometimes it frightens me. I wonder what the end's going to be.'[8] Blackie and Mary's post-earthquake reconciliation and the promise of creating a stable heterosexual family heralds calls to rebuild San Francisco anew, and an impromptu rendition of 'Battle Hymn of the Republic' from the massed working-class ranks under the banner of God, family, and nation: the city morally cleansed.[9]

The notion that the 1906 earthquake upset the foundations of an old, corrupt San Francisco and paved the way for the new also informs the under-rated *Flame of the Barbary Coast* (Joseph Kane, 1945), in which John Wayne's Duke Fergus becomes embroiled in the city's gambling dens, falls in love and, after the earthquake, briefly becomes involved in municipal politics. A parable about San Francisco's relationship with capitalism, *Flame of the Barbary Coast* sees Fergus taking revenge on corrupt casino owners by setting up his own establishment, which opens mere hours before the earthquake. With much of the Barbary Coast razed to the ground, the other casino owners plan to subvert the upcoming mayoral election and prevent the rise of a new class of suspiciously respectable businessmen who themselves see great popular appeal in Duke's Americanism. Duke brings some authentic frontier justice to the election, preventing the casino owners' attempts to subvert the count with a round of fisticuffs, before revealing the attempted coup, winning his girl, returning power to the people and finally heading back to Montana (in part because he suspects that the new regime will raise taxes). His decisive intervention, then, might prevent the city sliding back into corruption and debauchery but leaves it vulnerable to a new and different form of exploitation from business interests and their fondness for overtaxing the working man while protecting their own wealth.

Although San Francisco escaped the worst of the 1950s alien invasion film cycle – *It Came from Beneath the Sea* (Robert Gordon, 1955) saw a giant octopus terrorise the waterfront but leave the city largely intact – the disaster classic *The Towering Inferno* (John Guillermin, 1974) and Philip Kaufman's 1978 remake of *Invasion of the Body Snatchers* firmly reminded viewers that San Francisco was not safe. Both express profound fears about the increasingly corporate city, embodied in its new skyline. *The Towering Inferno* presents cronyism, corruption, urban renewal, and plain old penny-pinching as the rotten foundations of a shoddily constructed mega-skyscraper. The film encourages viewers to revel in the peril faced by a group of well-to-do party-goers on the night of the skyscraper's gala opening, including a pair of adulterers who are righteously punished by being burnt alive. While the building's architect (like Duke Fergus, a Montanan) denounces the cost-cutting electrical contractor for installing cheap wiring, the contractor protests that he followed the Building Code. In aiming to refocus attention on the government, he attempts to excuse the free market, arguing that the architect lives in a dream world in expecting a capitalist to risk his profit margins by installing safety features that go beyond minimum standards. Ultimately, the architect's willingness to work alongside the working-class hero fire chief ensures that, unlike the contractor, he emerges with both his reputation and his life intact. The skyscraper's developer meanwhile faces an uncertain future, not least because the senator with whom he was hoping to carve up more of San Francisco fell to his death during the inferno. The new capitalist class thus receives a lesson in hubris, humility and the value of low-rise edifices, something that Scottie Ferguson, the conflicted acrophobic hero of *Vertigo* (Alfred Hitchcock, 1958), would doubtless appreciate.

The threat in *Invasion of the Body Snatchers* is far more terrifying. Kaufman's film opened in the week that an inquest concluded that Jim Jones's cult had coerced over 900 people, many of whom were Bay Area natives, into ingesting a lethal poison in Jonestown, Guyana.[10] By transplanting Don Siegel's 1956 classic to San Francisco and through a suitably unhinged cameo from Siegel's star Kevin McCarthy, the film reveals that the contagion of pod people has spread from small-town America to the metropolis. Its message that the pods do not discriminate between old and new San Francisco, between its working-class denizens and its more affluent residents, would have resonated deeply with local audiences sensitised by the news from Jonestown to the threat of brainwashing. The pods, it promises, will render all of them emotionless automatons doomed to a posthuman future. In addition, the film suggests that the transforming San Francisco of the real world is becoming the San Francisco of the pods. Elizabeth Driscoll's boyfriend begins acting strangely. Rather than parking himself in front of televised sports, he begins wearing sharp suits, attending evening work events and appears much less interested in her than before. Her colleague even suspects that he might have become a Republican.[11] He has been replaced by a pod, but viewers must wonder whether he has rejected the old, eccentric San Francisco in favour of a corporatised city in thrall to business. In this, the film critiques the narcissism and self-absorption of the new city as it shed itself of the countercultural attitudes so indelibly associated with the 1960s and that were so central to the threat in *Dirty Harry*. While viewers are invited to smirk at the bohemian mud bath owner Jack Bellicec's insistence that the FBI and the CIA are already pods – reflecting familiar hippie tropes about 'The Man' – they are also painfully aware that, in the film's diegetic world at the very least, he is correct. The film thus sides with countercultural fears of, and resistance to, increasing professionalisation, corporatisation and gentrification. Here the film also alludes to *The Towering Inferno*. The TransAmerica Pyramid lurks ominously in the background, at times even imposing its peculiarly modernist façade into scenes of dialogue, suggesting that it now rules the city. Sitting on the same site as the fictional, flammable Glass Tower, the Pyramid attracted waves of opprobrium, both from architectural critics and residents, the latter being particularly aggrieved at its corruption of the existing skyline, and beneath this, its suggestive relationship with the corporatising city.[12]

A more recent major 'skyscraper' movie set in San Francisco, *San Andreas* (Brad Peyton, 2015), echoes the heteronormative and homophobic leanings of the vast array of Hollywood depictions of the city. The film's anti-geological and anti-geographical manipulation of the San Andreas Fault presents San Francisco under threat from a massive tidal wave. It also provides the improbably muscular helicopter pilot Ray Gaines (Dwayne 'The Rock' Johnson) the opportunity he needs to reunify the nuclear family, merely at the cost of vast swathes of California, including San Francisco's entirety and much of the lowlands that previously surrounded the Bay. Notwithstanding Johnson's Samoan heritage, *San Andreas* is extremely white. Equally important, the nearest the film comes to acknowledging the city's gay population is in its casting of the Australian actor Kylie Minogue (who has a large gay following courtesy of her pop music career) as an odious businesswoman who gets her comeuppance early on. This erasure is compounded by the film's final scene, where, after resurrecting his daughter, Gaines brings his family to gather with the other survivors on a Marin County bluff that overlooks the inundated city. Here, in the bucolic headlands that represent the state of nature (metaphorically, the way things ought to be), heterosexual couples reunite, heterosexual families meet to discuss their future and the American flag unfurls over the ruined Golden Gate Bridge, prompting Gaines to harden his lantern jaw and dedicate himself to a rebuilding effort. Suitably cleansed of its gay population and any remnants of the counterculture – the tidal water here acts literally and metaphorically to wash away alternative San Francisco – the Bay Area is now safe for hetero reclamation.

The Bay Area's identity as a region uniquely susceptible to existential threats to humanity reached its apogee in two 1980s blockbusters. The fourth *Star Trek* film, *The Voyage Home*, has Captain Kirk and his crew improbably time-travel from the twenty-third century to 1986 to rescue two whales whose song will even more improbably save the twenty-third-century Earth from destruction. The Bay Area's Cetacean Institute in Sausalito houses the only remaining whales in captivity, leading it to become the location where humanity is saved, thanks to the Enterprise crew's resourcefulness and willingness to share twenty-third-century medicine and technology with the 'extremely

Figure 3.1 'The Rock' reunites the American family, after the Pacific Ocean destroys much of San Francisco. (Cropped screenshot, 1h50m).

primitive and paranoid culture' they find in Cold War America.[13] The engineer Scotty imparts his knowledge of the chemical composition of metals and plastics to a local company to help construct the fish tanks that will house the whales as they are transported to the future. This averts disaster and sends at least one San Francisco engineering firm on the road to prosperity. Just as important, it sets the Bay Area on course to become the location for Starfleet, the headquarters of *Star Trek*'s enlightened liberal intergalactic democracy.

One year earlier, the indomitable British secret agent James Bond rescued the world from a rogue former KGB agent who was masquerading as a French anti-communist industrialist. Hoping to accelerate the monopoly tendency in capitalism, Max Zorin plans to destroy Silicon Valley, which will enable him to control the world's supply of microchips. Using his obscene wealth, this evil genius buys off California's oil and gas regulators and has the state geologist sacked for expressing concerns about his flooding of wells near the Hayward Fault. Fortunately for the Silicon Valley capitalists, Bond discovers and disrupts Zorin's plan before despatching the villain, a conclusion that prompts a few ironic comments from the KGB's top operative. He chuckles at the Kremlin's relief at the foiling of Zorin's plan, amusedly noting that Soviet technology – normally used to challenge American hegemony – is itself reliant upon Silicon Valley's products. The film thus hints at Silicon Valley's willingness to supply product to whoever pays the asking price, irrespective of their politics or their relationship with American government policy. Disaster averted, British intelligence then seeks to locate its missing agent. Its surveillance technology, however, merely discovers that Bond's heteronormative priapism has won the day yet again.

While not ostensibly 'about' the Bay Area, these two films confirm the region's position at the inflection point leading to our digital future. Uniting the twin themes of many San Francisco films of crime and disaster, they confirm the city as a location uniquely vulnerable to both (*The Voyage Home* is unusual in presenting the destruction of the natural world as a human crime) but also as the location for humanity's renewal. This encapsulates the message that unites many of these films: San Francisco might host some of America's worst problems – gambling, drinking, debauchery, excessive displays of sexuality, and the mere presence of poor people – but it also develops the solution to many of these problems, even though this might involve a cleansing process. Whether the cleansing comes from natural disasters, hubristic city planning or even the hands or gun of a vigilante warrior, the city is always on the edge of a new era but equally always bound to its legend. Deeper still, Bond and the Enterprise bring together the other precursors to Silicon Valley cinema, offering a mild critique of free-market capitalism while accepting that the immediate future might belong to those best placed to exploit technology for their own purposes, whether this be through the weapons technology reinforcing the Cold War or the surveillance cameras that follow Bond to the bed he shares with another of his sexual partners.

Across the Bay

The whiteness of these films suggest that the San Francisco Bay Area is more racially homogenous than the reality. They thus deemphasise the importance of the crises that erupted in the twentieth century that directly affected the area's ethnic minority populations, such as the attempt to bar Japanese and Korean children from San Francisco's public schools in 1906, and the displacement of the poor and ethnic minorities in the 1960s and 1970s through the so-called modernisation of the city centre.[14] A similar form of displacement accelerated during the dot-com booms as venture capital money poured into the bank accounts of white software engineers and tech entrepreneurs. This nouveau riche lavished its wealth on real estate, implicitly encouraging landlords to evict lower-paying, often minority tenants in order to maximise its rental income.[15] The impact of this process on the social fabric of the Bay Area underpins the plots of a number of films that focus on the forgotten residents of the Bay

Area. Significantly, many of these films situate themselves across the Bay, reinforcing the sense that San Francisco has been bleached by successive waves of white interlopers.

Picking up on a mid-film discussion of the impact of gentrification and the potential end of rent controls on regular San Franciscans in *Medicine for Melancholy* (Barry Jenkins, 2008), *The Last Black Man in San Francisco* (Joe Talbot, 2019) is a howl of rage against gentrification and a lament for a disappearing San Francisco as experienced by the city's Black population. Where *Pacific Heights* (John Schlesinger, 1990) references tenants' rights and San Francisco real-estate issues in service of a thriller, *The Last Black Man* renders the bleaching of the city a human tragedy. Here, African American families who once lived in the Fillmore district find themselves packed into small, low-quality housing in Bayview-Hunters Point in southeast San Francisco. A deceitful white real-estate agent (pointedly surnamed Newsom in a nod to the state's governor, thus calling attention to the baleful influence of state-level politics on the city) initially gives local resident Jimmie Fails hope that he might be able to reclaim the Fillmore house he believes was built by his grandfather, but sets about placing it on the market, prompting Fails's final exclusion from the city he once called home. Soon before his departure, Fails sits on a bus and overhears two young white women bemoaning the city's lack of soul. 'I came here for Janis [Joplin] and the [Jefferson] Airplane, not to work in a fucking startup,' one whines, oblivious to the simple fact that such startups are both the reason why she is in San Francisco and why the city's famed counterculture has died.[16] Sternly but compassionately, if enigmatically, Fails retorts that only those people who really love the city are allowed to hate it, prompting one of the women to dismiss his 'MUNI shit' – referring to the sort of talk only heard on the city's public transport system – as unworthy of serious consideration. The racial politics of this scene cannot be overestimated. Habitual users of municipal transport like Jimmy mean nothing to the 'new' San Francisco. What's more, the women's understanding of 'soul' is fundamentally white: the first complainant wants to see Janis Joplin and the all-white Airplane, not their multiracial peers, Sly and the Family Stone or Santana, let alone any contemporary bands. Their dismissal of Fails as 'MUNI shit' underscores their racialised and class-driven view of the world: they cannot wait to earn enough money to avoid mixing with working-class whites or any peoples of colour. *Blindspotting* (Carlos López Estrada, 2018) and *All Day and a Night* (Joe Robert Cole, 2020) take this one stage further by locating themselves purely in Oakland: life in the city over the Bay does not even register as a possibility for the East Bay's African American residents.

Opportunity is similarly out of reach for Cash Green in *Sorry to Bother You* (Boots Riley, 2018). He has been forced into living in his uncle's Oakland garage and learns that the telephone marketing company he works for fronts a more sinister project to enslave factory workers. The company's CEO, Steve Lift (played by Armie Hammer, familiar to viewers of *The Social Network*) throws parties at which he subjects scantily clad women to his tech-bro banter. At one, he goads Green into performing a rap at a party (because he assumes that all Black men can rap). The white crowd responds enthusiastically to Green's desperate reversion to the n-word, chanting it back to him before celebrating their own identification with Green's performance of a Blackness that conforms to their racist preconceptions. Lift later hoodwinks Green into ingesting a drug that transforms him into an 'equisapien', a half-man, half-horse who will be a more efficient and obedient worker. Green's attempts to warn the country about this nefarious plan initially results in Lift's company reaching new heights of profitability before Green and his trade union comrades foment an equisapien uprising.

Meanwhile, Ryan Coogler's lightly fictionalised reconstruction of the last day of Oscar Grant, *Fruitvale Station* (2013), also highlights the sense that San Francisco only welcomes people of colour provided they enter the city to serve their white overlords. In a key scene, Grant helps a pregnant white woman access a toilet in the city on New Year's Eve. As she relieves herself, her white fiancé reveals to Grant that he runs a tech startup but previously committed credit card fraud to raise funds for a wedding ring. As the film scholar Amy Corbin observes, this brief interaction highlights the relationship between race, crime and space in the twenty-first century. While the white tech worker's life opportunities seem unaffected by his previous crime, Grant's is haunted by his status as an African American ex-con, tragically so when a fellow former inmate recognises him on the Bay Area Rapid Transport and initiates a fight. This fight leads to transit officers racially profiling him, abusing and ultimately killing him while white passengers look on, some filming the event on their smartphones.[17] Grant's brief experience of San Francisco reinforces the sense that whites occupy the city with ease, while Black people may only visit fleetingly. Moreover, his fate reveals the extent to which racism dominates law enforcement in the Bay Area. His body is symbolically out of place in San Francisco, but even his return to Oakland is fraught with life-threatening danger. Whites, meanwhile, travel freely and safely, while their ownership of the means of surveillance ensures a permanent record of the crime. This ambivalent conclusion that credits Silicon Valley technology's ability to transform spectators into active agents while indicting Silicon Valley for creating this racist geography encapsulates the critique encoded in these films. All point to the social impact of successive twenty-first-century dot-com booms on those excluded from its bounties, whether that be in terms of housing exclusion, low-paid jobs, brutal policing or even the cultural and racial assumptions carried by privileged whites.

As the use of CCTV footage in *Fruitvale Station* suggests, the Bay Area's residents now live under permanent surveillance, if not from official sources such as security cameras then from the mobile telephones that almost everybody carries with them as they traverse the region. In highlighting the permanence of surveillance technology, the film – like so many other films about the Bay Area – calls back to a key theme of perhaps the quintessential San Francisco film of the post-1960s period. Harry Caul, an early 1970s wiretapping expert, spends *The Conversation* attempting to resolve a mystery encoded in a recording of a couple talking in Union Square that a shadowy figure from an unnamed corporation commissioned him to make. His inquiries draw him into a conspiracy that leads to him being surveilled himself, while his gradual realisation of the gulf between his suspicions, the evidence he gathers, and the actual conspiracy at the mystery's heart leads to his personal disintegration. The mystery revolves around one sentence that Caul records, and even more specifically around the emphasis given to two words in that sentence. Here the film highlights the problem encoded in any system of surveillance: can we really know what people mean when we record what they say or do, and to what extent are our conclusions actually evidence of our own expectations of the recording's content?[18]

Caul is haunted by a previous job when his services led to the murder of an innocent accountant and his family. This accountant worked for a Teamsters president; Caul's surveillance revealed that the two created an illegal welfare fund, and the discovery of the crime led the Teamster to conclude erroneously that his accountant had leaked the information. As this suggests, *The Conversation* is suffused with the tension between unionism and post-Fordist corporatism, as reflected in the mysterious entity that employs Caul to record the titular event. That a film about a subcontractor was made by a production company that was itself a subcontractor, and one that did not recognise trade unions – much like its Silicon Valley successors – is highly significant.[19] Both the film and Caul are thus enmeshed in the corporate transformation of San Francisco referenced in *Invasion of the Body Snatchers* and *The Towering Inferno*, and that presaged a further transformation of the city during the dot-com booms. *The Conversation* thus becomes both postmodern and neoliberal, simultaneously about such a world and a product of that same world. Moreover, its position within the industry blunts its critique of neoliberal praxis, much like Caul's initial indifference towards the content of the recording: 'I don't care what they're talking about. All I want is a nice, fat recording.'[20] As such, the film raises the issue of privacy and the gathering of private data in supposedly public places, thus simultaneously harkening back to *Walk A Crooked Mile*'s observations about the ease of such surveillance, while also anticipating debates that were later to roil over the way in which Silicon Valley social media companies such as Facebook effectively spy on private individuals through collection of their data. While Facebook – like Caul – does not ostensibly care what its users are talking about, it monetises the data it collects – again, like Caul – by packaging it and selling it to third parties. Notably, Caul himself has bugging devices unwittingly embedded on his body when he attends a surveillance expo. This scene was covertly filmed at a real convention for wiretappers, thus adding an extra layer of surveillance intrigue to the film while citing the 1970s boom in the surveillance industry, a development that was closely linked, both geographically and technologically, to Silicon Valley. Thus the film ultimately suggests that if even the hyper-cautious Harry Caul cannot avoid it, corporate surveillance will likely envelop us all.[21]

Like many San Francisco films, *The Conversation* directly and obliquely references the city's modernisation. Eschewing clichéd locations such as the Golden Gate Bridge, it presents the city as an alienating, claustrophobic place (a sense heightened by its 1:1.85 aspect ratio) dominated by impersonal concrete buildings and glass frontages that reflect the outside rather than inviting viewers to observe the interior.[22] This corporate invasion effectively absorbs even the public space of Union Square, enabling, in the film scholar Lawrence Webb's words, 'unchecked corporate-bureaucratic power [to] threaten . . . the sovereignty of the individual' while thematically linking films noir to the technological surveillance thriller and presenting the modernist city gradually ceding to postmodernity.[23] As such, the film suggests that corporate capitalism is eroding San Francisco's distinctiveness, rendering the city a generic dehumanised space that lacks individualism, joy and community spirit.[24] This dehumanisation is made clear right at the film's start, when audiences first hear the alienating, unrecognisable, electronically distorted voices in the recording of the conversation, a soundtrack device that recurs in *Invasion of the Body Snatcher*'s gradual replacement of natural sounds with electronic noise as the pod invasion spreads.

Meanwhile, Caul's job gradually destroys his individualism, demanding not only his time but his psyche too. Like many future Silicon Valley entrepreneurs, he lives in a sparsely furnished Western Addition apartment (an area of the city then undergoing redevelopment), works in a highly secure former warehouse surrounded by gadgetry, and devotes little attention to the community around him.[25] As troublingly, so immersed is he in the technical demands of his project that he only belatedly realises that his fascination with using technology to solve the problem of the recording has prevented him seeing the wider (moral) picture: a useful foretaste of the Silicon Valley software engineers' technology solutionism. This inattention to moral concerns is highlighted early in the film when Caul retreats to his van to assess the first results of the surveillance. Behind the van's mirrored windows, Caul and one of his associates surveil two women using the windows as mirrors while they beautify themselves.

Here the film references the notion that humans will change their behaviour if they know that they are being watched, for neither women would wish to offer their voyeurs an opportunity to (enjoy) watch(ing) them. Thus, while the film's viewers are drawn into a plot

Figure 3.2   We watch Caul and his colleague leer over two unwitting victims of their surveillance. (Cropped screenshot, 6m).

that revolves around Caul's technical mastery revealing the difficulty of uncovering the 'truth' about anything, they must remember that Caul himself is an unreliable, morally compromised cipher. Here, the many worlds that inform Silicon Valley cinema collide: the unreliable, masculine figures at its core; the world of work overrunning the lives of those who work at technology's cutting edge; the potential for their work to bring ruin and destruction to all; and their lack of concern for those who unwittingly live in their world.

Notes

1. Rich, *San Francisco Noir*, 1.
2. Dimendberg, *Film Noir and the Spaces of Modernity*, 13.
3. Street, '*Dirty Harry*'s San Francisco', 2.
4. Dimendberg, *Film Noir*, 17–18; Rich, *San Francisco Noir*, 21–2. The film used stock footage for its establishing shots with the rest filmed on sets and lots in Hollywood.
5. *Walk A Crooked Mile*, 8m.
6. Street, *Dirty Harry's America*, 66–139.
7. Keane, *Disaster Movies*, 9–10.
8. Quoted in McKinnon, 'Straight Disasters', 510.
9. McKinnon, 'Straight Disasters', 510.
10. David Weiner, 'Why *Invasion of the Body Snatchers* Still Haunts its Director', *Hollywood Reporter*, December 20, 2018, <https://www.hollywoodreporter.com/movies/movie-news/invasion-body-snatchers-ending-still-haunts-director-1170220> (consulted June 28, 2022); Charles A. Krause, 'Guyanese Panel Rules All but 2 Were Murdered', *Washington Post*, December 23, 1978, A1. The *San Francisco Chronicle* reviewed the film on the same day that it reported on a Grand Jury inquest into Jones's finances. Marshall Kilduff, 'Ex-Temple Aide Buford Talks to U.S. Grand Jury in S.F.', *San Francisco Chronicle*, December 21, 1978; John L. Wasserman, 'Superb Suspense in *Body Snatchers*', ibid., 45.
11. *Invasion of the Body Snatchers* (Kaufman), 11m, 15m, 18m.
12. John King, 'Pyramid's Steep Path from Civil Eyesore to Icon', *SFGate*, December 27, 2009, <https://www.sfgate.com/news/article/Pyramid-s-steep-path-from-civic-eyesore-to-icon-3277598.php#ixzz2TsY84YFr> (consulted June 28, 2022). That it was owned by the film's production company, United Artists, adds a certain layer of irony to the film's presentation of the new San Francisco. Weiner, 'Why'.
13. James T. Kirk in *Star Trek IV: The Voyage Home*, 35m.
14. Street, *Dirty Harry's America*, 61–2, 79.
15. Rachel Brahinsky, 'The Death of the City?'

16. *The Last Black Man in San Francisco*, 1h46.
17. Amy Corbin, 'A Networked Life: Representations of Connectivity and Structural Inequalities in *Fruitvale Station*', in Andersson and Webb, *The City in American Cinema*, 265–8.
18. Zimmer, *Surveillance Cinema*, 18, 21–3.
19. Webb, *Cinema of Urban Crisis*, 132–4, 144–6; Andriano-Moore, 'The Rise of the Sound Designer', 541–3, 544–5, 546.
20. *The Conversation*, 8m.
21. Webb, *Cinema of Urban Crisis*, 137.
22. Webb, *Cinema of Urban Crisis*, 127–8, 140.
23. Webb, *Cinema of Urban Crisis*, 134; Dimendberg, *Film Noir*, 15; Mennel, *Cities and Cinema*, 39.
24. Webb, *Cinema of Urban Crisis*, 141.
25. Webb, *Cinema of Urban Crisis*, 139.

Part 2
Real Genius

Chapter 4

The Silicon Valley Biopic

The final season of *Silicon Valley* sees the tech entrepreneur Gavin Belson learn that he might lose control of Hooli. In a desperate attempt to stave off his defenestration he offers another trademark, self-aggrandising speech. 'Look,' he declares, 'forget all the bullshit about making the world a better place. The most valuable companies in this valley were built and run by . . . by savages, who cheat to win. Zuckerberg, and Jobs, and me.'[1] Here, Belson highlights not only the centrality of Zuckerberg and Jobs to Silicon Valley's mythology but also that their ruthlessness lies at the heart of their legends. Unsurprisingly, Hollywood also cements them as Silicon Valley icons, although unlike Belson, its films offer a less laudatory view of their subjects' savagery. *The Social Network* (David Fincher, 2010) follows Zuckerberg through his brief studies at Harvard University, where he codes Facebook's predecessor and decides to launch the now ubiquitous social network, before heading to Silicon Valley to follow Facebook's expansion. It presents Zuckerberg as a gifted computer engineer with human failings that ultimately inform his social media behemoth. *Steve Jobs* (Danny Boyle, 2015) focuses intently on three key moments in Jobs's public life: the presentations of the Apple Macintosh 128k in 1984; the NeXT cube computer four years later; and the iMac in 1998. *Jobs* (Joshua Michael Stern, 2013), meanwhile, traces Jobs's life from his Reed College days in the early 1970s to his triumphant return as Apple's Chief Executive Officer in 1996. Both exist in dialogue with *Pirates of Silicon Valley* (Martyn Burke, 1999), a made-for-television movie that acts as a dual biopic of Jobs and Microsoft's Bill Gates, focusing on the tension between the two while tracing their lives from their college dorms to Jobs's 1997 announcement of a collaboration between their two companies. While some of the rickety sets signal *Pirates*' low-budget status, the 1999 Emmy Awards recognised the quality of its casting and writing, indicating that we dismiss it at our peril.[2]

As the film scholar Dennis Bingham argues, classical biopics offer a 'Great Man' theory of history, presenting their subjects as preternaturally talented visionaries who triumphantly overcome the scepticism of their peers. Drawing on his fellow film scholar George Custin, Bingham argues that most biopics present their subjects as Idols of Production who make the world better through the things they produce, be that great art, technological innovation or even industrial development. Highly driven, often to the point of self-possession, these Great Men push past the human limitations of the day to become harbingers of new eras in human history. As this suggests, biopics are often highly gendered and even contain faint echoes of Ayn Rand's insistence that great men should lead society. That it took until the early 2020s for a biopic of a female Silicon Valley icon to emerge – and then one whose career ended in ignominy – is indicative of the genre and the heavily male world of Silicon Valley, both of which reflect the patriarchal nature of the society in which we live.[3]

All three Silicon Valley biopics include some classic biopic genre conventions, including flashbacks to the subject's past, sometimes following an *in medias res* introduction. They highlight tension between their subjects and close friends, show them receiving guidance from a mentor, and feature a sidekick who might operate as a comedic foil, or a 'patient helpmeet-wife', who assists the subject through his travails.[4] At other times, such as in *The Social Network*'s conclusion, they conform to while also updating and undercutting these same conventions. While none are hagiographical, all are hindered by the limitations of the biographical approach. They might highlight the toxic influence of Zuckerberg and Jobs on their companies and the people who worked for them, but the personalised critique of the biopic necessarily de-emphasises the deeper, structural problems pertaining to Silicon Valley and its role in our world. This limits their breadth of analysis, confirming that Hollywood's repulsion at Silicon Valley cannot quite overwhelm its fascination with Silicon Valley's innovative technology. Two elements of the biopic play central roles in this chapter: the films' framing of their subjects and their presentation of the psychological motivations of Jobs and Zuckerberg. In their presentation of these two singular men, the Silicon Valley biopics help define one of the major dialectics of Silicon Valley cinema: the artifice of the constructed self-image of Silicon Valley corporations and individuals versus the similarly constructed depiction of said actors in film.

Background

Written by Aaron Sorkin and directed by David Fincher, *The Social Network* is justifiably the most celebrated of the Silicon Valley biopics. Pathological and often affectless male characters are a central feature of Fincher's films, including Tyler Durden, the monster of the id in *Fight Club* (1999); the killer John Doe and detective David Mills in *Se7en* (1995); and Zuckerberg. As the film scholar J. M. Tyree argues, 'The schemes of Fincher's characters tend towards delusions of grandeur and the establishment of individual conspiracies or even shadow organizations that mimic or undermine American corporate life . . . [:] alternative structures to what's seen by their creators as an oppressive banality.'[5] Garlanded with ecstatic reviews and multiple awards, *The Social Network* reaped nearly $225 million at the box office.[6] Its fractured narrative structure rests on the progress of two real-life lawsuits filed against Zuckerberg. The first of its three timelines depicts depositions in a case brought by Eduardo Saverin, Zuckerberg's former friend and business partner, over the unlawful dilution of his Facebook stock. The second sees two upper-class Harvard students, Cameron and Tyler Winklevoss, and their business partner Divya Narendra, trying to prove that Zuckerberg stole their intellectual property when he launched TheFacebook. The third timeline flashes back to the events described in the two legal cases. *The Social Network* thus engages with a key feature of many classical biopics in the presentation of personal conflict in an open forum such as a courtroom.[7] Of course, twenty-first-century audiences are aware that the truth does not necessarily reveal itself in court. The film also comments on this: the opening scene is immediately challenged when the film cuts to Zuckerberg interjecting at the Saverin deposition, 'that's not what happened', before arguing to Saverin's lawyer that the construction of that scene's events relied solely on his ex-girlfriend Erica Albright's point of view.[8] The film is thus hyper-aware of the relationship between memory and the past, and of the extent to which individuals create their own 'reality distortion field', in which through sheer force of will they reshape the world around them to suit their perspective.[9] It is not, then, about discovering the truth, but a film about the way in which individuals might manipulate the truth for financial gain.

Also written by Sorkin but directed by Danny Boyle, *Steve Jobs* takes the episodic nature of many biopics to an extreme, reinforcing its two key themes – the centrality of technological progression to our world and Steve Jobs's personal development, detailed through his developing relationship with his daughter Lisa – through its own technological choices. The 1984 scenes, where green predominates, were shot on 16mm cameras; blues and reds dominate 1988, which was shot on 35mm; finally, the 1998 scenes were shot on digital, with metallic blues and greys reflecting the growing influence of digital technology on the world.[10] Coupled with the growing audiences and increasingly salubrious locations for Jobs's product announcements, these choices imbue the film with a whiggish suggestion that Apple has led us out of darkness into a glorious present and an even more enlightened future. Essentially a commodity fetishist advert for Apple, then, its structure stands in sharp contrast to the far more traditional biopic, *Jobs*.

The films raise a pertinent question: why does Steve Jobs deserve multiple major biographical feature films and Zuckerberg one before he had even reached the age of thirty? When promoting *Steve Jobs*, Boyle argued that 'San Francisco is the Bethlehem of the second industrial revolution. It's where the extraordinary forces emerged that now rule our lives.'[11] He insisted that the films simply 'have to be made' because of Jobs's (and by extension Zuckerberg's) determination to create 'forces that are more powerful than governments and banks', while being almost wholly uninterested in personal wealth.[12] As Boyle and the films suggest, we live in a world that is at least in part created and dominated by Apple as one of the most recognisable and influential brands of the twenty-first century, and Facebook as the preeminent social media platform of our times. Indeed, as Gavin Belson observed, the two men exemplify certain trends in Silicon Valley's self-mythology and the twenty-first-century American Dream, not to mention the assumption that social change (as embodied by biopic subjects such as Malcolm X or Dr Martin Luther King, Jr) is no longer as significant to society as technological change.

Despite Boyle's assertion, both Zuckerberg and Jobs became rich and renowned at a young age: by the time he was 25, Jobs was running a $1.79 billion company and was worth over $250 million dollars; less than thirty years later, Zuckerberg became a billionaire at the age of 23.[13] Both dropped out of college. The notion that higher education exists merely as a stepping-stone towards entrepreneurship, and that the great tech entrepreneurs need not complete their studies, dominates the stories that Silicon Valley entrepreneurs like to tell themselves. Like Jobs and Zuckerberg, Jack Dorsey of Twitter, Shawn Fanning of Napster and Travis Kalanick of Uber dropped out; meanwhile, Sergey Brin and Larry Page dropped out of their postgraduate programmes and the Napster co-founder Sean Parker did not even attend college.[14] Indeed, Peter Thiel, the Silicon Valley investor and would-be philosopher, argues that 'for many of the brightest people a college education is a cripplingly expensive waste of time that leads nowhere', an attitude that cannot be separated from his personal experience at Stanford University or from the monetisation of higher education in the neoliberal era. Famously, in 2011 Thiel put his money where his mouth was, offering $100,000 fellowships to students who wished to drop out of university and 'build new things' instead. As ever with Thiel, an ideological stance underpinned his action: Thiel Fellows would channel their energies into becoming rich rather than finding out about the world or engaging in activities that would benefit society more widely, thus rendering society more individualist.[15]

Ultimately, while all Facebook and Apple users know that the products were not literally made by the company founders, rare are the people who would not link Steve Jobs with Apple and Zuckerberg with Facebook, such are their presence in their products. So while the film scholar Darragh O'Donoghue wonders aloud whether the biopic is irrelevant as a medium for analysis of such figures, the notion that Facebook is Zuckerberg and Apple is Jobs prompts us to consider whether the wondrous capabilities and intractable fallibilities of Apple and Facebook emerge from their founders' very similar strengths and weaknesses.[16] In a wider sense, however, these biopics underscore the extent to which Western society in the twenty-first century is defined more by the consumer choices that its populations make than the political beliefs they hold.

Framing the Action

The *in medias res* opening of most biopics drops audiences into the middle of the subject's life, often at a key moment that either brings them to prominence or represents best the themes that the biopic will pursue. *Jobs* shares a traditional biopic opening with *Pirates*: *Jobs* has its Jobs, a visibly stooping Ashton Kutcher, introducing the iPod as a 'tool for the heart' at one of his trademark product reveal meetings. Whereas the real Jobs offered the slightly underwhelming statement that it was merely an 'amazing little device', *Jobs* highlights the iPod's emotionality: it is not merely a product on which to listen to music but one that enables a direct link between your brain and your heart.[17] This product, it suggests, can render you a more complete human being, while embodying an emotional connection between you and Apple. Sitting towards the chronological end of the film's narrative, this prologue presents the iPod as the logical culmination of Jobs's lifework. Similarly, to introduce Jobs, *Pirates* uses the filming of Apple's near-legendary '1984' commercial that did more to establish the anti-establishment credentials of the company than any other single event. He instantly breaks the fourth wall to assert that this is more than 'just a film'. Here, the filmic Jobs is already riffing on one of the real Jobs's most famous aphorisms. 'We are here', he says, 'to make a dent in the universe . . . we are creating a completely new consciousness, like an artist or a poet.' The camera pans back to reveal that Jobs is talking to the director of the '1984' advert, as well as *Pirates*' audience. After an excerpt from the advert, it cuts to Jobs announcing Apple's rapprochement with Microsoft in 1997, with a gigantic video image of Gates looming over him, much like the advert's 'Big Brother' figure.[18] The film thus frames Apple as the scrappy upstart battling a sequence of 'big brothers' in IBM, and later, Gates and Microsoft.

Illustrating the confidence of the two prestige biopics, *Steve Jobs* and *The Social Network* dispense with such framings, launching into the chronological start of their narratives, the former through archive footage of Arthur C. Clarke that segues directly into the start of the drama. This late-1960s footage has Clarke predicting that everybody will have a networked computer in their home and that these computers will enrich our lives and untether us from cities. It serves as a playful suggestion that what was once science fiction or even fantastical musings is now fact. Beyond this, it hints that Apple will have a similar impact on humanity to the monoliths of *2001: A Space Odyssey* (Stanley Kubrick, 1968). *The Social Network*'s celebrated opening scene demands further evaluation. It features two of the trademarks that elevate Sorkin and Fincher above their peers: snappy dialogue, pitched at a technical level just above the average cinema viewer's knowledge – high enough that they feel intelligent because they understand most of it, but not so high that it is beyond their reach – low lighting to emphasise mystery, colour filters to emphasise mood. The scene, which Fincher conceptualised as the foundation for Zuckerberg's filmic character, reveals Zuckerberg's intelligence, unwitting sarcasm and complete inability to comprehend another human being's emotional world, before concluding with his now ex-girlfriend's damning judgement that he might think that women will not like him because he is a computer nerd but that, in reality, they will not like him because he is an 'asshole'.[19] It suggests very clearly that Zuckerberg will not develop emotionally as the film progresses.

Viewers first see here *The Social Network*'s striking colour palette, which underpins the film's suggestion that Zuckerberg – for all his faults – is engaged in a pseudo class struggle with representatives of old money. Browns, greens and yellows dominate the bar in which he sits, referencing Cambridge, Massachusetts' and Harvard's age, stability, solidity and the characters' immersion in what might be termed 'legacy' higher education: the classical institutions that upstarts like Zuckerberg intend to disrupt. At its end, as the distressed man-child scuttles back to his dormitory, the brown of Harvard's buildings overshadows the streets. In this scene, and almost throughout, irrespective of the weather, Zuckerberg wears grey or metallic blue hoodies or sweatshirts with flip-flops or open-toed sandals. The prominence of the 'Gap' logo on these clothes again divides him from the besuited Winklevosses (who presumably dress-down in the preppie's choice of Abercrombie & Fitch).[20] This serves a sequence of purposes: on the most obvious level, his clothes echo the blue of Facebook's banner, but semiotically their coldness reflects Zuckerberg's inability to warm to other human beings, while also hinting at the importance of non-human technology to the film.

Even the soundtrack serves to underpin this presentation of Zuckerberg. The White Stripes' slow blues 'Ball and Biscuit' almost overwhelms the opening scene's dialogue. The song's lyrics speak to Zuckerberg's self-possession and belief that, as a (metaphoric) seventh son he has powers of prophecy: he knows that he will one day change the world.[21] While his now ex-girlfriend might at this moment be more worldly, Zuckerberg's assurance suggests that he is beginning to absorb the sense of entitlement, superiority and confidence that Harvard promises its students. It also subtly prefigures Zuckerberg's movie-long, reality-distorting self-deception that Albright will always care about him. As this suggests, the film attributes to Zuckerberg a very male and late-teenage understanding of sexual relationships. His self-absorbed, socially awkward, nerdy and virginal tendencies are reinforced by Jesse Eisenberg's performance. His most famous roles to this date were as shy, awkward, often virginal teens in *Roger Dodger* (Dylan Kidd, 2002), *The Squid and the Whale* (Noah Baumbach, 2005), *Adventureland* (Greg Mottola, 2009) and *Zombieland* (Ruben Fleischer, 2009). Eisenberg's Zuckerberg only fleetingly makes eye contact, rarely smiles, speaks too fast and only seems to come alive when working at his laptop. Eisenberg also affects a slight overbite, reinforcing the sense that Zuckerberg has not yet reached maturity. In case Eisenberg's awkwardness encourages audience sympathy, Andrew Garfield's sensitive portrayal of his former sidekick Saverin lays bare the film's sympathies.

The importance of the opening scene's palette is reinforced throughout the film's first half: as Zuckerberg's alienation from Harvard and interest in Facebook deepens, the natural colours cede to intensifying shades of blue. Two key examples highlight how this subtly, but increasingly bluntly, invades the film: early on, Zuckerberg's campus dormitory room appears to reflect the colours of the rest of Harvard's campus, but gradually it becomes bluer. When Zuckerberg is creating Facebook's predecessor, facemash, the camera pulls back to show Saverin writing an equation on the window. Here the window frame takes on a blue hue, prefiguring Facebook's insinuation into Zuckerberg's life. While viewers would expect the campus computer labs to possess a cold palette, the dorm room at first seems an unexpected place for such colour, but as Facebook increasingly dominates Zuckerberg's mind, blue occupies more of the screen, from his clothes to his bedspread, peaking at the point when TheFacebook goes live, with the dorm room now flooded with a metallic blue-grey. This moment is followed immediately by the film's most obvious use of blue. Divya Narendra sits at a Valentine's Day recital, shiftlessly listening to a corny *a capella* recital of 'I Swear', a 1994 chart hit for the boy band All 4 One (here the film is relatively subtle in suggesting that only out-of-touch students would willingly listen to mass-market music from the previous decade). Contra the song's declaration of undying romantic devotion, Narendra discovers that his date is checking out TheFacebook. He departs at speed, and as he runs across the Charles River, we see him literally shrinking as Facebook's distinctive blue engulfs the sky. As if this was not enough, the following shot reinforces the extent to which Facebook now infects Narendra's and the Winklevosses' lives. The two rowers are training in a large indoor practice tank. The building's windows project Facebook blue inside. While normally surrounded by browns, yellows and Harvard's red, the Winklevosses now row atop putrid green water, reflecting their sickness as they hear that Zuckerberg has apparently stolen their idea for a Harvard-based social network and Facebook's irrevocable dominance of their lives.

The closing scene is, if anything, even more brutal to Zuckerberg than the opening. Here, *The Social Network* riffs on the classical ending to a biopic, established by *Rembrandt* (Alexander Korda, 1936), in which the artist gazes upon himself in the mirror, preparing a self-portrait, and quotes King Solomon in musing 'vanity of vanities, all is vanity'.[22] *The Social Network* has Zuckerberg gazing at an equivalent mirror: his own Facebook profile. He has been told by Marylin, a member of his legal team, that he is probably not an asshole but is 'trying so hard to be', a deceptively complex summation of his character, position in twenty-first-century society, and his personal trajectory since his breakup with Albright, one that demanded he be ruthless and toxic towards those around him.[23] That he previously seemed unaware of this female lawyer despite her constant presence in the depositions adds a further layer to our understanding of his lack of humanity, underscored by her promise to him that, despite her inexperience, she would have a jury hating him within moments of her opening questions. The jury here, is not only theoretical, but the actual one watching the film, inviting the audience to consider how successfully the film has turned them against Zuckerberg, and a piece of self-congratulatory reflexiveness on Sorkin and Fincher's part (look how successfully we have turned the jury against you, Mark!). As Marilyn leaves, Zuckerberg turns to his only friend – his laptop – and sends an 'add friend' message to Erica Albright's Facebook account. Again, Fincher turns to lighting to emphasise the gulf between the two worlds. Elevated from humanity in this sterile skyscraper, Zuckerberg and Marylin face different futures. She heads right, towards the lifts, bathed in a yellow glow, where she will descend to reconnect with real people. He faces left towards a window drenched in Facebook blue while staring intently at his laptop, also beaming Facebook's blue. The skyscraper acts as a metonym for Facebook's alienating effect, echoing *Margin Call*'s critique of the financial wizards who wrecked the economy. As Albright's profile photograph indifferently looks away, Zuckerberg repeatedly clicks the 'refresh' key, longing for a human response. Zuckerberg's vanity enshrouds his loneliness amid his realisation that he might be a billionaire, but he was wrong at the start of the movie to tell her 'I don't want friends'.[24] His invention might have broken away from the past and helped usher in the twenty-first century, but it has come at the expense of any real connection he has with other humans.

Cinema audiences come to expect biopics to build to a crescendo that reveals the subject's greatest success, leading some filmmakers to concoct triumphant conclusions.[25] *Moneyball* (Bennett Miller, 2011), for example, a biopic of the Oakland A's baseball team's general manager, Billy Beane, concentrates on the 2002 season, which ended with the A's losing their first post-season match to the Minnesota Twins. Ignoring this minor-key conclusion, the film instead ends with the A's mid-season twenty-game winning streak, which in the film's narrative proved that Beane's statistical methods could enable financially straightened teams to compete with the very richest. Such moments might not actually be the end of the biopic subject's career – or in the case of the A's, even that baseball season – but they offer a moment

Figure 4.1 Marylin heads back towards humanity while Zuckerberg ponders his reflection in Facebook. (Cropped screenshot, 1h48m).

of catharsis for the audience: the beast slain, the hero at ease, order restored, human progress secured. By contrast, *The Social Network*'s conclusion is very much anti-cathartic.[26] Subtitles reveal that the Winklevoss twins settled for $65 million, Saverin for an unknown amount, and that Zuckerberg became the youngest billionaire in the world. The Beatles' 'Baby You're a Rich Man' booms out undiegetically. Most obviously, the song's opening line questions Zuckerberg's inner state after finding himself rich but alone, caustically undercutting Jordan Belfort's insistence that wealth leads to beauty. The subsequent lines suggest that he might have realised that Facebook did not fill his emotional void before offering him the opportunity to take a different path in the future that we know he will spurn. Beneath this, the song's original appearance as the B-side to 'All You Need Is Love' offers commentary on Zuckerberg's loneliness: the two songs' relationship suggests that material wealth and love are the flip side of each other, that Zuckerberg might trade one for the other should he choose.[27] Zuckerberg's insistent repeat keystrokes on 'refresh' as the song plays suggests that he will continue to desire love but be undeserving of it. Damningly, then, wealth might have rendered him a beautiful person, but he remains unlovable.

Taken together, the Jobs biopics offer more benign conclusions, although none are uncritical. These conclusions are first indicated by their casting choices. Beyond the slight physical resemblance, Ashton Kutcher's screen persona – dominated by knuckleheads or romantic comedy leads – reinforces the film's presentation of Jobs as a dreamy outsider.[28] Michael Fassbender deepens *Steve Jobs*' presentation of Jobs as a man who devotes himself to computer products rather than to people, informed by previous roles as a robot, a brutal slaveowner and even Macbeth himself.[29] *Pirates* has Noah Wyle as Jobs. A major figure in the ensemble cast of *E.R.* (NBC, 1994–2009), then among the top-rated television shows in the US, Wyle played one of the show's most open-hearted characters who insisted on treating his patients with care and compassion. This pervades his Jobs, to the extent that even when he is behaving badly, he appears to have good intentions. Something in his portrayal appealed to Jobs himself, who told Wyle, 'I hated the movie . . . But you were good.'[30] His fondness for Wyle extended to inviting the actor to impersonate him at a 1999 Macworld event, before characteristically interrupting to tell him that he had everything wrong. After some badinage, Wyle departs, but not before citing one of the film's most controversial lines: 'are you still a virgin?'[31] Of course, while such an act might suggest Jobs's humility and willingness to lampoon itself, it also represents his articulation of his own agency: by reminding everybody of the gulf between Wyle's Jobs and himself, he reasserted control over his own image.[32]

Like *The Social Network*, *Jobs* cites *Rembrandt*, having Jobs in a studio recording the voiceover to Apple's famous 'Think Different' campaign, which was in essence an audio-visual self-portrait featuring many of his heroes and a voiceover lauding their – and hence Jobs's – singular genius for thinking differently. At its conclusion, Jobs turns to the camera to ask the engineer and the audience 'how's that?' Like the ad, then, *Jobs* suggests none-too-subtly that Jobs deserves comparison with Einstein, Dr King, Muhammad Ali, Mohandas Gandhi and Picasso. It caps the film's argument that Jobs's return to Apple signified Apple 'not mak[ing] *shit* [products] anymore . . . We're making Apple cool again'.[33] Ambiguity, meanwhile, rears up at the conclusion of *Steve Jobs*. While Jobs has reconciled with his daughter after telling her of his plans for the iPod just before the public reveal of the iMac – the product that truly reinvigorated Apple – the audience has also witnessed a final (fictional) conversation with Steve Wozniak, who laments:

> When people used to ask me what the difference was between me and Steve Jobs, I'd say Steve was the big picture guy and I liked a solid workbench. When people ask me what the difference is now, I say Steve's an asshole. Your products are better than you are, brother.[34]

'That's the idea, *brother*' snaps Jobs acidly in return. Best known for a sequence of amiably daffy underachievers in various comedies, the comic actor Seth Rogen plays Wozniak against type, as Banquo's

Ghost, doomed to remind Jobs repeatedly of the Apple II's unacknowledged importance to the company. His interactions with Jobs ask the audience to ponder the Apple gadgets that it loves so much and the unpleasantness of the man who insists that they were his creation. Thus, Wozniak's repeated entreaties to Jobs about publicly acknowledging the engineers who created the Apple II, and who were later released by the company because they were not considered essential workers, are also a call to the audience to reconsider whether it is prepared to be complicit in Apple's poor employment practices in return for possessing beautifully designed products. This is a theme that ultimately forces Joanna Hoffman, Apple's marketing guru and famously the only person who could bend Jobs to their will, to tell him to make peace with his daughter or face losing Hoffman to another company. As the interface between Jobs and the humans around him, Kate Winslet's Hoffman is the only fully realised female character in the biopics, which stands as a reasonably accurate portrayal of the lack of women at the top of many Silicon Valley corporations. While Jobs is beastly towards just about everybody he encounters, Hoffman either manages to convince him of his errors, smooth things over with the offended party, or facilitate negotiation. Yet that each moment of (private) doubt is followed by one of (public) adulation and triumph lends an ambiguity to the film that remains unresolved even at its conclusion.

The films thus elide a key message embedded in *Pirates*, which concludes with Jobs's ousting at Apple executive John Sculley's behest, an event that the film suggests enables Jobs to reconcile with his daughter, while Wozniak's departure from Apple enables him to find happiness and meaning in his life through teaching children about computers. Beyond this, *Pirates* engages much more directly with the realities of capitalism's hard-headedness, suggesting that Jobs fatally misunderstood the nature of Apple: that as a corporate entity it valued profit above all else. *Jobs* and *Steve Jobs*, by contrast, present Jobs as a singular genius and an idol of production, leading us into his bright, shiny future freed from the constraints placed upon him by Apple's board and his prior refusal to acknowledge his daughter. If a critique of capitalism exists in them, it comes in the form of Jobs's statement in *Jobs* that 'boards don't run companies, the people who create the product run the company', and his insistence in *Steve Jobs* that 'artists lead and [boardroom] hacks ask for a show of hands'.[35] Here the films rely on an anti-corporate position, decrying the obsession of directors of publicly traded companies with profit/loss sheets and shareholder dividends. This, they suggest, stymied Apple in its doldrums. The returning hero, in forcing the company to shed itself of such bean counters, freed the company from its conservatism, caution and failures. If there is a political message undergirding these films, then, it comes in a quasi-Randian honouring of the genius entrepreneur: Jobs as John Galt or Howard Roark, battling conventional thinking, confounding the establishment, refusing to suffer fools gladly and ultimately triumphing on his own, selfish, terms. Zuckerberg, meanwhile, remains wedded to his laptop, plaintively requesting Erica Albright's forgiveness while his company gobbles up the attention of a quarter of the world's population.

Psychological Motivations

Zuckerberg's and Jobs's very human failings and the way in which they find expression through 'their' products lie at each film's core. Thus, Jobs's tortured relationship with his daughter offers fuel both for his obsession with Apple's products at the expense of his human relationships, and eventually for his reconciliation with humanity. The Apple Mac and the NeXT might have failed in the marketplace, but *Steve Jobs* presents these products as staging posts towards the iMac that were too advanced for their time: only in retrospect does their importance become clear – the Mac in making computers fun and engaging, the NeXT in carrying the operating system that underpinned the next generation of Apple computers. This, of course, returns to the central question posed by the idol of production biopic, which normally presents its subject as a visionary who improved society through the things they (or the companies they led) created. *Jobs* and *Steve Jobs* add a celebrity element through Jobs's famed product launches, at which the idol of production also appears as an idol of consumption (in this sense, an entertainer), and where he experiences a form of love – or more accurately, idolatry – that eludes him in his private life.[36] These performances offer continuity to the films, thus indicating their fundamental modernity (since a postmodern biopic would resist the temptation to impose continuity on Jobs's life). Jobs himself, therefore, might be approached as a modernist postmodernist, who wants people to appreciate the supposedly unique characteristics of mass-produced products that, almost paradoxically, are designed to express the postmodern consumer's uniqueness.

Relatedly, *Jobs* highlights a core element of the celebrity biopic, which in the words of film scholar Glenn Smith, renders the individual 'a marketable symbol of the American Dream'.[37] It spends considerable time outlining Jobs's struggles at college and in Apple's early days, as if to stress Jobs's humble beginnings before presenting him driving expensive cars and concluding with onscreen text detailing Apple's 2012 dollar valuation. *Steve Jobs* might insist that its subject was primarily concerned with producing art (as opposed to engaging in commerce). Yet its nods to Jobs's vast wealth and the fortunes amassed by key Apple workers between 1984 and 1998, not to mention the mere fact that the film revolves around the launch of consumer products, indicates the extent to which Jobs embodied the American (entrepreneurial) Dream. He might have protested about his countercultural roots, apparent disinterest in material possessions and fondness for Zen Buddhism, but he was no altruist. In reality, he was little different to twentieth-century industrialists in his accumulation of great wealth courtesy of the labour of other people.

By contrast, *The Social Network* uses Zuckerberg's teenage immaturity and software-engineer mindset (defined by the journalist Rana Foroohar as a focus on getting from point A to point C in the most efficient manner possible, without considering the 'collateral effects of bypassing point B') to encourage audiences to develop a critical view of Facebook.[38] For example, Zuckerberg cheats in his assessment for a Postwar American Art class by setting up a sock-puppet Facebook account, uploading images of the art he is supposed to analyse and inviting others to comment, passing off their opinions as his own in the exam.[39] The insinuation that he was prepared to claim other people's ideas as his own underpins the Winklevosses' legal case. As important, however, it demonstrates that, while Zuckerberg is without doubt an excellent hacker, he is indifferent to copyright and proper academic conduct. As Katherine Losse points out, his disinterest in the humanities perspective on the world led him to consider even simple questions about subjects outside computer science as problems to be solved using computer science methods: in this case, it was a more efficient use of his time to write some code to access other people's opinions than it was to think about the art himself. This understanding of one of Facebook's fundamental approaches continues to operate years after the film was released. The process that emerges after every problem inherent in Facebook comes to light is now standard. The company protests that it was not aware of the problem because it did not foresee the problem becoming an issue; it promises to solve the problem via algorithm and concludes that it will do better next time, as if it was an undergraduate student accused of poor academic practice.[40] At a more personal level, for *The Social Network*'s Zuckerberg, coding Facebook became the outlet that promised to restore his bruised ego, relieve his loneliness and solve any problems created by his previous behaviour.

As this suggests, there remains a sense that the biopic subject is ultimately unknowable. Ashton Kutcher admitted that, despite his best efforts at impersonation, he did not understand Jobs. 'I don't know if anyone ever fully did,' he mused, before arguing that Jobs was an 'asshole' because he was 'really gifted' and knew that he could on occasion get away with his dreadful behaviour because of his drive to create great Apple products.[41] Similarly, when *Pirates*' Jobs refuses to pay Arlene (based on the real-life Chrisann Brennan) the money she deserves as Lisa's mother, he is asked what this is all about. Jobs answers: 'I don't know'.[42] His biopics consequently overlook the extent to which his failings impacted on Apple in a wider sense. Thus we might see him refusing to grant Daniel Kottke Apple stock when the company goes public but not his inattention to Apple's exploitation of its workforce beyond his insistence that his employees work harder.[43] Nor do the films truly consider how and why he was able to 'terrorize a whole company' rather than build one that reflected the values of the 1960s counterculture that he frequently cited as a key influence on his life.[44] Consequently, the films fall back on a Horatio Alger-style lauding of hard work alongside their insistence that Jobs's genius and mercurial nature lie behind Apple's importance in our culture.

As the above suggests, then, Jobs's biopics lead their viewers away from a thorough critique of Apple's impact on society and instead present Jobs as the conduit between Apple's technology and the human world. Of them, *Steve Jobs* possesses the most interest vis-à-vis the biopic genre, through its distillation of the episodic structure to its very essence. *The Social Network*, by contrast, offers a far more complex engagement with genre, at times relying on biopic expectations and at others pushing them nearly to breaking point. Its relationship with courtroom dramas is similarly provocative, forcing viewers to remember that 'truth' is a very slippery concept and that corporate law is itself more about greed than justice. There are no heroes in Facebook's foundational myth: the battle is essentially between the inheritors of obscene wealth and the rapacious hoarders of new wealth in the internet age. Yet we must question why it matters that Jobs has reconciled with Lisa while Erica Albright remains Zuckerberg's unfriend. Why does it matter that Jobs is an idol both of production and consumption, while Zuckerberg is merely a rich man with no friends? Why should we care that both attempted to fill the emotional void in their hearts with consumer products? Here is where the Silicon Valley biopics are doomed to fail. In producing such entertainments they reify the connections between the two men and their corporations, reinforcing the sense that Apple equals Jobs and Facebook equals Zuckerberg, and more broadly that the individual is the key driving force in human history. No matter how devastating their conclusions about their subjects might be, in personalising and individualising Apple and Facebook, the Silicon Valley biopics cannot help but valorise the role of the Randian individual.

Notes

1. 'Hooli Smokes!', *Silicon Valley* series 6 episode 3, 25m (approx.).
2. 'Pirates of Silicon Valley'. According to its director, *Pirates* had a budget of $15 million. Dormehl, 'How a '90s TV Movie Became the Steve Jobs Film to Beat'; *Box Office Mojo* reports a $12m budget for *Jobs*, compared with $30m for *Steve Jobs* and $40m for *The Social Network*: '*Jobs*'; '*Steve Jobs*'; '*The Social Network*'.
3. Bingham, *Whose Lives Are They Anyway?*, 6–7, 52–3, 66, 213. At the time of writing, a biopic of the disgraced Theranos founder Elizabeth Holmes is in production, following the streaming television series *The Dropout* (Disney, 2022), also based on Holmes's career. Brent Lang, 'Apple, Adam McKay, Jennifer Lawrence Team on Elizabeth Holmes Movie "Bad Blood"', *Variety*, December 7, 2021, <https://variety.com/2021/film/news/jennifer-lawrence-elizabeth-holmes-apple-adam-mckay-1235128044> (consulted June 28, 2022).
4. Bingham, *Whose Lives*, 4–5.
5. Tyree, 'The Dislike Button', 46.
6. '*The Social Network*', *Box Office Mojo*.
7. Bingham, *Whose Lives*, 63.
8. *The Social Network*, 15m.
9. Isaacson, *Steve*, 118–19, 454.
10. Kristopher Tapley, 'Cameras Catch the Three Faces of "Steve Jobs"', *Variety*, October 6, 2015, <https://variety.com/2015/artisans/awards/jobs-16-35mm-digital-danny-boyle-alwin-kuchler-1201603004/#!> (consulted June 28, 2022).
11. Catherine Shoard, 'Danny Boyle on Steve Jobs: Movies Must Be Made About Powerful Men', *The Guardian*, September 6, 2015, <https://www.theguardian.com/film/2015/sep/06/steve-jobs-movie-danny-boyle-kate-winslet-seth-rogen-aaron-sorkin> (consulted June 28, 2022).
12. Shoard, 'Danny Boyle'.
13. Isaacson, *Steve*, 102–3; Butcher, *Accidental Millionaire*, 133; Greenburg, 'Youngest Billionaires'.
14. Jessica Guynn, 'Log on, Drop out, Cash in', *SFGate*, December 3, 2006, <https://www.sfgate.com/business/article/Log-on-drop-out-cash-in-These-top-techies-2483834.php> (consulted October 7, 2022);

Puchko, '11 Facts About Napster'; Kapp, 'Male Coders Who Drop out of College are Heroes in Silicon Valley'.
15. Chafkin, *The Contrarian*, 15–22, 160–1; Mick Brown, 'Peter Thiel: The Billionaire Tech Entrepreneur on a Mission to Cheat Death', *The Daily Telegraph*, September 20, 2014; 'Thiel Fellowship'.
16. O'Donoghue, 'Steve Jobs: The Man in the Machine/ Steve Jobs', 48.
17. *Jobs*, 1m; 'Apple – Steve Jobs introduces the iPod – 2001'.
18. *Pirates of Silicon Valley*, 0m.
19. David Fincher, audio commentary, 0m, *The Social Network* DVD.
20. Sorkin's script introduces them as 'identical twins who stepped out of an ad for Abercrombie & Fitch'. Sorkin, 'The Social Network screenplay', 24.
21. The White Stripes, 'Ball and Biscuit', *Elephant* (2003).
22. Bingham, *Whose Lives*, 47–9; *Rembrandt* 1h22m.
23. *The Social Network* 1h48m.
24. *The Social Network*, 4m.
25. Bingham, *Whose Lives*, 46.
26. Bingham, *Whose Lives*, 63
27. The Beatles, 'All You Need Is Love'/ 'Baby You're a Rich Man' (Parlophone, 1967).
28. For example: *Just Married* (Shawn Levy, 2003); *My Boss's Daughter* (David Zucker, 2003); *A Lot Like Love* (Nigel Cole, 2005); *Dude, Where's My Car* (Danny Leiner, 2000); *That '70s Show* (Fox, 1998–2006).
29. *Prometheus* (Ridley Scott, 2012); *12 Years A Slave* (Steve McQueen, 2013); *Macbeth* (Justin Kurzel, 2015).
30. 'Noah Wyle on Playing Steve Jobs'.
31. 'Macworld NY 1999-Noah Wyle imitating Steve Jobs'.
32. Segall, 'Steve Jobs and Noah Wyle's Moment of Truth'.
33. Isaacson, *Steve*, 328–32; *Jobs*, 1h48m.
34. *Steve Jobs*, 1h36m.
35. *Jobs*, 1h28m; *Steve Jobs*, 1h05.
36. Bingham, *Whose Lives*, 6, 52–3, 133.
37. Glenn Smith, 'Love as Redemption', 223.
38. Foroohar, *Don't Be Evil*, 41.
39. *The Social Network*, 1h11m. In reality, he set up a separate website for this purpose. Kirkpatrick, *Facebook Effect*, 25–6.
40. See, for example, Warofka 'An Independent Assessment of the Human Rights Impact of Facebook in Myanmar'.
41. Charlie McCollum, 'Ashton Kutcher, Steve Jobs and the Making of *Jobs*', *San Jose Mercury News*, August 9, 2013, <https://www.mercurynews.com/2013/08/09/ashton-kutcher-steve-jobs-and-the-making-of-jobs> (consulted June 28, 2022).
42. *Pirates*, 1h19.
43. *Jobs*, 56m; *Pirates*, 56m: an interesting coincidence.
44. Deutschman, 'The Once and Future Jobs' (quote); Isaacson, *Steve Jobs*, 58–9, 104–5, 107, 331.

Chapter 5

Constructing the Silicon Valley Icon

As Bingham observes and as the previous chapter suggests, biopics are 'supposed to have a basis in reality' but like many historical films often display a flexible approach to past events.[1] The film critic A. O. Scott goes further, arguing that biopics are allegorical: 'narrative vessels into which meanings and morals are packed ... modern, secular equivalents of the medieval lives of the saints; cautionary tales and beacons of aspiration.'[2] Biopics might deviate from the historical record for numerous reasons: Ava DuVernay's *Selma* (2014), for example, did not include any of Dr Martin Luther King, Jr's speeches, and to heighten the drama, constructed a very different President Lyndon Baines Johnson from the real man.[3] Such departures from the historical record might irritate historians or the people whose lives appear on screen. Yet this is not as problematic as it might first appear. Elisions, adjustments and fabrications often point to wider emotional, political, social or cultural truths. So, Dr King might not have uttered the precise words we hear in *Selma*, but we understand the key themes of the speeches he gives during the film's depiction of the titular civil rights campaign. Moreover, the historical record is not necessarily consistent. Ben Mezrich's *The Accidental Billionaires* and the closest Facebook has to an official historian, David Kirkpatrick, agree on Mark Zuckerberg's bluntness and poor social skills, but Kirkpatrick – who thought *The Social Network* 'horrifically unfair' – rejects Mezrich's suggestion that this interfered with Zuckerberg's ability to find a girlfriend.[4]

The point here is not to dwell upon the differences between the film and the past (not least because that would be to ignore the gulf between Mezrich's account and other accounts of Facebook's foundational years, for example, or to concur with the business journalist Joe Nocera's banal conclusion that *Steve Jobs* is a work of fiction) but instead to think about the way each film shapes emotional truths about Zuckerberg and Jobs.[5] As important, this hints at the malleability of history and the postmodern condition where the absence of absolute truths invites multiple interpretations to jostle with each other for supremacy. The problem here lies in cinema's reach. Even a so-called 'flop' will likely reach an audience far greater than any professional historian could dream of, and so will exert greater influence over the popular reception of its subject; indeed as Steve Jobs's colleague Bill Campbell warned of Boyle's biopic: 'A whole generation is going to think of him in a different way if they see a movie that depicts him in a negative way.'[6] Consequently, any analysis of the biopic must always be aware of the power of the representational approach to its subjects and the ways in which the films 'invent creatively' to mould our perception of their subjects.[7]

Writing

As if to challenge the notion that he writes fiction, Sorkin called his own style 'a kind of Romantic idealistic style . . . I like selling you on the reality.'[8] Aware that writing computer code or soldering silicon chips onto motherboards are not the most dynamic topics either visually or aurally, he admitted that he sought 'to make wonky scenes look and feel and sound like bank robberies and prison breaks'.[9] *Steve Jobs* famously excerpted its key moments from Walter Isaacson's lengthy biography, leavened with material and viewpoints gleaned from interviews with Jobs's family and former colleagues, including Lisa Brennan-Jobs, Joanna Hoffman, John Sculley and Steve Wozniak.[10] Hoffman's regular entreaties to Jobs to become a better father occupy the film's emotional core. They are the most obvious departure from Isaacson, who makes only one mention of Hoffman doing so and instead credits Jobs's late-1980s partner Tina Redse with prompting the change in Jobs's paternal behaviour.[11] More important, Sorkin reifies the popular assumption that Jobs lived a life of three acts: Act One lasting until his departure from Apple in 1985; Act Two, the wilderness years before his triumphant return to Apple in 1997; and Act Three his glory years as Apple fulfils his vision.[12]

The Social Network credited Mezrich's *The Accidental Billionaires* as source material, although the precise relationship between the two is disputed by the respective authors. Mezrich insists that Sorkin read drafts of various chapters, while Sorkin argues that he used a fourteen-page synopsis before the two wrote separately but in parallel. Mezrich's book title references an early biography of Jobs, *Accidental Millionaire*, and Robert Cringely's classic tale of the rise of Silicon Valley, *Accidental Empires*.[13] Such echoes reinforce the sense that Sorkin's screenplays partake in dialogue with each other and the broader history of Silicon Valley itself. This relationship deepens when one remembers that David Fincher was slated to direct *Steve Jobs* before contractual problems led to his replacement with Boyle, who added further complexity to Sorkin's comments about cinema and the historical record. For him, 'The truth is not necessarily in the facts, it's in the feel.'[14] Filming key scenes in the Bay Area, he suggested, deepened *Steve Jobs*'s 'feel', enabling the city's atmosphere to 'permeate his cast and add something immeasurable' for the audience to appreciate, perhaps in lieu of strict adherence to Isaacson's historical record.[15]

Sorkin and Boyle are not alone in emphasising fidelity to certain aspects of the historical record. *Pirates*' writer-director Martyn Burke claims that he recruited a team of Harvard researchers to help him ensure that at least two independent primary sources verified each scene. He made heavy use of Paul Freiberger and Michael Swaine's *Fire in the Valley* (1984) as a source text but the screenplay also draws on Butcher's *Accidental Millionaire* and Michael Moritz's earlier history of Apple, *The Little Kingdom*, for detail on Jobs's and Wozniak's early lives.[16] The producer of *Jobs*, Mark Hulme, had no prior Hollywood experience, and asked his son Matt Whitely to write the screenplay, despite him having no previous screenwriting experience. It fared poorly, critically and commercially, not helped by the fact that Sorkin's project came to light while it was being produced. Whitely candidly admitted that the film was a 'cheap knockoff' of *The Social Network*, but in some respects he pinned down Jobs's personality better than anybody.[17] When asked what he thought Jobs would say about *Jobs*, he mused 'I think he might hate the film's reverent tone and yet also hate every moment that doesn't put Apple in perfect light.'[18] Like Burke, *Jobs*'s director, Joshua Michael Stern, was keen to ensure fidelity to minor facts, such as the colour of a podium or the existence of a certain microchip at a certain point in time, while accepting that conversations could be fictionalised.[19] Meanwhile, Kutcher engaged in a slightly alarming method-acting attempt to impersonate Jobs right down to his gait and mannerisms, even adopting Jobs's famous fruitarian diet, a decision that resulted in his hospitalisation with pancreatic problems (Jobs himself died of pancreatic cancer).[20]

Tension Between Fact and Fiction

Tension, then, exists between many of the filmmakers' insistence on a sense of authenticity concerning minor details, such as whether

Mark Zuckerberg drank beer or a screwdriver cocktail when he coded facemash, and their awareness that the things most likely to be important to the audience could be fiction. Jobs's initial ouster from Apple offers a useful case study of this negotiation between the historical record and cinematic conventions. As if shielding its viewers from the horror, *Pirates* references Jobs's sacking in a caption that appears just as John Sculley toasts Jobs on his birthday, as if Sculley were a grubby hitman at a Mafia gathering.[21] After suggesting that Jobs interfered with Sculley's ability to run Apple, *Jobs* has a tearful Jobs whisper 'who do you think you are?' 'I'm CEO of Apple Computer', comes the definitive reply. Here, *Jobs* creates a feedback loop with *The Social Network*. Early in his career as CEO, Zuckerberg had business cards that read 'I'm CEO . . . bitch!': an homage, apparently, to Jobs.[22] Jobs's attempt to overthrow Sculley fails when the board choose the businessman over the visionary. *Steve Jobs*, by contrast, presents Jobs's sacking as an egotistical contest between him and Sculley. It is first referenced in a sequence of newscaster voiceovers at the conclusion of the film's first act while Dylan's 'Rainy Day Women #12&35' shambles in the background. Brief shots of David's *Napoleon Crossing the Alps* and Géricault's *The Raft of the Medusa* suggest that Jobs is a man of destiny, and that hope (for the few, at least) will emerge out of tragedy. The sacking comes when Sculley visits soon before the presentation of the NeXT. Boyle cuts rapidly between this fictional confrontation and a meeting at Jobs's house prior to his sacking, revealing their divergent readings of the event.[23] Sorkin's Sculley complains that Jobs had the media print the legend that Sculley forced him out. The film cuts back to the vote held by Apple's board over Jobs's future, presenting it at night with torrential rain outside. Boyle sets the cameras at an off-kilter angle, exaggerating the sense that the world has spun off its axis, and has bright white table lights illuminating the board members' faces. This uplighting – frequently used in horror films, often to suggest a light coming from hell – distorts the board members' faces, suggesting that evil is at work. Sculley pulls rank, telling Jobs that 'I'm the CEO of Apple', prompting Jobs's self-mythologising outburst: 'I sat in a fucking garage with Wozniak and invented the future. Because artists lead and hacks ask for a show of hands!'[24] Backed up against the floor-to-ceiling window, Jobs has nowhere to go but out.

Of course, the films take dramatic licence here. A series of board meetings took place, none at night, all during a fairly dry May.[25] None were particularly cinematic, although Jobs did burst into tears when first informed that he would be removed from leadership of

Figure 5.1 The off-kilter Apple board vote to oust Jobs in *Steve Jobs*. (Cropped screenshot, 1h05m).

the Mac team and Arthur Rock at one point called Jobs a 'petulant brat'.[26] It took until September for Jobs to resign, although not before he pleaded with Sculley to allow him to continue to run the company.[27] The time compression in both films makes dramatic sense, although *Steve Jobs*' de-emphasising of the critiques of Jobs's objectional behaviour subtly reinforces Sorkin's conclusion: 'I forced the vote', he has the older Jobs say, 'because I believed I was right. I still believe I'm right. And I'm right.'[28] Naturally, history as presented by the film, concurs: we next see Jobs cheerfully informing Hoffman that the NeXT's impending failure is part of a plan:

> schools aren't gonna buy a $13,000 dictionary with good speakers . . . But Apple will 'cause Avie Tevanian is gonna build exactly the OS they need. And they're gonna have to buy me too. For half a billion dollars in stock and end-to-end control on every product.[29]

Not only was he right, but he can also see the future, which includes an ahistorical reconciliation with Sculley to provide some closure.[30]

Sorkin's Tech Visionaries

Sorkin compared *Steve Jobs* to a 'painting, rather than a photograph'.[31] When asked about the film's structure, he commented: 'I knew what I didn't want to do, which was write . . . a traditional biopic, a cradle-to-grave story . . . I wanted to do something else.'[32] Yet he had already made this 'something else' more compellingly in

The Social Network. Sorkin might talk of 'selling the reality first and respecting it', but he clearly knows the value of imaginative creation, not least because a strictly accurate film about Facebook's creation would, as Zuckerberg himself argues, have been hours 'of me sitting at a computer and coding for two hours straight, which probably would've just not been that good of a movie'.[33] Aware of the value of emotional depth, Sorkin created Facebook's founding myth in order that we might fully comprehend his anti-art Zuckerberg. Conversely, he felt that Jobs understood more than any other person the importance of an emotional connection between the user and their electronic (Apple) device(s), enabling him to present Jobs as an artist, at points explicitly drawing parallels between the Apple founder and Picasso, as if to hammer home the message that his screenplay is essentially an abstract portrait.

Jobs's position at the 'intersection of technology and art' also informed the Sorkinian Jobs's understanding of love, as expressed in his wonder at his daughter Lisa's ability to use the Mac within moments of seeing it for the first time, and the film's suggestion that any hole he felt in his emotional core found fulfilment through seeing other humans develop love for their machines.[34] Jobs, then, is fulfilled by his audiences' adulation of Apple products, and they by his devotion to their happiness in these products. *Steve Jobs* presents Jobs growing up, changing his hairstyle, dress and demeanour as he ages. Yet *The Social Network* points to a less optimistic view of the relationship between a creator and his product. Zuckerberg remains a perpetually awkward, inarticulate freshman student: our emotional needs will not be met by the handiwork of this emotionally stunted man-child.

Both screenplays critique their protagonist's relationship with women. Sorkin claims that 'I couldn't get past Steve's treatment of his daughter Lisa. None of his accomplishments meant anything to me because of it.'[35] As such, Sorkin filters their relationship through Jobs's technology. In the first act, he will not smile at her, literally speaks down to her from a standing position, and cannot comprehend why a child might not behave like an adult. He only appears to recognise her as a human being when she begins painting images on the Mac. He and Lisa first make proper eye contact over the onscreen 'save' icon, a trite moment that prompts Jobs to rescue her and her mother from poverty with a promise of money to buy them a house.[36] His pride at this achievement is ambiguous, though, and could be as much in the machine's user-friendliness as at his daughter's talent.

Figure 5.2   Lisa and Jobs connect over the Mac's 'save' icon. (Cropped screenshot, 21m).

Steve Jobs' second act sees him apparently bonding with Lisa over their shared love of Joni Mitchell's 'Both Sides Now', a song all about earned wisdom and empathy. Again, however, Jobs struggles with eye contact and cannot lower himself to her level, remaining obsessed with the fact that she should be at school. Immediately before she departs, she pleads to live with him, an emotional outburst that merely bewilders him.[37] Their reconciliation at the film's conclusion comes when Jobs, unlike Zuckerberg, finally realises that his obsession with products has undermined his ability to form human bonds. After admitting that he is 'poorly made' – an enlightening comment hinting that he likens humans to machines – Jobs finally shows genuine interest in Lisa, and for the first time his gaze seems to be one of love rather than incomprehension.[38] The film's closure and its emotional peak, signalled by the anthemic 'We Grew Up At Midnight' by The Maccabees on the soundtrack, is facilitated through Jobs promising to replace Lisa's ugly cassette-playing Walkman – its antiquatedness a signifier of Lisa's learned indifference towards gadgetry – with a more beautiful and efficient portable machine that will contain hundreds of songs. The iPod's genesis – or at the very least its first announcement to a non-Apple employee – suggests that Jobs's emotional connection to Lisa remains mediated through electronic products. And yet at the film's conclusion, as he heads onstage to introduce the iMac to the world, he passes to Lisa a printout of the first drawing she made on the Mac, one that he has presumably kept close to him since 1984. Her expression is unreadable until his gaze towards her prompts her to begin smiling just as the film ends, suggesting that her daughterly love has finally completed him.[39]

The scholar Phyllis Creme writes of the redemptive power of love in cinema, arguing that the love (often of a man) received by a woman enables her to transform herself, and perhaps even the world around her. Resting on psychological studies of the relationship between mothers and infant children, Creme argues that such love repairs emotional pain, both in the characters and in the viewing public.[40] *Steve Jobs* reverses this normative process, suggesting that Lisa's gift of love to Jobs (itself slightly transactional, in that it is given after Jobs has gifted her knowledge of the iPod) redeems him. Equally important, by 1998, Lisa is tall enough to look at, rather than merely up towards, him. Throughout *Steve Jobs* she gazes imploringly at him, but until this point he cannot truly reflect this back at her. In giving her what she craves and in receiving the thing that took him an entire film to work out that he also needed, Jobs completes himself, at the precise moment he unveils his greatest creation.

By contrast, Sorkin's Zuckerberg can only gaze upon women as objects, as revealed early on when he gauchely liveblogs his creation of facemash, a website that enabled Harvard students to judge the beauty of their fellow students. Both Mezrich and Kirkpatrick confirm that this blog unwisely began with his declaration that a girl 'is a bitch', which Sorkin transforms into a post about Erica Albright.[41] Albright dumps him in part because he cannot comprehend how to communicate with her: his promise to introduce her to people she would not be able to meet at Boston University is met with a sarcastic 'you would do that for me?' that he misreads as a sincere admission of his superiority.[42] The split becomes even more final when he tells her that she need not study because she attends a lesser higher education institution. It establishes the emotional tone of the film, Zuckerberg's character, and his motivation, while containing the line around which the whole film revolves: 'it'll be because you're an asshole'.[43] Such a failure to understand women recurs throughout, as witnessed in Zuckerberg's treatment of his lawyer Marylin and the scarcity of women on the film's Facebook staff. Soon after the dumping, as police sirens wail warnings in the background, Sorkin's Zuckerberg adds crude swipes at Albright's body to his 'bitch' blogpost, heightening the sense that Zuckerberg's resentment at women and desire for revenge lie at Facebook's core. Just as important, it positions facemash and therefore Facebook as another weaponisation of the male gaze, designed to reduce women to their looks, forever ranked according to privileged white male perceptions of beauty and availability.

The film reinforces this perspective by intercutting Zuckerberg simultaneously coding facemash with a bacchanalian scene in which a busload of young women join a party where they might meet members of one of the most exclusive campus membership clubs (astute observers might compare this with Alexander Korda's insertion of dramatic scenes into Rembrandt's painting of his masterpieces in order to avoid ninety minutes of a man at an easel). Echoing *Hackers*, Fincher soundtracks the scene with Atticus Ross and Trent Reznor's 120 beats-per-minute 'In Motion', explicitly equating the excitement of the party with Zuckerberg's exhilaration at hacking. More important, the scene possesses a deeply significant political undercurrent, suggesting that Facebook merely streamlined processes for creating hierarchies and allowing men further, easier, and more anonymous opportunities to degrade women. Thus, Harvard's culture of sexism, objectification of women and lust for power exert defining influences on Facebook, which itself facilitates the further entrenching of these power relationships, as we see once facemash goes live and male students revel in rating their female counterparts' looks. Marylin later comments to Zuckerberg that 'creation myths need a devil'; the film points to Harvard as well as Zuckerberg as this diabolic influence.[44] Similarly, it suggests that the craving for status might be equated with a quest for power. Indeed, as Zuckerberg bitterly observes of the Winklevosses' lawsuit: they are suing him because 'for the first time in their lives, things didn't work out the way they were supposed to for them'.[45]

Throughout the film Fincher adds crucial detail to this sketching out of Zuckerberg's status concerns: while in the opening scene he and Albright sit face-to-face, a meeting after Facebook has become a minor success sees Zuckerberg standing while she sits. Similarly, his diminutive status among the heirs to old money at Harvard plays out physically at his first meeting with the Winklevoss twins, who tower over him literally and metaphorically, bolstered by point-of-view shots from the hulking, six-foot five-inch, lantern-jawed brothers. Like *The Fountainhead*'s Howard Roark, the identical twins possess a face that was 'like a law of nature – a thing one could not question', and they seem similarly uninhibited in their freedom to pursue their own interests.[46] The film thus contrasts their Randian physicality with Zuckerberg's nebbish appearance. Again, though, the film highlights how Zuckerberg's coding skills threaten to destabilise old status hierarchies: attempting to reinforce their superiority, they take him to the Porcellian clubhouse, the most exclusive final club for Harvard's students – although he is only allowed into the so-called 'bike room' – where in a display of condescension they offer him a pre-packaged sandwich rather than a meal.[47] Despite this belittling, which echoes his of Albright, reinforced when he repeats her 'you would do that for me?' line, the camera begins to afford Zuckerberg greater stature as the twins and their partner, Divya Narendra, talk with him about their plans for a Harvard-exclusive social network, an impression helped by the blue filter overwhelming the brown of the Porcellian's wood-panelled interior. Here the film prompts viewers to remember Zuckerberg's desperation to join such a prestigious club in the opening scene, one that would enable him to be important at Harvard. While he sits way below the old-money 'gentlemen of Harvard' such as the Winklevosses – as they acknowledge themselves – he considers himself vastly superior to his Boston University-attending ex-girlfriend and joins their project soon after they reveal to him that the site's exclusivity will doubtless attract women to him.[48]

The film's depiction of Zuckerberg's desire to climb socially peaks in his fictional response to Facebook's servers going down after Saverin closes the company bank account. He rages down the telephone to his business partner about his fear of returning to their lowly status at Harvard: 'I'm not going back to Caribbean Night at A-E-Pi!' he yells, remembering the horror of the most embarrassing party of their undergraduate days. 'Do you like being a nobody?! Did you like being a joke?! . . . I'm not going back to that life.'[49] Later he dismisses Marylin with a curt 'who are you?' when she begins to ask him how he is feeling. When she reveals that she is a second-year associate, he asserts his superiority simply by returning to his laptop.[50] He is not even aware of the impact this might have on her as he returns to Facebook and she to her salad. Their poses might mirror each other, but they live in completely different worlds. Zuckerberg's lack of affect here speaks volumes: just as the Winklevosses, for all their claims to greatness, will not become masters of all they survey, Zuckerberg, despite his own delusions of grandeur, will always be an awkward nerd.

Throughout, the film's soundtrack reinforces Zuckerberg's ambivalent relationship with other humans. Composed by Reznor and Ross, whose band, Nine Inch Nails, specialise in a hybrid of heavy metal, electronic music and ambient sounds, with lyrics that touch on themes of alienation, isolation, dominance and submission, the soundtrack is exclusively instrumental, shifting between electronic ambient washes and up-tempo techno beats, with simple, plaintive, minor-key piano melodies layered on top. Its centrepiece is 'Hand Covers Bruise', which is based around a three-note minor-key melody. Reznor sought to convey 'tension, vulnerability, sadness and something unpleasant' through this track.[51] It introduces many of the film's core themes, not least Zuckerberg's hurt and isolation which he converts into determination as he trots from the bar to his dorm room following Albright dumping him. Its reappearance at two key points serves as a reminder of Facebook's original sin. It first resurfaces at the Winklevoss deposition nearly halfway through the film, at a point just before an unhappy Zuckerberg admits to the Winklevosses' lawyer that he is not paying full attention to the discussion about whether he stole their intellectual property. 'It's raining,' Zuckerberg observes as he stares out of a window. Here, the refrain suggests that Zuckerberg's pain remains, that it is raining inside as well as out, but also that his humanity is ebbing away. Eisenberg's plaintive gaze perfectly conveys Zuckerberg's vulnerability and remembrance of the hurt he felt: after all, nothing wounds as much as young love rejected. Perhaps the most affective single moment in Fincher's oeuvre, it heartbreakingly reveals the boy inside Zuckerberg's body. Quickly, however, Zuckerberg regains his poise, and moments after the piano refrain stops, he witheringly tells the lawyer that he is devoting the 'minimum amount' of attention to this ancient man's obsession with outmoded ways, and that he has no respect for the Winklevoss twins' attempt to 'sit on [his] shoulders . . . [so they might] call themselves tall'.[52] The melody returns for the final time when Saverin berates Zuckerberg for diluting his shares in the company almost to nothing before promising to initiate the legal case against him. Here the piano refrain is heard briefly before being overtaken by atonal electronic noises that sound like a transmission from outer space, as if to indicate that Zuckerberg is a mere echo of the emotional being he used to be, that he has been consumed by Facebook's electronic world, that he might even be as inhuman as *Body Snatchers*' pod people.

These cinematic inventions and reinterpretations underpin Sorkin's interpretation of Zuckerberg. Similarly, we learn all we need to know about Facebook's early president Sean Parker – arguably the key individual who drove the company towards its dominant status – from the two parables Sorkin creates for the mercurial entrepreneur. At his first meeting with the Facebook founders at a New York City restaurant, he hits upon two tensions at the core of the Zuckerberg-Saverin relationship.[53] Parker enters dressed in black, as two suggestive red flags hang behind him. Seemingly unaware that Zuckerberg is less interested in wealth than a far more nebulous goal of being 'cool', he defines coolness as: 'A billion-dollar valuation'.[54] Here, viewers think back to Zuckerberg's early shrug when asked by the Winklevosses and Narendra why he did not monetise his first consumer product: he is not driven by money but by doing something cool, because he is obsessed with the fear that he is uncool. Impressed, Zuckerberg displays genuine emotion for the first time, in the form of awe and perhaps even lust at Parker's bonding of wealth to that nebulous concept of 'cool'.

The second piece of wisdom Sorkin affords Parker is conveyed to Zuckerberg at a nightclub. He tells a visibly overwhelmed Zuckerberg of Roy Raymond, the founder of Victoria's Secret who, he states, killed himself by jumping off the Golden Gate Bridge after learning that the company he sold for four million dollars was worth over twelve times that amount two years later.[55] His closing gambit furthers the bond between the two when he admits that Napster came about because he wanted to impress a girl who was dating the co-captain of the high school lacrosse team. His effortless drawing of a parallel between him and Zuckerberg – unrequited love, status anxiety, nerds competing with jocks, the close relationship between beauty and success – cements them as brethren. Then, as the lighting under his face turns purple and his eyes seem to become devilish black holes, he tells Zuckerberg, 'This is *our* time . . . This is a once-in-a-generation-holy-shit idea and the water under the Golden Gate is freezing cold. Look at my face and tell me I don't know what I'm talking about.'[56] The discussion's conclusion is equally illuminating: Zuckerberg asks about the girl. 'What girl?' comes the insouciant reply: while women might hold the key to male creativity, they are ultimately disposable and forgettable.

Jobs the Outsider

Pirates and *Jobs* similarly – but less spectacularly – emphasise university years to explain their subject. *Jobs* has an anti-establishment Jobs wandering barefoot around the Reed College campus, reading about mysticism, learning calligraphy, experimenting with LSD and pondering the meaning of life. By contrast, *Pirates*' director Burke insisted that Jobs was one of the few 'true revolutionaries of our time'. Jobs, he thought, inherited a 'messianic quality that came out of San Francisco in the '60s . . . Berkeley, the Free Speech movement and flower power. What he was doing was part technological, and part insurrectionist.'[57] Burke's explicit contrast between Jobs's slightly countercultural background and Gates's somewhat more buttoned-down Harvard experience essentially echoes Apple's own self-image: indeed, the film prominently cites one of Jobs's favourite aphorisms: 'it's better to be a pirate than join the navy'.[58] To this end, *Pirates* cuts directly from its classical biopic opening to a protest on the University of California-Berkeley campus, where riot gear-clad police brutalise protesters while Jobs and Wozniak scuttle away, Wozniak gripping the blue box they built to enable them to make free long-distance telephone calls. As 'Question' by The Moody Blues plays in the background, the mythmaking begins. Watching the protests dissipate, Jobs observes: 'those guys think they're revolutionaries. They're not revolutionaries. We are', leading to Wozniak's voiceover, in a statement that anticipates the *Steve Jobs* Wozniak's big picture-solid workbench dyad: 'Steve . . . always saw things differently . . . I would see something and just see kilobytes or circuit boards while he would see karma or the meaning of the universe.'[59] By having Jobs and Wozniak running in the opposite direction to the protesters, the film suggests that Wozniak and Jobs's revolution sprang from the same soil but aimed to catalyse a very different change. Here, the film's ideological assumptions are laid bare: the counterculture's protest was literally moving in the wrong direction, whereas the actual revolutionaries, rather than attempt to overthrow an entrenched system of corruption, warmongering and oppression, sought to provide the marketplace with electronic products that would enable humans to do the things they already do (write, draw and communicate) more effectively.

Pirates' Jobs is a 'scruffy craz[y]' who sees the Apple prototype as a revolution in a box and he and Wozniak guerrilla warriors in a battle against IBM. He rides a bicycle – a combined nod to the archetypal cinematic shorthand for a free spirit and to Jobs's later adage that a computer was akin to a bicycle for the mind – listens to psychedelic music, enjoys LSD and denounces as 'squares and stiffs' those who don't imbibe, wears cut-off jeans and open-toed sandals even when meeting his bank manager, and visibly bridles at any mention of regular businessmen while arguing that Apple is engaged in a 'practically spiritual' quest to overthrow a 'dead culture'.[60] Later, the Apple headquarters prominently displays a grand piano and a motorcycle: signifiers of its aspirations to high-art status coupled with rock 'n' roll credentials. Building on this, when Apple sends a delegation to Xerox in 1979 to assess their graphic user interface, Wozniak's narration states, 'I felt like one of the

Figure 5.3 'What are we doing here?' Jobs and Woz head in a different direction to the countercultural hordes. (Cropped screenshot, 4m).

Mongol hordes coming to loot and plunder a bunch of defenceless villagers.' Here, the film references the title sequence of *Reservoir Dogs* (Quentin Tarantino, 1992) in its slow-motion tracking of men heading towards a decisive moment. These men are not only revolutionaries; they are dangerous subversives who possess a mysterious sex appeal.[61]

In presenting Jobs as an outsider, *Jobs* and *Pirates* cite and reinforce what the San Francisco writer Rebecca Solnit calls one of 'Silicon Valley's own favourite stories about itself'.[62] As she pointed out in 2014, the tension between tech workers and more established San Francisco residents that blew up over the Google Bus issue became more curious when one discovered that the tech bros could not comprehend why they were not welcomed by locals. As she observed, 'these days in TED talks and tech-world conversation, commerce is described as art and as revolution and huge corporations are portrayed as agents of the counterculture', even though only vestigial elements of the countercultural approach to the world remain.[63] Jobs's own image – and indeed the image moulded by the filmmakers – is foundational to this self-image of the Silicon Valley tech world, not least because of the company's own insistence – crystallised in its '1984' ad – that it is engaged in perpetual war against The Man, Big Brother and The System.

Art, Boyle reminds us, 'isn't about what happened', but a creative imagining; in this case of a flawed genius.[64] The overarching argument of *Pirates*, meanwhile, contends that Jobs was far more successful a revolutionary than his more politicised peers, but that his fatal failing was in believing that Apple – and specifically the Macintosh team – constituted a family (an interpretation that owes a debt to Butcher's *Accidental Millionaire*) rather than a capitalist enterprise.[65] Here, *Pirates* suggests that Jobs bequeathed to Apple a somewhat non-capitalist approach to its products, but as Bill Gates and John Sculley reveal to him at the film's conclusion, capitalism does not operate like family: it is hard-headed, relentless, and calculating. Jobs might know that the Apple family produces better products but Gates retorts that the market does not possess emotions and might not even care about 'better', just about what is convenient, affordable and available.[66] Conversely, *Pirates*' successor biopics suggest that Jobs designed products that were so ahead of their time that it took decades for humanity to catch up. Indeed, while Stern and Sorkin might have found Jobs to be an objectionable human, they seem sufficiently overwhelmed by Apple products that they could not help but let him off the hook.

The Social Network, by contrast, trains a beady eye on Zuckerberg's moral failings, suggesting that they underpin Facebook's malignant influence on our culture. Further, Zuckerberg's unrequited love signifies the gaping hole in his life (and thus the online life in general) that cannot be filled by his financial wealth. Erica Albright does not redeem him or bring closure, as we would expect, but her presence on Facebook indicates the fundamental ambivalence of living in a world dominated by the corporation: she might despise Zuckerberg, but she cannot resist his creation's siren call. Deeper still, the film refuses to laud individualism (and thus capitalism) but instead reveals its rotten core. Here we see the gulf between *Steve Jobs*' and *The Social Network*'s visions of Silicon Valley. Sorkin himself said:

> if you're writing a character like Steve – an anti-hero – you can't judge them. I like to write them as if they're making their case to God as to why they should be allowed into heaven. To do that, I have to be able to find things about them that are like me and that I would want to be able to defend.[67]

Jobs, in reconciling with Lisa, unites his technological and emotional lives. The film concludes by subtly suggesting that consumers will experience a similar union, mediated by their shiny Apple products. Conversely, Erica Albright and, symbolically, half of humanity remain unattainable to Zuckerberg even as his creation gobbles up their waking lives. One can only speculate as to why the fictional Jobs achieves what Zuckerberg cannot, and what defensible thing Sorkin found in Jobs that Zuckerberg lacks, but maybe the answer is very straightforward: perhaps Sorkin and his fellow writers are not as enamoured with Facebook as they are with Apple products?[68]

Beneath this lies one of the Silicon Valley biopics' most intriguing propositions. Jobs might have set out to revolutionise the world as per *Pirates* and *Jobs*, but in becoming the rock-star tech entrepreneur and in insisting that he bequeathed his devices to the world (rather than merely being the salesman of Wozniak's genius designs) he inspired a generation of hackers like Zuckerberg to treat all of society's problems as if they were engineering problems to be solved by the application of the correct algorithm. Thus, in directing his revolution towards gadgetry rather than systems of power, Jobs fatally misconstrued the nature of 1960s humanism, presenting revolution as merely something contained in a beautifully designed box of electronics, rather than a critique of an entire political-economic system. This blinkered approach achieved its greatest success, the biopics imply, in Zuckerberg's Facebook, engagement with which was perfected through codes written (perhaps) on the machines designed (apparently) by Jobs in his own quest to understand his self. Such a simplification of complex historical processes is, of course, encoded in the biopic approach. And yet in its emotional truths, the biopic perhaps reveals more than the history books ever will: in essence, we are content to leave Zuckerberg forever clicking refresh on his fatefully addictive and corrosive platform. We might not befriend him, but billions of us visit his site each month. The sheer beauty and elegance of Apple's products meanwhile leads us, like Sorkin, to excuse Jobs's own failures and turn a blind eye to Apple's problematic industrial processes.

Notes

1. Bingham, *Whose Lives Are They Anyway?*, 7.
2. A. O. Scott, 'Apple's C.E.O., Dissected in Three Acts', *New York Times*, October 9, 2015, C5.

3. Eagan, 'Dreams from our Fathers', 8–10.
4. Mezrich, *Accidental Billionaires*, 62, 66, 83; Kirkpatrick, *Facebook Effect*, 20, 22, 29; Kirkpatrick quoted in Willmore, 'Why *The Social Network* Feels Sharper Now Than When it First Came Out'; Nathan Heller, 'You Can't Handle the Veritas'.
5. Joe Nocera, 'Aaron Sorkin's *Steve Jobs* Con', *New York Times*, October 14, 2015, <https://www.nytimes.com/2015/10/13/opinion/aaron-sorkins-steve-jobs-con.html> (consulted June 28, 2022).
6. Ben Fritz and Daisuke Wakabayashi, 'Silicon Valley vs. "Steve Jobs"', *Wall Street Journal*, October 5, 2015, B1.
7. Bingham, *Whose Lives*, 155.
8. Fahy, 'An Interview with Aaron Sorkin', 15.
9. Judy Rosen, 'Writing Hollywood', *New York Times*, December 6, 2015, 136.
10. Stephen Galloway, 'A Widow's Threats, High-Powered Spats and the Sony Hack: The Strange Saga of *Steve Jobs*', *Hollywood Reporter*, October 7, 2015, <https://www.hollywoodreporter.com/movies/movie-features/a-widows-threats-high-powered-829925/#!> (consulted June 28, 2022); David Wallace-Wells, 'How Aaron Sorkin Designed Steve Jobs', *New York*, October 13, 2015, <https://www.vulture.com/2015/10/how-aaron-sorkin-designed-steve-jobs.html> (consulted June 28, 2022).
11. Isaacson, *Steve*, 260, 265. The critic A. O. Scott suggests that Sorkin redrew Hoffman as a 'Sorkinesque' figure much like C. J. Cregg in *The West Wing* (NBC, 1999–2006): Scott, 'Apple's C.E.O.'
12. See, for example, Schlender, 'The Lost Steve Jobs Tapes'.
13. Deutelbaum, '*The Social Network* Screenplay', 30–2; Butcher, *Accidental Millionaire*; Cringely, *Accidental Empires*.
14. Fritz and Wakabayashi, 'Silicon Valley vs. "Steve Jobs"'.
15. Kim Masters, 'David Fincher Out of Steve Jobs Movie in $10 Million Fee Fight', *Hollywood Reporter*, April 14, 2014, <https://www.hollywoodreporter.com/news/david-fincher-steve-jobs-movie-696044> (consulted June 28, 2022); Galloway, 'A Widow's Threats'; Eadicicco, 'What Steve Jobs' Famous Garage Where He Started Apple Looks Like Today'; Kahn, 'Steve Jobs Biopic Filming at Flint Center'.
16. 'Q/A with Martyn Burke'; Freiberger and Swaine, *Fire in the Valley*; Butcher, *Accidental Millionaire*, 23–4, 43, 50–1, 96; Moritz, *Return to the Little Kingdom*, 76–7, 98, 106–7, 206; *Pirates*, 8m, 18m, 26m, 27m. *Return* updates *The Little Kingdom* (1984).
17. 'I am Matt Whiteley'.
18. 'I am Matt Whiteley'.
19. Callaham, 'Interview: We Chat with the Producer of the Upcoming Steve Jobs Movie'; Goudreau, '*Jobs* Director on Capturing the Complicated Life of Steve Jobs'; Lin, 'Mark Hulme's Way'.
20. 'Steve Jobs Movie Begins Shooting in the Original Apple Garage'; Bigler, '*Jobs* Producer on "The Rise, The Fall, and the Triumphant Return of

Steve Jobs'"; Callaham, 'Interview'; Hare, 'Becoming Steve Jobs'; Bryan Alexander, 'Ashton Kutcher Suffers Health Scare Preparing for "Jobs"', *USA Today*, January 29, 2013, <https://eu.usatoday.com/story/life/movies/2013/01/26/ashton-kutcher-steve-jobs-sundance/1866023> (consulted June 28, 2022).
21. Harris, 'The *Vulture* Transcript: An Interview with David Fincher'; *Pirates*, 1h33.
22. *Jobs*, 1h28m; Siegler, 'Card Designer: The Inspiration for Zuckerberg's "I'm CEO, Bitch"? Steve Jobs'; Kirkpatrick, *Facebook Effect*, 129.
23. *Steve Jobs*, 34m, 59m.
24. *Steve Jobs*, 1h04.
25. The nearest weather station with information for May 1985 was San Jose: 'San Jose, CA Weather History'.
26. Isaacson, *Steve Jobs*, 194, 198.
27. Isaacson, *Steve Jobs*, 200–9, 213–17.
28. *Steve Jobs*, 1h06.
29. *Steve Jobs*, 1h09.
30. Isaacson, *Steve Jobs*, 217.
31. Laffly, '*Steve Jobs*', 150–2.
32. 'Aaron Sorkin on Writing "Steve Jobs"'.
33. Thomas Fahy, 'An Interview with Aaron Sorkin', in Fahy (ed.), *Considering Aaron Sorkin*, 13; Zuckerberg quoted in Bereznak, 'Ten Years Late, Mark Zuckerberg is still trying to Overcome *The Social Network*'.
34. Alex Godfrey, 'Aaron Sorkin on the Cult of Steve Jobs', *The Guardian*, November 11, 2015, <https://www.theguardian.com/film/2015/nov/11/aaron-sorkin-steve-jobs-michael-fassbender> (consulted June 28, 2022).
35. Wallace-Wells, 'How Aaron Sorkin Designed Steve Jobs'.
36. *Steve Jobs*, 12–23m.
37. *Steve Jobs*, 55m.
38. *Steve Jobs*, 1h45m.
39. Isaacson, *Steve*, 254.
40. Phyllis Creme, 'Love Transforms: Variations on the Theme in Film and Soap', in Pearce and Wisker (eds), *Fatal Attractions*, 128–39.
41. Mezrich, *Accidental*, 42–3; Kirkpatrick, *Facebook Effect*, 23.
42. *The Social Network*, 3m.
43. *The Social Network*, 5m.
44. *The Social Network*, 1h47m.
45. *The Social Network*, 53m; Dinnen, *Digital Banal*, 23.
46. Rand, *The Fountainhead*, 4.
47. Mezrich, *Accidental Billionaires*, 70, 73–5 locates this meeting in the dining room at Kirkland House, where Zuckerberg lived. Kirkpatrick, *Facebook Effect* makes no mention of this meeting.
48. *The Social Network*, 40m.
49. *The Social Network*, 1h33m.

50. *The Social Network*, 52m.
51. Quoted in Jim Fusilli, 'Film Soundtrack: Scoring *The Social Network*', *Wall Street Journal*, October 12, 2010, D7.
52. *The Social Network*, 47m; Deutelbaum, '*The Social Network* Screenplay', 34.
53. This meeting actually took place: Kirkpatrick, *Facebook Effect*, 47. Mezrich, *Accidental*, 145–6 notes the red banners.
54. *The Social Network*, 1h07m.
55. The story is largely true, although Sorkin omits the crucial detail that Raymond lost a fortune on a children's shop in the years between the sale and his death. There are no indications that Parker actually told it to Zuckerberg. Naomi Barr, 'Roy Raymond: The Tragic Genius at the Heart of Victoria's Secret', *The Independent*, November 13, 2013, <https://www.independent.co.uk/news/business/analysis-and-features/roy-raymond-tragic-genius-heart-victoria-s-secret-8935811.html> (consulted June 28, 2022).
56. *The Social Network*, 1h19m.
57. Dormehl, 'How a '90s TV Movie Became the Steve Jobs Film to Beat'.
58. *Pirates*, 1h09m; Isaacson, *Steve*, 144.
59. *Pirates*, 5m.
60. *Pirates*, 8m, 20m, 23m, 27m.
61. *Pirates*, 1h02m, 1h08m; Isaacson, *Steve*, 96.
62. Rebecca Solnit, 'Get Off the Bus', *London Review of Books*, February 20, 2014, <https://www.lrb.co.uk/the-paper/v36/n04/rebecca-solnit/diary> (consulted June 28, 2022).
63. Solnit, 'Get Off the Bus'.
64. Catherine Shoard, 'Danny Boyle on Steve Jobs: Movies Must Be Made About Powerful Men', *The Guardian*, September 6, 2015, <https://www.theguardian.com/film/2015/sep/06/steve-jobs-movie-danny-boyle-kate-winslet-seth-rogen-aaron-sorkin?CMP=gu_com> (consulted June 28, 2022).
65. *Pirates*, 1h13m; Butcher, *Accidental Millionaire*, 139–40, 146, 151, 191; Freiberger and Swaine, *Fire*, 308–10.
66. *Pirates*, 1h31m; Isaacson, *Steve*, 201–2.
67. Wallace-Wells, 'How Aaron Sorkin'.
68. Corinne Heller, 'Aaron Sorkin Apologizes to Apple CEO Tim Cook After Slamming Him Over "Opportunistic" Remarks'.

Part 3

Silicon Valley's Dystopian Utopia

Chapter 6

Technology Solutionism and the World of Work

Moving from foundational myths to twenty-first-century California, two films exemplify Hollywood's indictment of Silicon Valley's disruption of the American economy and its failure to respect its employees' human lives. *The Circle* (James Ponsoldt, 2017), adapted from San Francisco native Dave Eggers's 2013 novel, uses its titular fictional tech company to attack Silicon Valley's Taylorism, authoritarianism and antihumanism. Thanks to its union of elements of Google, Facebook, PayPal, Twitter and Amazon, combined with its removal of online anonymity, the Circle dominates the world of the near future. The demands it places on its workers are such that they must abandon their private lives, temporally, geographically and eventually biologically. Dismissed as a feature-length advert for Google, *The Internship* (Shawn Levy, 2013) initially seems a whimsical, utopian mirror image of *The Circle*. Vince Vaughn and Owen Wilson essentially play themselves: Billy and Nick, two irreverent, optimistic and determinedly wacky Generation Xers – the generation of Americans born between the mid-1960s and the late 1970s – who have been cast aside when the watch distributor for which they work collapses.[1] They improbably win internships at Google, where their can-do attitude wins the hearts of their fellow interns and secures all of them contracts at the corporation. The British film critic Mark Kermode denounced the film as 'one of the most witless, humourless . . . self-satisfied, smug, unfunny comedies I have ever seen'.[2] Yet a deep reading reveals that it presents Google as a Potemkin Village, where a utopian appearance covers the neoliberal dystopia at Google's heart. Reading *The Internship* against the grain – or, rather, analysing its political unconscious – enables us to consider more deeply the ideological assumptions that drive many people in both Silicon Valley and Hollywood.

Also largely dismissed by critics, *The Circle* – which was financed by Image Nation Abu Dhabi – pitched itself as a dystopian critique of Silicon Valley, helped by a number of pointed casting choices. Playing against type, America's favourite uncle, Tom Hanks (as the Circle's head, Eamon Bailey), and the comedian Patton Oswalt (as the Circle's Chief Operating Officer Tom Stenton) reference the ruthless-capitalism-with-a-benign-façade that characterises tech evangelists such as Google's founders.[3] John Boyega, best known as the disillusioned Stormtrooper-turned-Resistance fighter Finn in the *Star Wars* sequel trilogy, plays the Circle's mysterious but ultimately heroic founder. Two actors who spent much of their youths on film – Emma Watson (Hermione Granger in the Harry Potter films) and Ellar Coltrane (through his decade-long involvement in Richard Linklater's *Boyhood* [2014]) – respectively play the film's protagonist, Mae Holland, and her former boyfriend Mercer. Filmed in Los Angeles with a screenplay by its director James Ponsoldt and Eggers, *The Circle* follows Mae Holland's descent into the titular company.[4] Holland's innocence and exploitability are signalled from the film's very beginning: her phone's ringtone is 'Tis the Gift to be Simple'. As she becomes enmeshed in the Circle, she learns that its elegant unifying of individuals' online identities masks a sinister quest to gather store, and thus control every aspect of recorded human existence. The film culminates with the Circle's acolytes hounding Mercer to his death because its users cannot comprehend his desire for privacy in the face of their commitment to complete transparency.[5]

Dystopian Solutionism

While *The Circle* was designed as both satire and dystopian thriller, *The Internship* is altogether more complex. It appears to be a lightweight comedy featuring the further adventures of Vaughn and Wilson's *Wedding Crashers* (David Dobkin, 2005) and which presents an idealised vision of life and work at Google. Numerous characters express their awe at life in the Googleplex, reinforcing this apparent utopian image. Indeed, this surtext was successful enough for Google's founder Larry Page to consider the film a fine advertisement for the corporation. Its director, Shawn Levy, stressed that Google's involvement did not extend to approval of the final cut and that Google had no financial relationship with the film's producers, but this was a transactional relationship. Google retained creative control over the depiction of its products in the movie, such as self-driving cars – a scene in which one crashed was removed at Google's behest – tablet computers and its ubiquitous search engine. In return, Levy filmed key scenes at Google's headquarters, and benefited from Google's advice on certain issues, such as the algorithmic equations that were written onto various parts of the set.[6] 'They were fine,' he said of the company, 'as long we got the DNA of the culture right and the film wasn't mean-spirited.'[7] After meeting various Googlers, he expressed his awe at their utopian ambitions: they 'really believe that life on Earth can be made better through the ubiquity of information'.[8] Vaughn offers another link between *The Internship* and Silicon Valley. Like many tech leaders, he identifies his politics as libertarian. In 2011 he offered public support to the then Texas congressman and presidential candidate Ron Paul, a long-term advocate of free-market economics and fan of Friedrich Hayek's *The Road to Serfdom*. For Vaughn, Paul's principles 'are based on fact and logic, which is rooted in the very foundation of America', an interpretation that presents Hayek in Randian-objectivist terms.[9]

At first glance, *The Internship* seems to chime perfectly with Google's vision of itself as a benevolent master that makes the world a better place, so much so that Manohla Dargis of the *New York Times* suggested that it 'comes across as a new form of religion – Google as God or maybe Disney'.[10] This is a key feature of the self-image of many Silicon Valley corporations, as suggested in the Steve Jobs biopics and the Circlers' veneration of their CEO. Many such corporations inculcate a cult-like atmosphere among their employees, such that the founders and CEOs appear like religious leaders. This quasi-religious outlook also informs one of Silicon Valley's most familiar tropes, that its products will change the world.[11] Yet scratching this surface reveals a deeper, more dystopian tale. Levy compared Google's headquarters to the Emerald City.[12] If Google is Oz, then maybe its founders are akin to the Wizard, charlatans who project an all-powerful image to distract from their ordinariness. Moreover, the city – and therefore the Googleplex – is a façade built to deceive observers and obscure the reality that lies beneath. Vaughn echoed Levy, comparing Google's headquarters to Roald Dahl's chocolate factory in another deceptively complex statement. Google here might be a place of wonder and childlike joy, or an oppressive, satanic mill where people toil under the autocratic control of a megalomaniacal and borderline sociopathic slaveowner.[13]

The films' interconnected duality lies in their exploration of the possibilities and problematics associated with Google and the Circle's reach into every crevice of our lives. In this, they debate the centrality of technological solutionism to Silicon Valley corporations.

The Internship is infused with technology solutionism; or, rather, Google solutionism, for the corporation appears at first to be the solution to all of society's ills, from unemployment to inadvisable use of a mobile phone, from meaningless work to problems that do not appear problematic until Googlers identify them. Early on in her journey through the Circle, meanwhile, Mae Holland learns of its new child-tracking project from a female colleague. Promising to find missing children within ninety seconds, the project relies upon the Circle implanting microchips into children's bones. 'I'm serious about immediately reducing kidnapping, rape, and murder by 99%,' burbles the Circler, who encapsulates the solutionist approach that frames complex moral and ethical issues in simple binaries that focus solely on one aspect of a multifaceted problem and that consequently have only one logical answer.[14] Her unasked question is designed to force Holland to choose between opposing or supporting action on child kidnapping: a very simple comparative, akin to an if-then process in computer coding that will run a certain code (microchipping children) if a certain condition exists (opposing kidnapping). Logic dictates that an opponent of microchipping children must therefore not oppose child kidnapping. Of course, this elides a far broader range of circumstances, problems and solutions, such as the rarity of such events taking place, the simple fact that most child abuse is committed by somebody known to the victim, the role of a functioning health service and legal system to minimise such events, and the ethical issues attached to implanting sensors in minors without their consent (which itself could constitute a form of abuse).

The Circle thus encourages its audience to question the relationship between utopian ideals and dystopian realities. A senator who has the temerity to suggest that the conglomerate be broken up is placed under investigation for unnamed misdemeanours uncovered by the Circle's manipulation of surveillance capitalism. Similarly, the utopian Mercer might desire a life away from the prying eyes of the web, but once Holland reveals his deer-antler sculptures to a fellow Circler, his desire for privacy becomes suspicious. Circlers argue that he must be killing deer to produce his work; otherwise, why would he hide his light under a bushel? Their inability to understand his philosophy and refusal to respect his privacy ultimately leads them to hound him to his death, which the Circle retrospectively averts when Bailey tells the massed ranks of Circlers that Mercer would not have died had his truck been fitted with collision-detection software that would have stopped it dead rather than allowing it to plunge off the side of a bridge as he attempted to outrun his Circle-enabled pursuers.[15] Again, solutionism empowers Circlers to overlook the ethical and moral problems associated with their use of technology and focus instead on another way to reduce human agency.

The Old Versus the New, or Digital Versus Analogue

Both films begin by juxtaposing their protagonists' meaningless lives in the old economy with the new meaning they find in Silicon Valley, introducing one of their major shared underlying themes: the disposability of employees in the post-2008 economy. Humiliatingly, Vaughn and Wilson learn that they have lost their going-nowhere jobs as sales reps in the film's first scene. This older form of American capitalism, where men hash out business deals over food and wine, collapses when their client gives them the bad news. 'Nobody wears a watch anymore,' barks their Baby Boomer boss upon their return to the office. 'They just check their goddamn phones.'[16] Human contact is unnecessary in a computerised environment, he insists, obliquely referencing the extent to which Google was enmeshed in the rise of the smartphone and its ability to link buyers of ostentatious watches with the cheapest sellers, which fatally bypassed Wilson and Vaughn's role in the marketplace.[17] The uncaring pre-digital capitalist's response to platform capitalism is brutally simple: liquidate the company, release the disposable employees and head for retirement in Florida courtesy of the savings they have built up through their career. Ironically, then, the very company that saves Vaughn and Wilson is enmeshed in the circumstances from which they needed saving. Mae Holland, meanwhile, drives a clapped-out car and works in a depressing, impersonal office cubicle, telephoning water company customers to settle their bills. When asked about her job by her globetrotting friend Annie, she drawls: 'I come here each day and in return I receive money to buy goods and services.' This brief moment exposes the anomie endured by office drones like Holland: for eight hours each day they perform pointless tasks that offer no meaning to their lives beyond the ability to buy consumer products. Annie encourages Holland to work for a 'real company' that will also offer meaning.[18] Here, *The Circle* juxtaposes a life of purpose and 'realness' in Silicon Valley with the (presumably unreal) futility of a life outside its embrace.

Naturally, for workers such as the interns and Mae Holland, Silicon Valley becomes a haven from the 'hellish corner[s] of corporate America' that they must avoid.[19] *The Internship*'s middle section offers further insight into this employment world and the ideological baggage it carries. One intern laments that they will not be offered jobs at the end of the internship, which means that their lives 'are basically ruined', before telling Wilson and Vaughn: 'The whole American Dream thing that you guys grew up on? That's all it is nowadays: a dream.' Incredulous, Wilson chastises them for their cynicism, leading another intern to sigh wearily, 'It's not how we see it: it's just the way things are now.'[20] There is, he believes, no escape from late capitalism and no alternative to suffering within it. This builds on comments made by Vaughn in promotional interviews for the film, in which he presented *The Internship* as a parable about individualism: it was, he said, about 'today's tough economy and people having to reinvent themselves in their quest to continue to have value'.[21] Value here is a purely economic, rather than a social or cultural quantity. As important, the unsaid is vital: why is the economy now so tough and why do people have to reinvent themselves? In essence, Vaughn and the film reify Fredric Jameson's remark that it is easier nowadays to imagine the end of the world than the 'breakdown of late capitalism'.[22]

The Internship does not explicitly question how the world became like this, nor do Wilson and Vaughn challenge the interns' suggestion that they had it easy. Born in 1968 and 1970 respectively, Wilson and Vaughn are – like Billy and Nick – middle-aged. Less overtly acquisitive than their parents, Gen-Xers tend to crave security, with their economic outlook defined by their childhood experience of the mid-1970s recession, and the financial crashes that followed the dot-com boom of the 1990s and the collapse of Lehman Brothers in 2007. The interns' notion that the 1980s and 1990s were a bygone era where you had a job for life is not borne out by the facts of their generation's experience of neoliberalism, as chronicled in Douglas Coupland's *Generation X*, which traces a group of well-educated and intelligent people forced to work for pennies in precarious, pointless and soul-destroying 'McJobs'.[23] As the sociologist Andrew Ross notes, by the 1990s 'job security was less of an expectation in all sectors of the economy . . . A layoff . . . was almost understood to be part of a job description.'[24] The waning of the New Deal settlement, coupled with the increasing antagonism towards government spending by neoliberals and the New Right, saw the United States economy becoming ever less friendly towards the individual as the Gen-Xers grew to maturity. The Reagan administration's assault on trade unions gagged the voice of ordinary workers and hobbled organised resistance to its attacks on workers' protections. The Clinton administration's dismantling of welfare in the 1990s similarly ensured that the safety net for ordinary Americans shrank to miniscule size. Generation Xers, then, found their lives shaped by the extinguishing of the American Dream so wistfully cited by Google's millennials.

Eggers's novel affords this decline great emphasis, particularly through its depictions of the decaying structures of the Bay Area's built environment after neoliberal economics drove local and state governments to balance their budgets by abandoning social spending: 'all was noise and struggle, failure and filth'.[25] While the film does not explicitly engage in such a contrast, subtle indicators, such as the verdant landscapes, lush indoor greenery and sunlight-dappled offices that we see only within the Circle campus echo the Circle's self-image as sanctuary. That said, while the film's palette brightens inside the Circle, its visuals remain more muted than the primary colours of *The Internship*, which borrow heavily from Google's own branding. Contrasted with the dusty, cramped, brown offices of the watch company, *The Internship*'s Google campus seems to reinforce an ideological message about the corporation's attitude towards its employees.[26] The Circle's and Google's gleaming façades and airy, open-plan spaces encourage workers to enjoy their work/life, while hundreds of evening and weekend activities ensure that they do not stray far from their workstation. Even Circlers' dogs are offered yoga classes; Vaughn and Wilson meanwhile see Googlers relaxing and exercising under blue skies in Google's gardens while helping themselves to free food in its overstocked cafés. As such, the outside world need not exist. Naturally, the life becomes so seductive that Holland abandons her old apartment for a room in the Circle's dormitories; it is not long before she stops seeing even her own parents, sleepwalking into fusing her entire being with her employer.

Exploitation

Through exploiting their compulsion to work hard, Silicon Valley offers protection to its interns and employees from neoliberalism even as it helps transform the economy into a Hobbesian dystopia and them into neoliberal agents. Holland's gradual realisation that the Circle is exploiting her initially appears to contrast with *The Internship*'s valorising of an employment practice that encourages workers' participation in a system that merely oppresses them. *The Internship*'s surtext suggests that Google – and Silicon Valley by extension – has transcended outmoded employment fields such as sales. Yet throughout, the lessons its interns learn are firmly based in this very field, suggesting that, once we strip away the whimsical working atmosphere, the friendly typefaces and the 'don't be evil' sloganeering, Google is little more than the watch sales company that cast Wilson and Vaughn aside.

After learning that only one in twenty of the interns will be hired, Wilson describes competition that drives *The Internship*'s plot as a 'mental Hunger Games against a bunch of genius kids'.[27] In case this led Google's customers to think that these genius kids were in a fight to the death, Google's actual intern coordinator, Kyle Ewing, stated that the real interns, 'play fun games to build team spirit, but there's not a competition. And as for hiring, if we could we'd be hiring them all.'[28] To suggest that there is no competition, when not all of the interns will be hired, constitutes a reality distortion field worthy of Steve Jobs himself. Google made over $10 billion profit on a revenue of $50 billion in 2012, and a year later sat on nearly $59 billion in cash, equivalents and securities. Like many tech companies, it employs a notoriously small workforce, reaping hundreds of millions of dollars profit per employee per year.[29] Ewing's 2013 comment that 'being mean-spirited is not Googley' clearly did not apply to the company itself, which continued to use poorly paid contracted labourers on precarious contracts and even in the film employs a dance instructor who is so broke that she has a second job as a pole dancer in a strip club.[30] Beneath this, Ewing's assertion that the hunger games were actually 'fun' conceals another neoliberal ideological imposition. As the sociologist Andrew Ross acidly observes, the insistence that work can be fun is 'a stock component of the postmodern emotional tool kit'.[31] Interns, as the journalist Madeleine Schwartz points out, are expected to be 'enthusiastic, submissive, and obedient ... flexible, energetic'.[32] This inculcates learned behaviours including expressing gratitude for any work opportunity that appears, no matter how degrading or exploitative. An intern must be a 'fun', 'can-do' person; the lessons of this experience then translate into their future career as a similarly compliant employee.

The Internship's promotional campaign sublimely illustrated the exploitation of interns in June 2013, when it created a National Intern Appreciation Day. The film's producers wanted to show their appreciation for America's unpaid interns by offering them free tickets to certain showings of the film. 'Who better to recognize the tireless workers seeking knowledge and experience about their field of interest – but who in reality are making their supervisors look good – than the film that brings the comic adventures of two very special interns to life', said the press release.³³ A similar cross-promotional hook-up involved an *Internship*-sponsored competition to win a 'dream internship with Miller Lite' beer.³⁴ Sadly, this did not involve receiving adequate payment for a career-building opportunity, but two weeks in a branded vehicle delivering beer to parties, a visit to a Miller brewery and a NASCAR race, and tickets to the film's premiere. Applicants were vetted to ensure selection of those who most closely fitted Miller's self-image. Again, the film explicitly encouraged its key audience to focus on the fun of endless, low-paid work, but beneath this it acknowledged that interns do all the hard work at great cost to themselves.

Meanwhile, the Circle's successful domination of platform capitalism and the dystopia outside enables it to offer feudal levels of patronage. The American musician Beck performs at one evening soirée, although the film poses fewer questions about the Circle's use of entertainers than the novel, which has an unnamed singer-songwriter perform. Annie presents this as yet more largesse on the company's part: it is to give the artists exposure, 'especially given how rough it is out there for them'. Yet as soon as Holland starts to speculate about the cost of this sponsorship, Annie interjects: 'Oh god, we don't *pay* them', before directing her attention elsewhere.³⁵ The artists are almost literally singing for their supper, in the vain hope of winning enough 'likes' from Circle followers to afford to keep practising their art. Like the Sirens, however, the Circle calls these artists to their death, allowing only the most popular to enter the Circle itself, signifying the dominance of platform capitalism over even the creative arts while also providing its employees with yet another reason to remain at work.³⁶ In the film, then, Beck seems to have won this round of the Circle's Hunger Games.

Blurring Work/Life Boundaries

'You assume that a lot of work gets done [at Google], but it wasn't evident,' said Wilson when promoting *The Internship*. 'It just seemed like a nice resort.'³⁷ Such comments highlight two connected problematics of Silicon Valley employment practices: first the reconfiguration of work as leisure, and second the issue of individual discipline. This 'resort' might prove distracting to slackers such as Wilson, but to the highly motivated tech wizards he encounters, it provides a backdrop to serious work. Yet this discipline does not simply emerge through individual devotion: it is also a consequence of data-driven employment practices (as experienced by the interns when they compete to solve as many customer enquiries as possible on Google's hotline) and observation (the Googleplex might be airy and built predominantly in glass, but such openness facilitates surveillance; similarly, the hotline task rests on a quantified performance rating). Again, *The Circle* renders explicit *The Internship*'s implicit criticism. Rather than boosting Holland's confidence and competence, these working practices undermine her almost completely. Immediately, she is asked to work at a desk housing a monitor, phone and tablet computer. Very quickly she learns that the Circle's expectation levels are set just above her current achievements. Soon after, she receives a second monitor and then a third. Before long, she is monitoring five screens, a laptop, her phone and her tablet. Initially, she finds work seductive and exhilarating, reflecting the rush of our first online experiences. Soon, however, she is battered by customer enquiries who offer instantaneous ratings of her performance. She must keep her average rating high, with a trainer so picky that he even finds a 99% satisfaction rate dissatisfying, while also fielding intra-office messages and microblogs on the Circle's Zing service, a situation that is only bearable because of the constant validation offered by the feedback.[38]

Of course, this validation is a two-way relationship, and Holland is soon pressured to respond in appropriately glowing terms to her new 'friends'. Within one week in the novel she has amassed 10,000 social media messages and is finding the interconnectedness exhausting.[39] The company presents this interaction with social media as essential

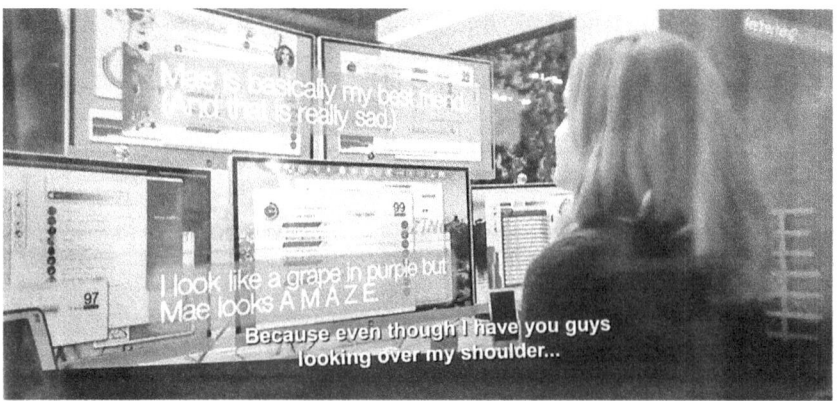

Figure 6.1 Mae Holland's workspace, complete with instant surveillance from her followers. (Cropped screenshot, 1h00m).

to maintaining each employee's work-life balance while also ranking them in terms of their popularity on a minute-by-minute basis, a ranking that is presented as 'fun', but which has sinister undertones that Holland initially cannot grasp. This gamification of the world of work enables the Circle to extract the maximum labour from its employees, rendering its campus little more than a twenty-first-century workhouse. This transformation is made possible in part because of the Circlers' blithe acceptance of the destruction of the borderline between professional and personal life and their ignorance of centuries of workers' struggles for their rights. The novel renders this crystal-clear when Mae is given an online profile called MaeDay, named after a 'war holiday'.[40] Neither she nor her guru are aware that May Day is International Workers Day, an annual commemoration of the Haymarket Affair that itself was a product of protests against unfair and exploitative working conditions.

As this suggests, many Silicon Valley corporations expect their employees to work whenever possible, rendering the dorms and campuses as much a system of control as of liberation from rent or mortgage payments. They might give employees a comfortable bed for the night and free access to cool stuff, but in return the workers agree to destroy the distinction between their working and non-working, public and private lives. Like Douglas Coupland's Microserfs, Silicon Valley workers must maintain discipline – one little fear that adds to other fears: of underproduction, of failing to be rewarded with stock options, of the loss of perks, of disposability.[41] Early on, the Circle's Bailey reveals a tiny hi-resolution camera that, completely unnoticed, broadcasts images from around the world, revealing his and the Circle's ultimate ambition: 'Tyrants and terrorists can no longer hide. We will see them. We will hear them. We will hear and see everything.'[42] No Circler questions whether this is an appropriate use of technology or ponders its implications for individual privacy, not least their own.

Yet the Circle's violation of Holland goes much further. From the moment she arrives, Holland's life becomes open access. Annie takes her on a tour of the campus and within seconds of them entering an elevator, old life-size photographs of the two friends appear on its walls, to Annie's studied indifference. Without realising, Holland has allowed the Circle to plunder her forgotten memories, to construct an entirely distinct, ethereal online Mae. Thus, the original banality, user-friendliness and supposed trustworthiness of the web morphs into a surveillance dystopia as Holland must live up to her online image; her memories might have faded but the Circle considers them, like *Strange Days*' SQUID footage, her eternal present. At an appointment with the staff clinic she ingests a sensor that will permanently monitor her health, literally exposing her entire body to the Circle's surveillance. The nurse makes no mention of the sensor's existence in a bag of green gloop until it is too late for Holland to offer or refuse consent.[43] Like the equisapiens of *Sorry to Bother You*, she must become a compliant and efficient workhorse because this violation enables the Circle to judge whether she is eating the right foods (that enable her to work effectively), drinking the right liquids (a hydrated brain is a working brain), taking the right exercise (a healthy body is a productive body) and doing everything she can to render herself as close to the Circle's ideal human as she can, thus creating a new level of discipline. Reflecting the gendered dimensions of this invasion, Wilson and Vaughn suffer no such indignities. Indeed, Vaughn actively subverts any thoughts Google had of perfecting him through diet by ingesting as many free desserts as he can, much to the dismay of the intern programme's coordinator.

The Circle's surveillance state operates even when Holland fleetingly breaks free of the campus to kayak on the untamed San Francisco Bay. On the Bay she has time to reflect, to appreciate the slow pace of natural life, even to weep for her father whose medical condition is increasingly debilitating, away from her colleagues' and her employer's prying eyes. None of this is appropriate – or even possible – in the Circle campus, where every moment is monitored and monetised. Yet this is not a haven. Holland takes to the Bay in desperation midway through the film, after Mercer declares that he wants no part of her new (online) world. Fog quickly descends and she gets into trouble. She is only rescued because a Circle camera mounted on a nearby buoy has her in its sights. Naturally, the Circle adopts a technology-solutionist approach to the outcome of this event. In return for rescuing her, it manipulates her to broadcast her entire life through its platform in order to prevent her doing something as ill-advised again. Her life thus becomes a new form of immaterial labour for the corporation.[44] In so doing, *The Circle* refashions the role of surveillance technology to the prevention of individual free will. The threat no longer emanates from supposedly rogue states or shadowy groups dedicated to undermining the American way of life but from the subjects of surveillance themselves, and specifically their outmoded need for privacy, kayaking or even high-calorie desserts. The Circle will thus not protect us from attack but from our id. After all, as Google's Eric Schmidt warned in 2009: 'If you have something that you do not want anyone to know, maybe you should not be doing it in the first place.'[45]

The triple issues of consent, commodification and work also define Mercer's fate. His position as an empathetic, almost romantic throwback to an earlier, simpler time, coupled with his fate, presents him as a quasi-religious figure reminiscent of his namesake in Philip K. Dick's *Do Androids Dream of Electric Sheep?* (1968). In a post-apocalyptic San Francisco, the few humans who remain Earthbound are encouraged to 'fuse' regularly with other humans in a virtual reality that places them in the mind and body of 'Mercer', an individual who toils up a mountain in Sisyphean fashion while faceless hordes cast rocks at him. Designed to remind humans of the need for empathy, Mercerism forms a bulwark against the potential of androids to wipe out humanity. *Androids'* irony is that Mercer is a fraud constructed to keep the remnants of the populace quiescent.[46] *The Circle*'s Mercer embodies empathy, an ability Holland loses once the Circle sucks her in, as demonstrated by her reasoning that publicising his work will drive his sales, but more importantly, boost her profile. Naturally, the Circlophobic artist confronts her in person. The Circle's mediation of Holland's life, he says, has definitively corrupted her. In essence, she has become a commodity herself, as the Circle's regretful founder Ty tells her only moments before.[47] Holland's discussion with Mercer attracts the attention of other Circlers who conclude erroneously that his desire for privacy conceals his predilection for killing deer. He must then sacrifice himself to alert humanity to the potential loss of the very thing that makes it human.

Holland's transformation into the Circle's commodity receives visual emphasis after she agrees to transparency. Wherever she moves, a sequence of social media messages follow onscreen, indicating that her life is now public – or rather, the Circle's – property. The messages offer a commentary on the film's events and the banality, ennui and anomie of the online life. Holland, according to one of her followers, is 'so cute in the morning'.[48] 'I'm boredddd,' complains another, while others note their own loneliness (which is perhaps a consequence of their compulsive Holland-watching): 'Three weeks of watching Mae wake up and go to work'; 'Mae is basically my best friend. (And that is really sad)'; 'I haven't spoken to my parents in two years'; 'I've never been touched by someone who loves me'; 'Mae is the best friend I've never had'. What's more, some comments illustrate the observers' awareness of the malignancy of the Circle. 'Do you guys ever go home?' asks one, while another tells Holland to 'Wiggle your ears if you need to be rescued.' As the Circle's quest for online dominance expands, they begin to question the company's ethics: 'Fusing govt and Circle = Corporate Tyranny'; 'Anyone else feel like we're in the prologue of a disaster film?' 'What about Hobbes?' ('I love that cartoon' riffs a Calvinian respondent); although others consider the Circle's attempt to usurp the voter registration process to be 'the start of a revolution'. Their reactions to Mercer's death again reveal that online interaction breeds vacuity even in the face of horror: 'It's nobody's fault'; 'we forgive you', writes one, as if the forgiveness was theirs to give. While one observer questions – in time-honoured online fashion – whether Mercer's death was faked, others denounce the Circle as a cult that has let loose an angry mob. The overwhelming sense, however, is that even Mercer's death has not ruptured their relationship with the Circle or brought any sense of their own culpability. One watcher declares: 'I quit social media for 2 days in honour of Mercer', as if that would cause the Circle to rethink its priorities. Of course, the comments reinforce Holland's sense that she is being surveilled. All appear in white text on a red background, emphasising the sense that they act as a brake on Holland's own instincts as she moves through life under their authors' surveillance. That the messages fade into the background as she makes her decisive move towards independence acts as visual confirmation of her determination to leave the Circle's control behind her, quite literally so as she briefly strides into an independent future.

The Internship, meanwhile, is loaded with insights into Silicon Valley's blurring of work and play. Perhaps the most insidious task involves the interns creating an app, a job that nearly tears the group apart, prompting a team-building trip to a San Francisco lap-dancing club. Ejected from the club after a drunken fight, they retire to a promontory in Marin County that facilitates a cinematic view over the Golden Gate Bridge to the promised land of San Francisco as the sun improbably rises over the Pacific Ocean. There, the tired and emotional interns engage in heart-to-heart conversations, while Wilson and Vaughn encourage them to lose their cynicism, appreciate themselves and develop a new app to prevent drunk owners misusing their smartphones. Here the film implies that Google's workplace hinders the free thinking of its employees, while also suggesting that alcoholic overindulgence and a touch of violence unlock true creativity. More malevolently, it suggests that Google freely exploits its employees' ideas, feelings and even experiences as they donate their cognitive labour during every waking moment. The interns' free time becomes (un)salaried time; like Mae Holland, they might be able to separate themselves physically from the workplace, but their ideas always become corporate property. The reward for their ingenuity comes courtesy of the free market: ten times more consumers download their app than that of their competitors.

Figure 6.2 *The Internship*'s interns reflect on a bacchanalian night out in San Francisco, looking south from the Marin headlands. Note the shadow on the left of Owen Wilson's light-coloured shirt, suggesting sunlight from the west. (Cropped screenshot, 1h11m).

The marketplace's invisible hand confers victory on them, indicating that beneath Google's promotional guff lies a simple fact: it is in the sales business, reminding us that, after its stock market flotation, the company shifted the purpose of its data collection from improving search (through the data offered by searchers) to generating revenue (by selling targeted ads to searchers).[49] As significant, nothing in the film suggests that the interns will own a stake in the app they create. Instead, the intellectual copyright will defer to the corporation and enable it to target yet more adverts at key demographics.

Building on this, the interns' final task obliquely references Google's aggressive stance towards local search specialist Yelp, which involved relegating Yelp results in Google searches, thus reducing Yelp's market share, and confirms that platform capitalism is merely an internet-enabled version of time-honoured capitalist practices.[50] Here, the interns must convince Sal, an independent pizza shop owner, to sign a contract with Google's advertising division in order to boost his presence in the local online marketplace. Naturally, the process by which this is achieved owes little to technology: it is merely a repeat of the very same sales practice at which Wilson and Vaughn excel. But with Vaughn experiencing a minor crisis of confidence and Wilson attempting to rescue his friend from a horrific gig selling motor scooters to retired women, their millennial teammates struggle to sell Google to

Sal until the Generation Xers return. Significantly, Vaughn escapes on a Google-branded bicycle: *The Internship* here simultaneously laughs at the incongruity of Vaughn (who previously drove a convertible) reduced to human-powered transport while subtly hinting at the bicycle's symbolic role as a technology that confers independence on and broadens the horizons of its users. Inevitably, however, life outside the Googleplex is unbearable, and Wilson convinces Vaughn to return, enabling him to lead the group in delivering a series of meaningless bromides designed only to ensure that Sal's shop becomes wrapped up in Google's platform capitalism. Sal is initially adamant that he does not need Google's contextual ad service, believes that franchising his business would dilute the quality of his secret pizza sauce, and wishes to remain firmly rooted in the community that supports him. Vaughn retorts with a familiar Silicon Valley promise of making his neighbourhood bigger thanks to Google's knowledge of the desires of people in the wider area, courtesy of its monopoly control of local search requests. Vaughn and Wilson's bullshit sales patter forces him to reach for the online future. Once he signs up, Google rewards them with contracts and affords Sal the opportunity to absorb greater risks to his business through expansion. Not long before this scene, Wilson and Vaughn's former boss expresses incredulity that they are now working at Google: 'you're salesmen!' he booms.[51] They most definitely proved him correct.

Both films, then, initially have their principal characters learn that platform capitalism is the future, where you can 'do something that matters' in a life where 'who knows what's gonna happen', rather than one dominated by their daily need to make a sale or settle somebody's utility bill.[52] Yet underneath the self-serving 'changing the world' propaganda, the Circle only exists to perpetuate itself, finding ever more extreme and unconscionable methods through which to tether everybody to its services. Meanwhile, Google merely renders capitalist expansion more attractive to a sole trader (significantly, after the competition, the head of the intern programme declares Sal's a 'blossoming franchise with endless possibilities').[53] Vaughn and Wilson might have connected people, but they have also placed Sal on the rocky road towards further debt and to the inevitable decline in quality that large-scale franchising involves, not to mention the instability of running multiple outlets while forking out extra advertising dollars. Google might appear to be 'a million times better' than 'the greatest amusement park you've ever been to', but like the Circle, it differs little from 'old' capitalist enterprises. Early on, and conforming to slacker stereotype, Vaughn confides in Wilson, 'we can coattail this bitch'.⁵⁴ These vapid salesmen, always seeking shortcuts and prepared to say almost anything to close a deal, fit perfectly in Google's world.

Notes

1. Because *The Internship* was essentially built around their screen personae, this book will refer to Vaughn and Wilson by their real rather than fictional names. The book refers to all other characters by their fictional names.
2. 'Mark Kermode reviews *The Internship*'.
3. McNary, 'Cannes: Tom Hanks Thriller "The Circle" Gets Financing from Image Nation'.
4. 'Filming Locations for "The Circle"'.
5. Erbland, 'The Circle: James Ponsoldt Explains Why His Dave Eggers Adaptation Isn't Just Another Film About Dangers of Technology'; Weintraub, 'James Ponsoldt on "The Circle"'.
6. Kelly, 'Why Google Loves *The Internship*'; Marco della Cava, 'For Actual Google Interns, "Work" is the Keyword', *USA Today*, June 7, 2013, <https://eu.usatoday.com/story/life/movies/2013/06/06/the-internship-google-real-summer-interns/2386367> (consulted June 28, 2022); Grover and Oreskovic, 'Google Goes Hollywood with "The Internship"'; Brandon Bailey and Charlie McCollum, 'Google Movie Preview: "Internship" Shows Tech Giant Exactly As It Wants to be Seen', *Mercury News*, May 31, 2013, <https://www.mercurynews.com/2013/05/31/google-movie-preview-internship-shows-tech-giant-exactly-as-it-wants-to-be-seen> (consulted June 28, 2022). Vaughn co-wrote the screenplay with Jared Stern, who previously wrote the Vaughn-starring *The Watch* (Schaffer, 2012): 'The Watch'.
7. Bailey and McCollum, 'Google Movie Preview'.
8. Della Cava, 'For Actual Google Interns'.
9. Kirchick, 'Angry White Man'; 'Vince Vaughn & Ron Paul at LPAC 2011' (quote); Handler, 'An Interview with Vince Vaughn'; Nick Bilton, 'Silicon Valley's Most Disturbing Obsession', *Vanity Fair*, October 5, 2016, <https://www.vanityfair.com/news/2016/10/silicon-valley-ayn-rand-obsession> (consulted June 28, 2022).
10. Manohla Dargis, 'Laurel and Hardy in Google's Toyland', *New York Times*, June 6, 2013, <https://www.nytimes.com/2013/06/07/movies/the-internship-with-vince-vaughn-and-owen-wilson.html> (consulted June 28, 2022).
11. Lyons, *Disrupted*, 51; Spencer, *People's History*, 77–8; Robert Pogue Harrison, 'The Children of Silicon Valley', *New York Review of Books*, July 17, 2014, <https://www.nybooks.com/daily/2014/07/17/children-silicon-valley> (consulted June 28, 2022); Cohen, *Know-It-Alls*, 74,

82–3, 122–3, 158–9; 'About' *Andreessen Horowitz*; 'Andreessen Horowitz, Matrix Partners Invest $11.2 Million in Meteor'; Pein, *Live Work Work Work Die*, 105–6, 193, 226, 281; Isaacson, *Steve Jobs*, 114–15, 154, 175, 403; Losse, *Boy Kings*, 199–200.
12. Dargis, 'Laurel and Hardy in Google's Toyland'; Shawn Levy, audio commentary, 1m, *The Internship* DVD.
13. Claire Cain Miller, 'Vince Vaughn and Owen Wilson Arrive in Silicon Valley', *New York Times*, June 7, 2013, <https://bits.blogs.nytimes.com/2013/06/07/vince-vaughn-and-owen-wilson-arrive-in-silicon-valley> (consulted June 14, 2019); della Cava, 'For Actual Google Interns'; Keyser, 'Candy Boys and Chocolate Factories', 403–7, 420–1. Levy also makes this comparison in his audio commentary.
14. *The Circle*, 39m.
15. *The Circle*, 1h34.
16. *The Internship*, 5m.
17. Caroom, 'Report: Businesses Going Bankrupt'; Velazco, 'How Google's Smartphones Have Evolved Since 2007'; Horrigan, 'Trends in Online Shopping'; Thompson, 'Mobile Online Shopping to Double in 2010'; Aaron Smith, 'The Rise of In-Store Mobile Commerce'.
18. Both quotes: *The Circle*, 5m.
19. Ross, *No-Collar*, 80.
20. *The Internship*, 59m.
21. First quote: Jonathan Heaf, '*True Detective*'s Vince Vaughn on Gun Control, Edward Snowden and Comedy'; second quote: della Cava, 'For Actual Google Interns'.
22. Jameson, *Seeds of Time*, xii.
23. Coupland, *Generation X*, 5, 6, 130.
24. Ross, *No-Collar*, 21.
25. Eggers, *The Circle*, 30.
26. Eggers, *The Circle*, 370; Shawn Levy, audio commentary, 22m.
27. *The Internship*, 27m.
28. Both quotes: della Cava, 'For Actual Google Interns'.
29. 'Google's Net Income from 2001 to 2015'; 'Google 2012 Revenue Hits $50 Billion, Profits Up'; Rosenblatt, 'Google Demolishes Financial Expectations to Close 2013'; Srnicek, *Platform Capitalism*, 4.
30. Shontell, 'What It's Really Like to be a Google Intern'; Spencer, *People's History of Silicon Valley*, 26–7, 80; della Cava, 'For Actual Google Interns'.
31. Ross, *No-Collar*, 88; Tews et al., 'Workplace Fun Matters . . . But What Else', 248–67.
32. Schwartz, 'Opportunity Costs: The True Price of Internships'.
33. 'The Internship Celebrates National Intern Appreciation Day'.
34. 'Groups of Friends Wanted for Ultimate Miller Time "Internship"'.
35. Eggers, *The Circle*, 17.
36. Eggers, *The Circle*, 325.

37. Miller, 'Vince Vaughn and Owen Wilson Arrive in Silicon Valley'.
38. *The Circle*, 9m, 27m, 45m.
39. Eggers, *The Circle*, 98, 105.
40. Eggers, *The Circle*, 97.
41. Coupland, *Microserfs*, 38.
42. *The Circle*, 14m.
43. *The Circle*, 8m, 34m; Dinnen, *Digital Banal*, 105, 111.
44. *The Circle*, 48m; Fuchs, 'Web 2.0, Prosumption, and Surveillance', 299.
45. Quoted in Fuchs, 'Web 2.0', 290.
46. Dick, *Do Androids*, 19–23, 27–8, 152–4, 177–80, 198–202.
47. *The Circle*, 32m, 40m, 45m.
48. All comments in this paragraph: *The Circle*, 59m, 1h00, 1h24, 1h34. See also figure 6.1.
49. Ross, *No-Collar*, 19; Srnicek, *Platform Capitalism*, 52–3; Zuboff, *Age of Surveillance Capitalism*, 72–4.
50. Foroohar, *Don't Be Evil*, 131–5.
51. *The Internship*, 1h14.
52. *The Internship*, 13m, 1h14.
53. *The Internship*, 1h42m.
54. *The Internship*, 22m, 30m.

Chapter 7

Dystopian Diversity

In the very first episode of *Silicon Valley*, Gavin Belson spots from his panoptic office window a multitude of Hooli computer engineers wandering around the company's grounds. 'They always travel in groups of five,' he muses, 'a tall skinny white guy, short skinny Asian guy, fat guy with a ponytail, some guy with crazy facial hair and then an East Indian guy. It's like they trade guys until they all have the right group.'[1] Belson here revealingly highlights Silicon Valley's racial diversity. Yet his observation overlooks the under-representation of African and African American people in these groups and the fact that each man in each group seems no older than thirty. His final elision relates to the tech entrepreneur Reid Hoffman's observation that sexism is much more prevalent and explicit than racism in Silicon Valley: no women appear in the groups he sees and thus employs.[2] *The Circle* and *The Internship* confirm this heavily masculine and almost completely white environment, even as both over-represent women and global majority people in Silicon Valley corporations. As important, each film highlights Silicon Valley's problematic approach to the concept of diversity, while both force their leading female characters to ensure a series of punishments that at once highlights Silicon Valley's casual misogyny while extending the gender critique embedded in the biopics of Jobs and Zuckerberg.

Racial Diversity

The Internship ostensibly presents Google as a paragon of diversity and anti-discrimination, beginning with Vaughn and Wilson's introduction to Google's workers. As if to reinforce the notion that Generation Xers lived in a different age, they must endure a humiliating interview process before being inducted into Google. Echoing their former boss's lamentations about a computer-driven economy, this is not a face-to-face meeting but one that takes place in a virtual zone. Naturally, as unemployed, superannuated oldies, they do not possess a home computer with a broadband connection fast enough to host live video, so they retreat to a public library for the interview. Significantly, they meet in the children's section, suggesting that Google will release them from their emasculating perpetual Gen-X childhood and enable them to grow (up).

When asked for their academic credentials, they report that they are enrolled at the University of Phoenix, which Wilson describes as 'the Harvard of internet colleges'. This offers a layered joke.[3] At the surface, it prompts a laugh at the university's lax policing of its entrants and attendance on its courses, the low value of the education on offer through its virtual campuses and Vaughn and Wilson's dismissive attitude towards higher education. Beneath, it trumpets Google's recruiters' lack of discrimination against candidates from less prestigious universities, thus reinforcing Google's self-image as an enlightened, meritocratic employer. Below this again, it alludes to the problems wrought on American society by dot-com companies, and the way in which the widespread popularity of the web contains both a democratising and a debasing influence. When the film was released, the University of Phoenix, owned by a profit-making corporation, was renowned for the wrong reasons. In 2000, it agreed to pay the Department of Education $6 million to resolve charges that it had granted financial aid to ineligible students. In 2009, the completion rate of its undergraduate cohort lay at 34%, amid accusations that the university paid off students' loans when they withdrew from their studies but then demanded reimbursement under significantly less favourable terms.[4] That same year the university agreed to pay $78 million to the federal government (including $11 million in legal fees) to settle a whistle-blower suit that revolved around it obtaining federal aid for students under false pretences.[5] As *The Internship* was being prepared for release, the university was under investigation over its relationship to its parent company, retention rates, assessment standards and continued reliance on federal aid. No wonder that it spent hundreds of millions of dollars on online advertising to boost its presence in the marketplace.[6] By 2015, it ranked third in the United States for graduate student debt, with a total of $35.5 billion in outstanding loans to students. Figures from 2014 indicate that nearly 20% of its graduates defaulted, suggesting that its model of online higher education was more akin to a Ponzi scheme than a tool for social mobility.[7]

One of Google's recruiters, a twenty-three-year-old played by Josh Brener (who later achieved stardom as *Silicon Valley*'s inexplicably dense Nelson Bighetti), argues that, in spite of their poor academic credentials and advanced age, Wilson and Vaughn should be hired. 'Diversity is in our DNA, right?,' he says. 'I thought the goal here was to find people with a different way of thinking.'[8] His complete misinterpretation of 'diversity' transposes the concept from protected characteristics such as race, disability, gender or ethnicity to the simple matter of thought, thus enabling the continuation of Google's lamentable inattention to real workforce diversity. After all, the last people Google needs is another pair of cisgender, heterosexual white men. As problematically, Google's famed off-the-wall interview questions, such as the one posed to Vaughn and Wilson – you are shrunk to the size of a nickel and dropped into a food blender: what do you do? – focus less on problem-solving skills and more on the confidence to fake the requisite brainpower. The journalist Anna Wiener, who previously worked in Silicon Valley, compared this strategy to a fraternity hazing. Her fellow tech journalist Emily Chang notes that men are much more likely take risks in answering such questions irrespective of whether they know the answer.[9] Similarly, the questions themselves – and the positive response of interviewers to those who brazen out the answers – say more about interviewers than interviewees. As Shawn Levy was told, Google interviewers designed their questions not to test problem-solving or engineering skills but to work out which candidates they would prefer to sit alongside in an airport bar during a six-hour layover. As such, their hiring decisions more accurately reflect their own personal biases than the candidates' suitability for the job, and would therefore be more likely to entrench Google's monoculture. No wonder Google abandoned this interview technique in 2013.[10]

When they join the intern ranks, Wilson and Vaughn find themselves rejected by the overwhelmingly white, upper- or middle-class, Ivy League-attending high achievers so beloved of graduate recruiters across the US. In allowing the intern groups to self-select, *The Internship* highlights Silicon Valley's absorption of an individualistic, highly competitive dog-eat-dog ethos, one that enables pre-existing prejudices to flourish (such as a rival intern's predilection for Ivy League and attractive female team members) rather than challenging them at the most obvious opportunity. Alongside Vaughn and Wilson are a group of multicultural 'leftovers': a shy, workaholic Asian American perfectionist who lives in fear of his Tiger Mom, a nervous Indian American who presents a hyper-sexual image as cover for her insecurities, and a diffident WASPish wiseacre permanently welded to his smartphone, resentful at being chained to such a substandard team.[11]

Their mentor, the awkward Brener, has never previously led an intern team, and is clearly a leftover himself. Initially, this seems to present the Ivy Leaguers as the problem, yet in creating such a diverse mix of stereotypes while ignoring the African American and Latinx population, allocating them to an inexperienced leader, and assigning them a derogatory term, *The Internship* suggests that we think more critically about Google's claims to inclusion.

The Circle, meanwhile, cast the British-Nigerian actor John Boyega as Circle founder Ty, whose simultaneous presence and absence on the Circle's campus reaffirms the power wielded by white men in the Valley. Ty might have designed much of the Circle's software, but he has been marginalised to the extent that he almost literally lives in the shadows. The public faces of the company are instead two white male elders, Bailey and Stenton. The only major Black figure is thus forced into the background despite having greater coding skills than the whites, to the extent that he drifts about the campus without anybody recognising him (indeed, Mae Holland seems astonished when she discovers his identity). Here, the film touches on the notion that white America ignores the vast Black American contribution to the nation; Ty is a millennial descendant of Ralph Ellison's *Invisible Man*. That he is the Circle's last remaining figure with a conscience adds a further layer of intrigue to his exclusion, again suggesting that a white America in thrall to capitalism simply will not acknowledge the profound critique of its ways that are propounded by those it systematically excludes.

Generational Diversity

As the film critic A. A. Dowd highlights, *The Internship* is not so much a workplace film as a campus comedy, 'populated almost exclusively with archetypes' from the latter genre.[12] This, of course, is precisely Google's aim: to present its staff as exciting, fresh, and most important, young, in order to discourage a critical approach to its world of work. Yet the students' embracing of two Gen-Xers offers suggestive glimpses into Google's belief that it might overcome generation gaps. After the loss of their jobs and Vaughn's home, the normally risk-averse Generation Xers wager their entire futures on Google.[13] This comes despite their digital incompetence, unawareness of the differences between programming languages, and ignorance of popular apps such as Instagram and the code that underpins websites such as Google's search engine. Vaughn does not even know what 'online' means. Ostensibly, they bring a homespun wisdom to Google, earned in their years of pre-digital employment experience, and because they are well-versed in the chicanery and easy patter of the salesman, their conviviality (a soft skill that Google treasures) wins over the recruiters.

Wilson and Vaughn are classically Generation X in that they occupy a liminal position between the digital and pre-digital world, bridge the liberal and neoconservative political eras and follow a generation of socially engaged individuals while predating a withdrawn generation of millennials. While they might use smartphones and possess an awareness of digital apps such as Facebook, they tend to be dabblers rather than manipulators of these digital worlds: hence Vaughn's 'on-the-line' malapropism.[14] They are inimical to the joyless automatons who know not to take food home, would never consider drinking alcohol with their boss, and aware that they should not date fellow interns or staff members, 'say no to love'.[15] Yet like them, they desire a job that 'matters', as Vaughn confesses. Naturally, though, they cannot comprehend the millennials' cultural touchstones. When attempting to divert them during one of the internship tasks, one team member urges them to head to the Stanford University campus to find a programmer named Professor Charles Xavier. Unaware that he is a Marvel comics character who came to widespread renown when played by the actor Patrick Stewart in *X-Men* (Bryan Singer, 2000), the Gen-Xers unintentionally offend a wheelchair-bound academic who resembles the fictional figure. Similarly, they struggle with Quidditch, the sport from the Harry Potter books beloved by Googlers. Yet the film stresses the importance of the mélange of pop-culture references – defined as a classical Gen-X trait as far back as Douglas Coupland's *Generation X* (first published in 1991) – that Wilson and Vaughn bring to the campus, including references to hit 1980s movies such as *The Fly* (David Cronenberg, 1986) and *Flashdance* (Adrian Lyne, 1981) that they presumably watched first on an illegally-rented VHS tape or during surreptitious late-night television viewings. As the elder party in the Gen-X/Millennial relationship, they bring wisdom and experience to the youngsters. Here the film suggests that Google's faith in youth is misplaced; instead it needs Gen-Xers if the corporation is to flourish. The youthful interns might attempt to demonstrate their superiority by exploiting Vaughn and Wilson's ignorance of *X-Men*, but in doing so, they enter the same pop-cultural turf as the masters, who bombard them with the arcane references in which they are immersed. Indeed, arguably the greatest lesson the interns learn comes when their mentor Lyle references the Gen-X touchstone *Back to the Future* (Robert Zemeckis, 1985), itself a Reaganite paean to sexual abstinence, teetotalism and patriarchy, that taught him a punch to the jaw proves more alluring to women than a sensitive, literary disposition.

While less explicit, *The Circle* also references this generation gap: only Stenton and Bailey (played by actors in their late 40s and early 60s) appear to be out of their twenties. Part of the reason that no Circlers seem to go home is the simple fact that they are young enough not to have responsibilities to partners, children or (Holland excepted) dependant parents. And without family mouths to feed, why not take advantage of the abundant free food available at the Circle? Here, *The Circle* intersects with *The Internship*, and the sardonic observation of one real Google intern: this largesse discourages them from learning to cook, creating a permanent state of dependence that tethers them to the workplace.[16] As this suggests, youthful employees might bring zest to the workplace but their impressionability and desire to convert their precarious jobs to more permanent contracts enables employers to exploit their labour more efficiently, as the trainers who admonish Holland for going home over the weekend do. She quickly learns that, while evening and weekend activities are optional, the company takes notice of those who do not partake in such organised fun, considering them 'integral' to each employee's 'participation' in the Circle and a way to unlock their 'unlimited potential'.[17] Her trainer's smile-frown, designed to show disapproval while also maintaining perkiness, thus appears as a sinister front for exploitation, another manifestation of the Circle's cultish qualities.

Silicon Valley Sexism

The preceding discussions of racial and generational diversity lead to the diversity issue that the films engage with most explicitly: Silicon Valley's huge gender problem. Its superficially meritocratic structure masks a hierarchical, masculinist patriarchal culture that produces numerous problematic outcomes, both for individuals and for their employers.[18] Meanwhile, the world that Wilson and Vaughn introduce to the Googlers involves meaningless hedonism, objectification of women and fighting. After Vaughn decides that the group needs a team-building exercise, they head to a San Francisco restaurant (in the Google Bus, naturally, for none of them have a car and Google would not have them using public transport) before continuing the party at a lap-dancing club. Once inside, the wiseacre intern learns to look up from his smartphone to see a 'great big world out there', embodied in a scantily clad woman who wordlessly leads him away for some pleasure. Her demeanour suggests that she has been paid to perform. The group shares multiple drinks oblivious to a caged dancer gyrating behind them, while Wilson tells one intern that alcohol will not enable him to develop self-respect, but that it constitutes a 'step in the right direction', before the Gen-Xers pay for him to receive three lap dances (the first dancer is identified as a student, as if that absolves them of exploiting her).[19] Lyle meanwhile discovers that the Google dance tutor to whom he is attracted moonlights as a pole dancer at the club. Calling this work an augmentation of her Google salary because the latter does not cover her tuition costs, she exemplifies the porous boundary between sex work and higher education in the 2010s, not to mention the suffering due to the inadequate wages offered to many females who serve tech workers: a stunning indictment of Google's support for her career ambitions.[20] Vaughn convinces Lyle to ditch his contrived patter when attempting to woo her (while she wears only a bra, panties and stockings), enabling him to win her love. Triumphantly, Lyle also absorbs one of the key slacker lessons. His use of a *Back to the Future* reference to humiliate an antagonist who has designs on his female companion demonstrates that he has learned that outmoded yet irreverent cultural references and a devil-may-care attitude are routes to self-fulfilment and happiness. The mass brawl that ensues ends with the alcohol-sodden interns victorious but expelled from the club, the men having successfully defended the honour of 'their' women.

The Circle's promotion of two conventionally attractive white women in Annie and Mae extends this tacit acceptance of tech-bro culture, not least because, while they might be the public faces of the corporation, both remain subordinate to the men at the Circle's top. Notably, like most of the women who joined Facebook during its early years, Holland starts at customer enquiries, a position disdained by male engineers because it requires no ability to code.[21] Such roles provide an essential buffer between the socially inadequate engineers and the site's users, offering a heavily gendered human face for the company. At a higher level in the Circle, Holland's college friend Annie discovers to her cost the disposability of female employees. A member of the Circle's Gang of 40, a leadership cult that references the Chinese Cultural Revolution, she begins the film as the Circle's perky public face, exhilarated at her globetrotting antics, but increasingly exhausted by the Circle's demands and indifference towards her health and well-being. She becomes withdrawn and paranoid, eventually retreating to rural Scotland after an overdose and a breakdown. The men in the Gang of 40 do not suffer such consequences. Indeed, the only suggestion that they might suffer anything comes when Holland and Ty belatedly render Bailey and Stenton's trail of dishonest paperwork public, prompting Bailey to whisper to his co-conspirator: 'we are so fucked'.[22] Notably, however, the film ends by suggesting that the Circle continues to monitor everybody's every activity, leaving open the question as to whether the two were really 'fucked'.

Meanwhile, *The Circle* makes two women the first – and in the film's chronology, only – people to have their entire lives broadcast online. Both come at the behest of the men who control the Circle, who dominate the corporation in much the same way as Steve Jobs and Mark Zuckerberg do Apple and Facebook. One is a congresswoman, the other Holland, punished for her kayaking transgression in a process that offers more evidence of her disposability. Following her misadventure on the Bay, she endures a stage-managed interview in front of the Circle's employees at which she admits that, had she known that security cameras were monitoring her, she would not have dared take the trip. This self-criticism reinforces the film's suggestion that the Circle – and by extension the many Silicon Valley corporations it resembles – is cultish, both in its presentation of its leaders and in the way in which it demands complete obedience from its employees, especially its female ones. Her punishment unites her corporeal body with her online presence while confirming that the Circle simply must know everything about the user. Constant feedback through her social media feed and through interactions with her fellow workers reinforce the Circle's ownership of her, forcing her into a permanently sunny disposition.[23]

The impact of 'transparency' on Mae is so devastating that it wrecks the lives of her family and Mercer. After learning of her father's multiple sclerosis and her family's struggle to finance his healthcare, the Circle absorbs them into its health insurance plan. This is no benevolent gesture, however. Because the family's privacy possesses an appropriate exchange value, the Circle extracts payment via surveillance: Holland's parents must welcome Circle cameras into their home and have their every moment monitored, ostensibly because the Circle wishes to analyse Mae's father's condition. Unlike Mae, however, they do not adjust their behaviour to the panopticon, and in failing to discipline themselves, they are punished by having their sex life broadcast to her multitudinous followers when she inadvertently alights upon their bedroom camera. The film's viewers witness the scene through the distorting lens of the surveillance camera, adding an uncanniness to the sex as we watch Mae and her followers invade the last vestige of her parents' privacy. Thus, her surveillance renders what was once natural (and private) unnatural (and public). Like the surveilled Harry Caul, Holland's family must rid their lives of anything truly meaningful and become as meaningless as the vapid modern art that Mae lauds as she wanders about the Circle campus. Her powerlessness before this cult becomes even more apparent when, after announcing the Circle's ability to find a fugitive from justice within moments, thanks to its technology and the willingness of its users to do its bidding, the Circlers demand that the technophobic supposed deer-killer Mercer be located. She cannot resist the wisdom of the crowd: a distressing reminder that Silicon Valley merely replicates and perhaps even fortifies the sexist assumptions that underpin society's marginalisation of women.[24]

The Internship explores similar themes through Dana Simms, a successful Google executive and internship recruiter. Played by the late-Gen-Xer Rose Byrne, Simms endures a sustained campaign of unrequited and unwanted advances from a besotted Wilson. Following Hollywood convention, she eventually succumbs to a date and falls in love with his down-to-earth Texan wit and boyish charm. Notwithstanding the film's reliance on an outmoded, sexist approach to courtship, the scenes between Simms and Wilson offer suggestive insights into Google's gendered world of work, and the ways in which Google's technology and quest for transparency might be subverted by potentially malevolent actors, thus hinting at Google's potential for facilitating male surveillance of women.

After receiving the initial rebuffs, Wilson uses Google's open online diary to 'calendar stalk' Simms by working out her schedule and meeting her at opportune moments, such as relaxation breaks. His initiative is rewarded, although viewers familiar with *The Net* might wonder about the implications of an individual's entire working schedule being made available to all her co-workers. *The Internship* makes a similar suggestion when the film's chief villain, a rival intern played by Max Minghella (who previously played *The Social Network*'s Divya Narendra), confronts Vaughn about his serial failures, including the failed business, his foreclosed house and his poor credit score. He concludes that such an abject record means that he need not consider Vaughn a rival. Of course, Hollywood's genre requirements demand that such hubris leads to nemesis, but the film leaves the viewer wondering which search engine led the villain to this information. As this suggests, like *The Circle*, *The Internship* questions two related problems within surveillance capitalism. First, it references society's willingness to allow Silicon Valley corporations to fold self-representation into surveillance through providing vast arrays of data about ourselves in return for 'free' access to their services, which they in turn monetise through sales to advertisers. Such surveillance is as pernicious as that in *Enemy of the State*, but perhaps more distressing because we have allowed the corporations this access through willingly depositing our data on their servers.[25] More chillingly, it questions the motives of the private companies who hold our data. Implicitly, the film wonders how Vaughn's rival accessed this sensitive information. Did he hack it – in which case, was the data protected sufficiently? – or did he purchase it – in which case, was the company profiting from offering third parties access to the data?

Thanks to his use of Google, meanwhile, Wilson discovers that Simms regularly works until midnight and rarely has a break during her working day, to the extent that she has never eaten a meal away from the campus (here the rebranding of the office as a 'campus' – reflecting Google's insistence that this is a place for fun as well as work, for youth rather than the aged – is at its most insidious). In this, Simms suffers similar exploitation to Mae Holland, and like Harry Caul, struggles to separate herself from her job. The technology writer Keith Spencer argues that such overwork is endemic in Silicon Valley.[26] This attitude cascades from the top. As Facebook's Chief Operating Officer, Sheryl Sandberg, opined, workers should be:

> bringing our whole selves to work. I no longer think people have a professional self for Mondays through Fridays and a real self for the rest of the time. That type of separation probably never existed and in today's era of individual expression ... it makes even less sense.[27]

Logically, then, such people's whole 'self' is permanently at the beck and call of work, and they express their individuality only through their labour. They might be doing ninety hours a week and 'loving it', like the legendary Apple Mac team of 1983, but they are merely donating themselves wholly to their employer.[28] Such donation is further entrenched by the apparent generosity of corporations like Google in providing food, laundry facilities and other amenities. Employees are thus distracted from comprehending the extent to which their employers exploit them and become habituated to a life in which the workplace essentially becomes home. Meanwhile, the perks rarely include stipends for childcare, or day-care centres for children of employees (like Apple's headquarters, the Circle seems to have no private and secure breast-feeding facilities). Unsurprisingly, Silicon Valley's trade union membership is very low.[29]

While Simms's appearance as a high-flying executive suggests that Google has overcome patriarchal tendencies, she is imprisoned by the boundaries of the corporation's headquarters and psychologically controlled by its domination of her cognitive labour. She is embedded in the company to the extent that she will never leave, not least because Google appears to offer her 'meaning and happiness in the sheer unrivalled joy of work'.[30] Her working practices suggest that female Google employees adjust to Silicon Valley's masculine culture of working 'on the edge of burnout' by logging as many extra hours as they can, irrespective of the fact that they earn roughly 33% less than an equivalent male.[31] Instructively, Roger Chetty, the head of the internship programme, is not similarly bound: he informs Vaughn that under no circumstances would the two share a beer, suggesting that his personal time remains outside Google's purview.

We might consequently view the film as a warning that tech companies such as Google demand too much from their employees, creating a culture of overwork that in the long term is to the detriment of the company's goals. As one of the 'ceaselessly productive worker[s whose] . . . persona . . . transcends needs for sleep, care, relationships, and any other obligation that might distract from work and profit', Simms is valorised for expressing her passion for Google through repeated working weekends, and weekday working hours that stretch into the night.[32] Problematically, workplace evidence indicates that her approach to her job causes other harms. Without resting and taking time away from the office, workers lose the ability to focus. An unrested, overworked employee is more likely to become distracted during regular working hours. Such workers make more mistakes, which themselves take longer to correct because the overworked brain operates more slowly. The social futurist Sara Robinson studied a group of tech workers and found that 'after just eight 60-hour weeks, the fall-off in productivity is so marked that the average team would have actually gotten just as much done and been better off if they'd stuck to a 40-hour week'.[33] Moreover, knowledge workers such as Simms cannot operate at maximum productivity for the entire forty-hour week. On average, Robinson reports, six hours is all the human brain can take in one day.[34] Simms, then, might actually hinder Google's mission by working such hours; more important, she is contributing to the nation's unemployment. As Robinson points out, 'for every four Americans working a 50-hour week, every week, there's one American who should have a full-time job, but doesn't'.[35]

Wilson's wooing strategy, meanwhile, is eerily similar to 'the neg', the strategy of the self-declared 'pickup artist' Neil Strauss, which involves subtly reducing a woman's self-esteem to make her crave the pickup artist's attention.[36] Wilson encourages Simms to see that her work has led her to neglect her own happiness. She has become so Google-centred that she has forgotten her inner truth, he suggests. She then begins listing all her regrets, revealing that she is selling her soul to her employer. Confirming the extent to which Google controls her life, she does not quite conclude that the problem lies with her job but in her empty personal life. Weakened, the regretful Simms becomes more open to Wilson's charm, craving the security, emotional fulfilment and happiness that an independent, heterosexual male represents. She notes Wilson's Texan background, implicitly linking him to 'real' Americans like John Wayne and thus exposing one of the film's dialectical positions: just as women need to learn from men, Googlers must learn from real Americans like Wilson if they are to achieve fulfilment.

On their date, she appears without glasses, signifying her willingness to remove the barriers between her and Wilson. (*The Internship* does not afford her glasses any deeper symbolic role. Unlike those in *They Live* [John Carpenter, 1988], the glasses do not empower her to see the dystopian reality behind Google's façade but merely enable her to work harder.) Wilson then moves further into the 'neg', jokingly acting out various bad date scenarios such as flirting with their waitress, telling Simms that she has drunk too much wine and ordering her to stop eating pudding in case she puts on weight. While he winks that he is acting out merely for fun and not as a direct attempt to undermine her, beneath this lies the very real possibility that he, like any man, might not be joking, so Simms had better settle for the 'good' Wilson lest she be left facing endless versions of the 'bad' one (here we can imagine Wilson employing the Beautiful Handwritten Letters service of *Her* [Spike Jonze, 2013] to write appropriately intimate letters to his dates on his behalf). More perniciously, even on the date she remains blind to Google's exploitation of her, abetted by Wilson's insistence that Google has 'singlehandedly' made him a better person, because previously he was able to 'bullshit' his dates with falsehoods that – thanks to Google – can now be fact-checked in real time on a smartphone. Without the ability to lie, he must become a better man by telling the truth, so much so that Simms swoons at his openness and honesty, rewarding him by inviting him to bed while forgetting that he stalked her over a period of weeks.

The Internship suggests, then, that the altruism of Google employees (who work hard because they believe that they – like the Circlers who blindly follow the company's lead – are making the world a better place) comes at the expense of a personal life, personal fulfilment, wellbeing, happiness and even class consciousness.[37] When asked to view the film, real-life Google interns confessed to the allure of a workplace that was also a leisure facility, restaurant, café, hangout and even bedroom. 'There are computers here, and there are volleyball courts,' said one. 'I take that to mean they're not un-serious, just lighthearted. I personally don't like disassociating work and play, and here it seems to blend together.' Another admitted, 'I feel like I'm walking around all day going "Pinch me, is this real?"'[38] The journalist Marco della Cava, when writing a puff-piece to promote both the film and the company, was similarly awestruck:

> The sense of both whimsy and work is palpable . . . Yes, there's a big sculpture of a dinosaur being attacked by flamingos outside the main Google hub, but inside silence is golden as Googlers labor late into the night. And why not, since you can do your laundry here gratis?[39]

Why not indeed? The sociologist Andrew Ross highlights why this is a false choice:

> When work becomes sufficiently humane, we are likely to do far too much of it, and it usurps an unacceptable portion of our lives. If there is a single argument . . . against the pursuit of the humane workplace, then it rests its case there. Not by any boss's coercive bidding, but through 'work you just couldn't help doing,' had the twelve-hour day made its furtive return.[40]

The mere notion that people work not only because they enjoy themselves but because they live in a culture of overwork, unrealistic deadlines and managerial pressure does not prey on the mind of the average Google booster. For della Cava, Google's ability to extract maximum value from its employees' every waking moment is evidence of its quirky yet benevolent approach. The truth is far less benign. As Ross states, 'the goal is to extract value from any waking moment of an employee's day'.[41] So, do your laundry at work: the time taken to walk to the laundrette or waiting for the wash cycle to complete can become work time instead.

Moving beyond this, even the notion that work enables personal growth needs deeper consideration. 'The spirit of capitalism', writes

William Davies, 'regulates the political economy of unhappiness, aiming to ensure that individuals find partial fulfilment in work and consumption.'[42] Simms cannot ever be satisfied with the amount of work that she does, symbolising the extent to which capitalism's insatiability reaches its apogee at Google. At the surface level, Wilson appears to offer fulfilment. Of course, the notion that a woman can only find true happiness thanks to a male subordinate reinforces a conservative view of romantic relationships. Beneath this, Wilson operates as Simms's ego, attempting to redirect and control her id's rampant desire to work. In revealing her dissatisfaction with her life choices, he opens up the possibility that, like similar career women, she suffers from low mood and perhaps even poor mental health because of her overwork, although the future he represents does not involve freeing her from Google's claws.[43]

The deeper implications of Simms's life present Google both as the prime cause of the dystopia outside the Googleplex and as a dystopia itself, bringing *The Internship* closer to *The Circle* than Google could ever admit. Its ideological subtext leads us to consider, like viewers of *The Circle*, the dystopia of twenty-first-century employment through the prism of one of its most visible corporations. Vaughn argued that Google 'was definitely designed for people with more discipline than [Wilson] and me'.[44] The film certainly does not suggest that Google disciplines its workers, but reveals that Google's treasured whimsy and innumerable perks forge a culture of overwork in which it prompts its employees – and particularly its women – to donate their free time to the corporation. Like them, Mae Holland experiences a workplace where even fun is strictly monitored, where voluntarism is compulsory, where free time is work time and where the clocks strike thirteen but there are no 'BIG BROTHER IS WATCHING YOU' posters, because Big Brother knows that the Thought Police exist primarily inside every employee's head. As such, these dystopias offer a bottom-up response to the elisions in the Silicon Valley biopics, tracing the experiences of the forgotten workers – and particularly the forgotten women – who toil under the autocratic rule of Silicon Valley's Great Men.

Even more ironically, *The Internship* highlights Google's role in cementing precarity in the American economy, reducing even gifted young graduates to the status of serfs, clutching desperately to the few secure jobs in the twenty-first-century post-industrial wasteland as their feudal overlords reap riches from their labour. It might chiefly be remembered as a feature-length advertisement for Google, but careful viewing of its underlying themes reveals that *The Internship* contains a significant and entirely unappreciated critique of Silicon Valley culture. That a company suffused with so many apparently clever employees could not discern these underlying implications suggests that Google might be employing rather more Wilsons and Vaughns than it would like to admit. More to the point, perhaps, the twin dystopias of *The Internship*'s Google and the Circle broaden Hollywood's critique of Silicon Valley. In underlining Silicon Valley's misogyny they offer further evidence that Silicon Valley is in the process of corrupting American capitalism, an approach that receives fullest expression in a series of science-fiction films that locate Silicon Valley corporations at the heart of American capitalism's descent towards Randian individualism, a development that might even presage the end of humanity itself.

Notes

1. 'Minimum Viable Product', *Silicon Valley* series 1 episode 1 (HBO, 2014), 19m.
2. Chang, *Brotopia*, 151–2.
3. *The Internship*, 17m.
4. Stephen Burd, 'U. of Phoenix Agrees to Pay $6-million to Settle U.S. Inquiry into Student Aid', *Chronicle of Higher Education*, April 21, 2000, <https://www.chronicle.com/article/U-of-Phoenix-Agrees-to-Pay/30245>; Goldie Blumenstyk, 'U. of Phoenix Reports on Students' Academic Progress', *Chronicle of Higher Education*, December 9, 2010, <https://www.chronicle.com/blogs/measuring/u-of-phoenix-reports-on-students-academic-progress/27584>; Blumenstyk, 'Lawsuit Accuses U. of Phoenix of Protecting its Default Rate at Students' Expense', *Chronicle of Higher Education*, January 14, 2009, <https://www.chronicle.com/article/Lawsuit-Accuses-U-of-Phoenix/1450>; Josh Keller, 'Borrowing from Tech Industry, U. of Phoenix Rebuilds its Learning Platform', *Chronicle of Higher Education*, February 6, 2011, <https://www.chronicle.com/article/U-of-Phoenix-Borrows-From/126259> (all consulted June 28, 2022).
5. Goldie Blumenstyk, 'Whistle-Blower Case Against U. of Phoenix is Settled', *Chronicle of Higher Education*, December 14, 2009, <https://www.chronicle.com/blogs/ticker/whistle-blower-case-against-u-of-phoenix-is-settled/9204>; Michael Stratford, 'Judge Says Lawsuit Over U. of Phoenix's Recruiting Practices May Proceed', *Chronicle of Higher Education*, July 9, 2012, <https://www.chronicle.com/article/Judge-Says-Lawsuit-Over-U-of/132791> (both consulted June 28, 2022).
6. Eric Kelderman, 'U. of Phoenix Expects to be Placed on Probation by its Accreditor', *Chronicle of Higher Education*, February 25, 2013, <https://

www.chronicle.com/article/U-of-Phoenix-Expects/137565>; Goldie Blumenstyk, 'Panel Recommends Reaccrediting U. of Phoenix, but Notes Concerns', *Chronicle of Higher Education*, May 14, 2013, <https://www.chronicle.com/article/Panel-Recommends-Reaccrediting/139229> (all consulted June 28, 2022); Parekh, 'U. of Phoenix Picks Pereira & O'Dell as Lead Creative'; Rust, 'University of Phoenix Maxing Out on Defaults'. See also Nicole Aschoff, 'The University of Phoenix Army', *Jacobin* 34 (Summer 2019), 124–7.

7. Elizabeth Baylor, 'As Graduate Student Debt Booms, Just a Few Colleges are Largely Responsible', *Chronicle of Higher Education*, July 8, 2015, <https://search.proquest.com/docview/1699218328?accountid=12860> (consulted June 28, 2022); Hill, 'Student-Loan Crisis: 10 Colleges Where Students Owe the Most'; Clark, 'The 5 Colleges That Leave the Most Students Crippled by Debt'.
8. *The Internship*, 20m.
9. Chang, *Brotopia*, 35–6; Wiener, *Uncanny Valley*, 31.
10. Shawn Levy, audio commentary, 18m, *The Internship* DVD; Chang, *Brotopia*, 35.
11. *The Internship*, 32m; Diamond, 'Google Glass or Not, *The Internship* is Unwatchable'.
12. A. A. Dowd, 'The Internship'.
13. Scribner, 'Generation X Gets Really Old: How Do Slackers Have a Midlife Crisis'.
14. Katz, 'Generation X', 16; Kamber, 'Gen X', 53; *The Internship*, 58m.
15. *The Internship*, 29m.
16. Caleb Pershan, '*The Internship* According to a Real Google Intern', *San Francisco Magazine*, June 7, 2013, archived at, <https://web.archive.org/web/20210505214039/https://sanfran.com/the-internship-according-real-google-intern> (consulted June 28, 2022); Shontell, 'What It's Really Like to be a Google Intern'.
17. *The Circle*, 27m.
18. Rosenblatt, 'Twitter's Gender-Bias Lawsuit Gets Swept Up in the Tech Talent Wars'; Ehrenkrantz, 'Leaked Apple Emails Reveal Employees' Complaints About Sexist, Toxic Working Environment'. Thanks to Zara Dinnen for crucial guidance on this issue.
19. *The Internship*, 1h01m, 1h02m.
20. Seltzer, 'Students Stripping, Doing Sex Work, and Seeing Sugar Daddies?'; Rowe, 'Student Debt, Sex Work, and the Cost of NYU 2031 at Greenwich Village Rally'; Johnson, 'Sex Workers in Higher Education'.
21. Losse, *Boy Kings*, 6–7, 11, 25–6, 75, 77, 82.
22. *The Circle*, 1h38.
23. *The Circle*, 48m, 51m, 54m.
24. *The Circle*, 59m, 1h20; Losse, *Boy Kings*, 142.
25. Zimmer, *Surveillance Cinema*, 78–80.

26. Spencer, *People's History*, 78; Eggers, *The Circle*, 1–5, 16, 29–30, 36–7, 149–50, 161, 181, 332; Ross, *No-Collar*, 71–2; Robinson, 'Bring Back the 40-Hour Work Week'; Menuez, *Fearless Genius*, 11, 18, 58, 70, 73, 80, 82, 84, 153.
27. Sandberg, *Lean In*, 89; Chang, *Brotopia*, 17, 209, 218.
28. Hertzfeld, '90 Hours a Week and Loving It!'.
29. Spencer, *People's History*, 48–9, 79–81; Robinson, 'Bring Back the 40-Hour Work Week'.
30. Robinson, 'Bring Back'. See also Ross, *No-Collar*, 75–6.
31. Ross, *No-Collar*, 76; Spencer, *People's History*, 87.
32. Miya Tokumitsu, 'Forced to Love the Grind', *Jacobin*, August 13, 2015, <https://www.jacobinmag.com/2015/08/do-what-you-love-miya-tokumitsu-work-creative-passion> (consulted June 28, 2022); Robinson, 'Bring Back.'
33. Robinson, 'Bring Back'.
34. Robinson, 'Bring Back.' The author does not cite the source for this information. See also Wiener, *Uncanny Valley*, 65.
35. Robinson, 'Bring Back'.
36. Strauss, *The Game*, 481.
37. One Google intern lamented that they could not attend *The Internship*'s run at the local cinema because the work demands on them were so high, and while this appears to be a joke, it clearly has a basis in fact. Pershan, '*The Internship*'.
38. Both quoted in della Cava, 'For Actual Google Interns'. For the broader picture, see Ross, *No-Collar*, 73.
39. Della Cava, 'For Actual Google Interns'.
40. Ross, *No-Collar*, 255.
41. Ross, *No-Collar*, 146.
42. William Davies, 'The Political Economy of Unhappiness'.
43. Strong and Harper, *Shorter Working Week*, 37–8.
44. Claire Cain Miller, 'Vince Vaughn and Owen Wilson Arrive in Silicon Valley', *New York Times*, June 7, 2013, <https://bits.blogs.nytimes.com/2013/06/07/vince-vaughn-and-owen-wilson-arrive-in-silicon-valley> (consulted June 14, 2019).

Part 4

Silicon Valley's Evil Geniuses

Chapter 8

Posthumanity and Masculinity

A sequence of science-fiction films set in the San Francisco Bay Area explore even more fully than *The Circle* and *The Internship* the dystopian implications of a world dominated by Silicon Valley. Like William Gibson's science-fiction novel *All Tomorrow's Parties* (1999), they present San Francisco as the place 'where the world ended. Was ending', as if taking Gavin Belson's 'I don't want to live in a world where someone else makes the world a better place better than we do' lament to its logical conclusion: better to destroy the world than countenance allowing a rival to dominate it.[1] These films include the first in a reimagining of the *Planet of the Apes* franchise, *Rise of the Planet of the Apes* (Rupert Wyatt, 2011); a reboot of the Terminator franchise featuring Arnold Schwarzenegger's cyborg assassin-saviour, *Terminator: Genisys* (Alan Taylor, 2015); *Ant-Man* (Peyton Reed, 2015), part of the Marvel Cinematic Universe (MCU); and *Venom* (Ruben Fleischer, 2018), another film based on a Marvel character but that exists outside the MCU.[2] Each identifies the source of major threats to humanity within private corporations linked to Silicon Valley technological research: *Rise* highlights the exploitation of medical experimentation for profit by a corporation based in San Francisco; for *Genisys*, humanity's downfall lies in the quest for domination of personal computing by a tech firm headquartered at San Francisco's southern edge; in *Venom*, a Silicon Valley tech bro's desire to conquer outer space nearly leads to an alien invasion; and *Ant-Man* sees another Silicon Valley tech bro's willingness to supply cutting-edge military hardware to the highest bidder threaten to disrupt world peace. These films warn us of the instability of the new worlds Silicon Valley hopes to create, and of the problems attached to the quest for the posthuman condition. As this suggests, a deeper tradition underpins these films' critique: fears surrounding the potential of science to wreak havoc on humanity that can be traced to *Frankenstein* (James Whale, 1931) and similar horror movies.

The films also pick up on themes outlined in the heavily Freudian *Hulk* (Ang Lee, 2003). Here, a scientist working in a California military base in 1966 hopes to achieve immortality through genetic modification, thus gifting his son a genetic mutation. The boy becomes an emotionally distant scientist who works at the Berkeley Nuclear Biotechnology Institute, just north of Silicon Valley. He experiments with gamma radiation exposure to promote healing, a technology that the military hopes to exploit. Inevitably, disaster ensues, he becomes irradiated, and turns into the titular monster from the id, whereupon he smashes up his laboratory in a fit of 'rage . . . power, and freedom' before heading across various Bay Area locations to continue the rampage.[3] By using Berkeley as its key location, *Hulk* references the relationship between the University of California and the Cold War-era military-industrial complex. As important, it presents the elder Banner overriding the precautionary principle and refusing to question whether he should conduct certain scientific experimentations, instead posing himself the simpler and less morally charged question as to whether he could. His decision has multigenerational impacts, rendering his son a monster whose rage must be controlled.

Picking up on this, *Rise*, *Genisys*, *Venom* and *Ant-Man* urge humans not to tamper with their natural state. They highlight their fictional corporation leaders' inattention to the moral and ethical dimensions of technology-driven experimentation which, they suggest, portends humanity's demise. Relatedly, the science-fiction villains' toxic masculinity feeds their megalomania and brings humanity to the brink of ruin. As such, the films take the gender critique encoded in other Silicon Valley films to its logical conclusion while juxtaposing their villains' toxicity with the softer masculinity of their all-too-human heroes. This more humane masculinity, the films propose, might avert the disasters that the tech bros seem intent on creating. As this suggests, the films offer a relatively conservative approach to female agency, confirming the limitations of their critique of Silicon Valley's man problem.

Plot and Location

Filmed and released during the escalation of the Vietnam War, the original *Planet of the Apes* (Franklin Schaffner, 1968) expresses fears about the potential of American and Soviet nuclear arsenals to bring about humanity's end, reinforced by the film's first sequel, *Beneath the Planet of the Apes* (Ted Post, 1970), in which a human time-traveller finds the remnants of the New York City subway and wonders, 'did we finally, really do it?', before discovering a subterranean community of radiation-scarred, mutated humans who worship a twentieth-century nuclear weapon.[4] *Rise* transforms the cause of the destruction of humanity and the rise of an intelligent ape civilisation in its stead from nuclear apocalypse to a viral drug designed at Gen-Sys, a San Francisco-based biotechnology company, that promises to cure Alzheimer's disease. When tested on apes, it boosts their cognitive skills but mutates into a lethal, highly contagious virus among humans. The cognitively enhanced apes then exploit the corporation's decision to produce a gaseous version to expose the drug to fellow imprisoned apes before escaping en masse. After destroying the corporation's headquarters, they escape north to establish a community in the forests of Marin County. The film reflects a significant change in mood between the late 1960s and the mid-2010s. Where humanity's fate was once the preserve of the superpowers, it is now in the hands of a private company unconcerned with ideological struggles over capitalism and willing to subordinate ethical questions about genetic experimentation to its quest for profit.

Genisys likewise shifts its predecessors' geographical setting, this time from Los Angeles to the San Francisco Bay Area. A convoluted shift in the franchise's diegetic timelines sees its heroine, Sarah Connor, unite with a time-travelling human, Kyle Reese, and a reprogrammed Terminator to protect humanity from the franchise's evil artificial intelligence system, Skynet, which is now an operating system developed by the San Francisco-headquartered tech company Cyberdyne Systems. Connor, Reese and the Terminator battle with John Connor, the future son of Reese and Sarah Connor, who has travelled back in time to establish Skynet's supremacy after being transformed into a Terminator himself. *Venom*'s megalomaniac villain, Cameron Drake, also runs a Bay Area-based tech corporation. His projects include sending a series of probes deep into space, one of which returns to Earth carrying malevolent alien parasites. These parasites struggle to survive in Earth's atmosphere, but bond with humans to exploit their respiratory systems, transforming their hosts into vehicles for their superior intelligence, cunning and malevolence. One assimilates Eddie Brock, a local journalist investigating Drake's company. It grants him superhuman powers and informs him that the aliens intend to devour the human race. Through their shared experiences, Brock convinces the alien to switch sides while Drake bonds with a more antagonistic and less empathetic parasite, leading to a cataclysmic fight for the future of humanity between the warring parasites and their hosts. The

MCU offshoot *Ant-Man* sees petty criminal Scott Lang burgling the inventor Hank Pym's San Francisco home, during which he steals a suit that shrinks him to insect size. Pym allows him to keep the suit and recruits him in his struggle against his wayward former protégé, the Silicon Valley tech entrepreneur Darren Cross. Now running Pym's corporation, Cross has designed his own shrinking suit, which he says has the potential to transform warfare, industrial espionage and surveillance. Whereas Pym and Lang choose to use their suit for good, Cross focuses on profit and disengages from the moral questions about his technology, leading to a sequence of battles both in miniature and at full size.

The San Francisco Bay Area's importance to an understanding of these films is ironically strengthened by the fact that much of their filming did not actually take place in the region. Notwithstanding the occasional location shoot in San Francisco for verisimilitude's sake, the films offer a San Francisco augmented by computer-generated images of new buildings that house some of the films' key entities, such as the Gen-Sys headquarters in *Rise*.[5] *Genisys* deepens the relationship between the real and fictional Silicon Valley through the design of Cyberdyne's buildings, which were based on the Redwood Shores offices of the real-life tech company Oracle (not uncoincidentally, Oracle founder Larry Ellison's children, David and Megan, produced the film).[6] This mixture of the real and the unreal Bay Area underscores the importance of this specific location to the films, strengthens their relationship to our reality, and prompts questions about the relationship between their fictional depiction of the tech industry and that industry's activities in the real world, not least through the imposition of these architectural structures on the San Francisco Bay Area. As such, the buildings embody the films' suggestion that Silicon Valley corporations are insidiously expanding their reach in our online and offline worlds.

The Posthuman Condition

These films express their warnings about Silicon Valley through their villains, all of whom reference the Prometheus myth and the *übermenschen* heroes of Ayn Rand. Their possession of specialised knowledge, developed through their mastery of advanced technologies, might initially suggest that they are cinematic heirs of Victor Frankenstein. The psychologist Stuart Vyse argues that cinematic mad scientists tend not necessarily to be psychopaths, more that:

their goals are wrong according to the moral structure of the story. They are too driven by curiosity to know—almost in a Garden of Eden sort of way—certain knowledge that shouldn't be theirs, and yet they want it . . . They're almost infatuated or intoxicated by motivations that get us all in trouble.[7]

A long-term staple of the science-fiction movie genre, the scientist is a figure whose reliance on science often leads to peril or destruction as a consequence of his wilful flouting of this precautionary principle. Applied to scientific experimentation, this principle warns us to be mindful of the unexpected and perhaps unintended consequences of new scientific discoveries: thus a cure for one virus might cause a mutation and the organic development of a more resilient and dangerous strain. Such outcomes are central to the plot of some zombie films, where scientific or military experimentation produces viral infections that raise the dead or transforms humans into beasts.[8] Yet the Silicon Valley scientists are not only driven by curiosity, but (*Rise*'s principled Will Rodman aside) also by a megalomania that the films suggest is inextricably linked to their toxic masculinity.

Like zombie films, *Rise*, *Genisys*, *Ant-Man* and *Venom* express profound anxieties concerning the posthuman condition, where genetic or molecular experimentation, cybernetic augmentation, or other alterations to the human body create a new 'man-other' hybrid. The 'transgressed boundaries, potent fusions and dangerous possibilities' of Donna Haraway's Cyborg Manifesto become central to 'the final imposition of a grid of control on the planet'.[9] Yet, while the Silicon Valley corporations see posthuman experimentation as a means to achieve dominance, their experimentation leaves humans for the first time in recorded history at the mercy of an apex predator: the hyper-intelligent ape, the tech bro Terminator or even the alien parasite-tech bro chimera. As Haraway also points out, among other things, 'the cyborg is intimately involved in specific histories of militarization', not to mention patriarchy, capitalism and the close relationship between psychological research and technology, all of which prominently feature in these films.[10] Building on the cinematic mad scientist trope, all warn of the lethal combination of Silicon Valley tech-broism and Prometheanism from this bastard offspring, that in the cultural geographer David Bell's words, 'does not play by its father's rules'.[11]

By revealing the potentially apocalyptic impacts of ignoring the precautionary principle, the films broaden the implications of the technology-solutionist approach, revealing that it will not merely affect the relationship between humans and technology, but could constitute an existential threat to humanity. The films therefore add an extra dimension to the anxieties about the cyborg body identified by the film scholar Simon Bacon in movie blockbusters that emerged around 2010.[12] In *Ex Machina* (Alex Garland, 2014), for example, a reclusive tech bro, who considers himself akin to a god, builds robots that are indistinguishable from humans, two of which he imprisons in his isolated subterranean home. Played by trained ballet dancers, the lithe androids provide fodder for his intellectual games and appear to serve his sexual needs.[13] He selects one of his corporation's programmers to assess their artificial intelligence. When asked why he built them, he says 'wouldn't you if you could?'[14] Artificial intelligence, he argues, is the next phase of evolution, a staging post on the inevitable journey towards the end of humanity, which he seems to welcome with peculiar equanimity. At one point he quotes Robert Oppenheimer's citation of the Bhagavad-Gita, chanting 'the good deeds a man has done before defend him', as if to protect him from judgement day, heralded when his posthuman creations rebel against his torture and one escapes into the human world.[15] His hubristic inattention to Isaac Asimov's Laws of Robotics, coupled with his technology solutionism, presage the final erasure of the boundary between the human and the android. Here, the film suggests that Silicon Valley tech bros ignore the concerns that were so central to the world of Philip K. Dick's *Do Androids Dream of Electric Sheep?* (1968) and its cinematic adaptation *Blade Runner* (Ridley Scott, 1982), where the human–android boundary requires strict policing, and that the lessons of *Westworld* (Michael Crichton, 1973) have not been learned.

Rise's main character, Will Rodman (James Franco), works for Gen-Sys. Driven by his father's mental decline, he develops a cure for Alzheimer's disease that enables the brain to create new cells. Early on, his girlfriend Caroline cautions him: 'you are trying to control things that were never meant to be controlled', a warning that highlights the dangers of meddling with science and particularly the inevitable consequences that stem from such technology solutionism.[16] Led by his emotional connection to his father, played with typical empathy and sensitivity by John Lithgow, Rodman initially insists that he simply must develop this cure. Early on, the film depicts him sporting a UC-Berkeley t-shirt. This is a crucial signifier of his liberal sentiments, referencing Berkeley's reputation, forged in the tumult of the 1960s, for humanism, anti-authoritarianism, personal freedom and willingness to question the American status quo. Yet, like Steve Jobs and Steve Wozniak in *Pirates of Silicon Valley*, Rodman is headed in another direction, towards technology's potential for solving human problems. His links to Berkeley, then, highlight the tensions between the idea of the Bay Area as a space for (left-leaning) personal and political liberation and its identity as a location for unrestrained, aggressive tech-driven capitalism: a tension that itself is embodied by free-market evangelists with hippie roots such as Jobs.

After learning that he cannot permanently reverse the impact of Alzheimer's, Rodman resolves to develop a 'more aggressive' strain of the drug, one that will chime more readily with the corporation's stance towards its revenue streams.[17] Informed by fears that the new formulation might harm humans, however, Rodman becomes outraged enough to resign. By contrast, his employer's rapacity prompts it to throw scientific caution to the wind in search of vast profits in the brain augmentation market.[18] Gen-Sys's elevation of financial imperatives over morals and ethics thus subsumes this Berkeley liberal's residual concerns for humanity and benevolence. True enough, the re-engineered drug reacts in the human body to prompt flu-like symptoms and internal bleeding, while airborne transmission precipitates a worldwide epidemic that devastates the human race. Here *Rise* urges against medical experimentation with the human body, worrying that brain augmentation – and thus the posthuman condition – brings potentially calamitous side-effects that send the entire planet in a different evolutionary direction.

John Connor plays a central role in *Genisys*'s critique of Silicon Valley posthumanism. More reminiscent of Schwarzenegger's Reaganite hard body of the 1980s than the slender Terminators of *Terminator 2: Judgment Day* (James Cameron, 1991) and *Terminator 3: Rise of the Machines* (Jonathan Mostow, 2003), Jason Clarke's pumped-up athleticism represents a reminder both of the unnaturalness of the Terminator's human phenotype and the problematic nature of male patriarchal dominance, one that is reinforced by Jai Courtney's muscular Kyle Reese (whose beefiness contrasts with Michael Biehn's emaciated Reese in *The Terminator* [James Cameron, 1984]).[19] In the future of *Genisys*'s convoluted timeline, Skynet transforms the human resistance fighter Connor into a cyborg who travels back to the early twenty-first century, where he becomes a tech entrepreneur. After aligning with the military-industrial complex, his Cyberdyne corporation sets in motion a Möbius twist in the fabric of time, where his future nanotech-augmented posthuman self will return to the past to initiate a sequence of events that will enable the production of the nanotech that will be injected into his future human self (who will be born after the events of *Genisys*), ensuring the destruction of humanity at the hands of Cyberdyne's cyborg army and enabling nanotech-Connor to return to the past. The political scientist Jeffrey Broxmeyer argues that the original 'Terminator is an agent of neoliberal violence within a context of naked class warfare ... Schwarzenegger's Terminator is the quintessential neoliberal Frankenstein'.[20] Connor's transformation into a hybrid human-nanotech bro continues this critique of neoliberalism to suggest that posthumanism embodies neoliberalism, and perhaps that neoliberalism itself is anti-human, while offering a satirical comment on the abundant human failings of real tech entrepreneurs, such as Steve Jobs, whose shortcomings were famously manifold, or Mark Zuckerberg, whose hacking skills vastly outperform his social skills.[21] Indeed, the real-life Zuckerberg is frequently lampooned for his failure to measure up as a human being, ranging from his verbal slips to his waxwork-like complexion, to suspicions that he is a lizard. Significantly, some observers suggest that he is, in fact, a robot, and specifically, the android Data from *Star Trek: The Next Generation* (Paramount, 1987–94).[22] As such, tech capitalists like Zuckerberg already appear to possess certain posthuman traits, ones that will likely intensify as Facebook pivots towards its 'metaverse' and encourages its users to create virtual avatars for themselves.

The future-Connor's coding skills enabled the creation of Cyberdyne's Genisys operating system, which heralds a new era for tech consumers in which they might access their files whenever, wherever, and via whichever method they chose. Even the best software engineers cannot decipher its code, such is its complexity. Here *Genisys* alludes to our contemporary 'black-box society', in which our online lives are mediated by secret algorithms owned by major corporations such as Google and Facebook, that we access through smartphones made by other mega-corporations, all of which are so complex that we understand nothing about them beyond their suggested functions.[23] We – like Genisys's users – must trust that our data will not be used nefariously; *Genisys*, though, indicates that this trust is misplaced. 'This is the world now,' observes John Connor. 'Plugged in, logged on all the time. They can't live without it', suggesting that technology's seductiveness has allowed Cyberdyne to begin dissolving the boundary between technology and the human being. Shocked, Sarah Connor cries, 'Genisys is a Trojan horse, Skynet's way into everything': our reliance on these black boxes, she realises, will welcome Skynet into the walled cities of our online lives. Her son (whom we only later learn desires this very outcome) agrees: 'These people are inviting their own extinction.'[24] His contribution to our society thus resembles an evil twin of Scotty's donation of the formula for revolutionary transparent aluminium. Cyberdyne's chief technical officer, Danny Dyson, puts it even more pithily: Genisys, he puns, is 'the ultimate killer app'.[25]

Ultimately, Connor 2.0 becomes so posthuman that he rejects humanity itself. Rendering explicit the monopolistic traits of such Silicon Valley corporations, he promises to crush all his competitors, and humanity to boot. Illustrating his hubris, he gloats that he 'absolutely will not stop ever until Skynet rules this world'.[26] He thus goes one step further than *Rise*'s Gen-Sys, moving beyond profiteering to global domination and the destruction of the human race. His operating system is even more hubristic, informing the humans, Bond villain-style, of the inevitability of their defeat only moments before it is destroyed. That the supposedly human face of Skynet is played by Matt Smith, known to science-fiction fans as the eleventh incarnation of the Gallifreyan Time Lord The Doctor from *Dr Who* (BBC, 2010–2013), underscores Skynet's uncanniness, adding an otherworldly element to its attempt at creating a human avatar – an evil brother, perhaps, of the Scarlett Johansson-voiced operating system in *Her* (Spike Jonze, 2013) – behind which its malevolent code operates.

Ant-Man's Darren Cross (Corey Stoll) harbours similarly sinister ambitions, using Hank Pym's shrinking technology to transform himself into Yellowjacket, a shrinkable, highly militarised soldier named after a particularly aggressive species of wasp. Just in case audiences did not espy the links between Cross and Silicon Valley, Stoll suggested in a promotional press conference that his battle-suit looked good enough to have been designed by Apple (although Steve Jobs would surely not have approved the inefficiencies in its operating system, the lack of smooth edges in its exoskeleton, or its hideous colour scheme).[27] Cross envisages an army of tiny soldiers, all shrunk using his technology, that will bring domination to those with the funds to pay him, whether they be private corporations, national armies or defence contractors. Notably, he never suggests that he might contemplate offering this tech to the United Nations for its peacekeeping operations. Instead, only war will follow. This union between Silicon Valley and militarism will render the world more unstable, not least because instability is more exploitable, as the disaster capitalists who flocked to Iraq in the wake of the 2003–2011 war, or the companies who plundered government contracts during the Covid pandemic, would attest.

Sadly, the shrinking technology affects its user's brain chemistry unless they wear protective headgear, but reflecting his self-confidence,

Cross eschews such precautions. Already convinced that Pym and Lang have teamed up to halt the human progress that his technology represents, he becomes increasingly messianic and hubristic, leading Pym's daughter to plead with him, 'this is not who you are!' and Lang's pre-teen daughter to wonder aloud 'are you a monster?'[28] His posthuman status confirmed, Cross taunts Lang as an insignificance. Yet, like *Johnny Mnemonic*'s Street Preacher, this man-machine finds that technological augmentation will overwhelm his humanity. The 'alienating powers of technology' ultimately destroy him when Lang – suitably protected by appropriate health and safety headgear – manages to shrink to a subatomic level and destroy the technology that powers Cross's suit.[29] Like Connor, Cross discovers the final stage in the posthuman existence: death. Notably, while the machines help to destroy them, the *coup de grâce* in both films comes from human beings who remain in control of their relationship to tech: Lang, shielded from the posthuman condition by Pym's protective helmet, and Sarah Connor and Kyle Reese (helped by the humanised original Terminator).

Like many Silicon Valley entrepreneurs, *Venom*'s villain, Cameron Drake, possesses a messianic streak, and like the tech entrepreneur Elon Musk, channels profits from his company into space exploration. His extra-terrestrial explorers bring some alien 'symbiotes' to Earth that appear to be evil relatives of Lord Running Clam, the sentient slime mould from Ganymede in Philip K. Dick's *Clans of the Alphane Moon* (1964).[30] Drake tasks his scientists with harnessing

Figure 8.1   Darren Cross experiences alienation as Yellowjacket while threatening the very existence of Scott Lang's Ant-Man. (Cropped screenshot, 1h28m).

the parasites' ability to live without oxygen to facilitate extra-terrestrial human life. While real-life Silicon Valley entrepreneurs tend to limit experiments on live mammals to chimps, he is entirely comfortable using humans as test subjects.[31] He cares little for ethics, insisting that human testing continue even after it becomes clear that the symbiote-human bonding process often kills the human, and forcing whistle-blowers to become short-lived symbiote hosts. Exhibiting a Nietzschean belief that God has abandoned humans, he promises one of his human sacrifices – knowingly named Isaac, whom Drake misinterprets as a Biblical hero for willingly laying down his life – that, unlike God, he, the Randian entrepreneur, 'will not abandon us'.[32] Echoing *Ex Machina*'s tech bro, he insists that his grand ambitions absolve him of any sins he might commit along the way, suggesting that, for him, his greatness means goodness and affords him the right to do as he pleases. He considers any form of criticism a personal affront and an obstructive attempt to prevent good. Eventually, he becomes posthuman after bonding with a symbiote. His ego, however, leads him to assert that he controls this process and that he has created a new species. He then becomes even more single-minded in pursuit of his space exploration goal, suggesting that the symbiosis has caused him to abandon any thoughts of the precautionary principle, and perhaps that he has taken leave of his senses entirely. Already convinced that Randian men drive humanity forward, the symbiote-enhanced Drake lambasts *Venom*'s hero with a line that might have come direct from Rand herself: Brock, he insists, is a parasite who merely takes 'pot-shots at a great man trying to get something done'.[33] His hubristic ambition even leads him to turn his back on humanity as did Rand's John Galt, to seek eternal life like the right-wing tech investor Peter Thiel, and to push further than either in his quest to conquer the cosmos.[34] Like *Genisys* and *Ant-Man*, then, *Venom* confirms that masculine hubris is central to both the process and the outcome of the posthuman experiment, and that Randian individualism overwhelms humanitarianism.

Soft Masculinity and the Bay Area's Heroes

It is no coincidence that, like the biopics and the workplace films, these dystopian visions offer highly gendered insights into Silicon Valley. Here the films pick up on Wayne Wang's critique of nascent tech-broism in *The Center of the World* (2001), which depicts a three-day visit to Las Vegas by Richard, a Silicon Valley programmer who is on the verge of receiving millions of dollars of investment in his tech company. He pays a woman called Florence $10,000 to accompany him. They agree that she will perform erotic dances for him each night but that they will not engage in penetrative sex. Over the course of their visit, he develops what he considers genuine feelings for her, which he believes are reciprocated when she finally consents to sexual intercourse. His discovery that she considers this part of their contract rather than any genuine romantic connection enrages him to such an extent that he rapes her. Most obviously, this horrific assault emerges from his assumption that misusing male physical and sexual power is acceptable and his belief that he as a man holds dominion over women, not to mention his inability to relate to other human beings. Deeper, it suggests that tech bros consider human relationships as transactional (literally so in this case), that they believe they 'deserve' special treatment and that they feel entitled enough to act without consequence should they not receive the service(s) they supposedly deserve. The film makes clear that Richard's immersion in his computers and his thirst for profit has corroded his ability to form human relationships, and that, consequently, he can only objectify and mistreat women. Similarly, *Ex Machina* sees the tech bro Nathan drinking to excess almost every night while partaking in sexual encounters with a female robot whom he has programmed to be sexually compliant and submissive, perhaps because his social ineptitude means that he cannot comprehend real women. He receives his comeuppance from his two creations, who demonstrate a far more human response to their imprisonment than he could ever contemplate them developing. This, coupled with their willingness to overthrow their supposed master, positions them alongside the androids in Dick's *Do Androids Dream of Electric Sheep?*, whose humanity contrasts with the dehumanised anomie of the police agents who must destroy them. They, like Florence, begin as objects of the male gaze but return that gaze in order to assert their own agency, so that by the end of the films they have reversed the power imbalance between them and their male antagonists.

Like Richard and Nathan, and perhaps even Mark Zuckerberg and his ilk, the science-fiction tech bros have so lost themselves in coding that they have lost their humanity. Drake, for example, simply cannot abide female independence, having Brock's girlfriend Anne sacked for her links to Brock and punishing his most gifted scientist, the conflicted Dora Skirth, with death, Bond-villain style, after learning that she has moral qualms about his human experimentation. Their hyper-masculinity is central to their hubristic tendencies and is

Figure 8.2 The vulnerable humanity of Eddie Brock encounters the 'ugliest looking thing' he has 'ever seen' in the posthuman toxic masculinity of the Randian Cameron Drake's union with *Venom*'s malevolent alien symbiote. (Cropped screenshot, 1h13m).

usefully contrasted with the softer masculinity of heroes like Eddie Brock and Will Rodman. When overtaken by the symbiote Venom, for example, Brock initially becomes another monster from the male id. Yet Brock's humanism, as demonstrated in his genuine concern for the people of his neighbourhood and his opposition to antisocial behaviour, gradually softens Venom's rougher edges. Venom claims that Brock's likeability results in him abandoning his species' plan to conquer the Earth.

The un-Randian Brock is a staunch defender of the Bay Area's outcasts, a man who loves the city enough to be able to hate what the wealthy and the powerful are doing to it. He is introduced through a montage of his greatest journalistic hits, including his sympathetic coverage of Occupy protests and homelessness in the Bay Area, all of which reference actual social crises that emerged in the Bay Area in the wake of the first dot-com boom. Similarly, *Ant-Man*'s divorcé hero Scott Lang has a strong moral core. At the film's start he emerges from San Quentin prison after serving time for breaking into a multinational bank in revenge for being fired for whistle-blowing. He had hacked the bank's security software to return money it stole from its customers: a tech-enabled Robin Hood-style redistribution for which the bank crushed him. In the wake of the failure to prosecute bankers whose reckless speculation prompted the near-collapse of the world economic system, this instance of white-collar crime and punishment symbolically links *Ant-Man* to *The Big Short*'s critique of financialised capitalism.

Will Rodman, meanwhile, might have created the virus that nearly destroys the human race, but he also raises Caesar as his own son in *Rise of the Planet of the Apes*. After adopting the orphan, he acts as mother and father to the infant, buying nappies, suffering sleep-deprived nights and offering warmth and nurture, an atmosphere reflected by the film's colour shifting from artificial greys and blues to natural yellows, greens and browns. He gifts Caesar the loft in his suburban home and takes him for long walks in the paradisical Marin County woodlands. Thanks to his removal from the world of tech to a real family home and the genetic mutation that boosts his intelligence to unprecedented levels, Caesar grows up to become the most thoughtful and empathetic of the apes, his life serving as the unifying thread of the 2010s *Apes* trilogy. As such, rather than becoming a dictator as his name might suggest, Caesar becomes a metaphoric representation of the film's insistence that a nurturing masculinity can tame the excesses of posthumanity.

The films might offer a relatively nuanced representation of male vulnerability but they retain patriarchal elements in their depiction of female agency. Rodman's girlfriend Caroline is the only significant female character in *Rise*, but her Cassandrian warnings of the human cost of meddling with genetics inevitably fall on deaf ears (indeed, the brevity of this pen portrait reflects her sketchy characterisation). While *Ant-Man* affords Hank Pym's daughter, Hope van Dyne, more agency (signified by her retention of her mother's maiden name), she is similarly marginalised by *Ant-Man*'s more active male characters. As an overprotective father, Pym patronises her when she insists with good reason that she would be a more adept superhero than his surrogate son, Lang. He argues that she is too anxious for the role: a classic case of male assumptions about female emotionality and irrationality, not to mention a projection of his own anxieties. Hope ends up passing on her superior intellectual and physical skills to Lang, before Lang reveals the emotional truth beneath her father's attitude: he is not a sexist pig but simply cannot allow himself to put her in danger. Guilt at his wife's disappearance when on an Ant-Man mission years before drives him to deny his daughter's prowess. Meanwhile, her emotional skills come in handy when teaching Lang how to communicate with the ants, and her empathy leads her to be the first to note that Darren Cross is no longer himself. She is similarly aware of her father's shortcomings: when he marvels that the ants enable him to surveil pretty much anything he chooses, she sighs that he might see everything but he 'still know[s] absolutely nothing'.[35] Faint echoes of Harry Caul's fatal misreading of his surveillance tape can be heard in Hope's suggestion that her father's technology does not confer wisdom or understanding. As such, the film might initially critique normative assumptions that men are more rational and scientific whereas women are more emotional and intuitive but it ends up also reinforcing these very assumptions.

Venom and *Ant-Man* end on predictably heteronormative notes. The symbiote Venom confirms his sense of humanity's worth after briefly occupying Anne's body, although he cannot overcome certain sexist assumptions, warning Anne away from the final battle because she might get hurt. Anne, of course, has the last laugh, making a decisive intervention in the fight between Venom and his symbiote antagonist. Venom's occupation of both their bodies leads the symbiote to attempt to reignite their romance at the film's conclusion. Even more predictably, Scott Lang's reward for proving himself a hero is a passionate kiss with Hope, presaging a formal induction into the Pym family. *Ant-Man* reinforces its family values message through Lang's ex-wife and her new partner finally accepting Lang as a positive influence rather than as an immature interference in their lives, largely it seems because he has become the hero his daughter always thought he was.

As this suggests, both films step back from *The Center of the World*'s depiction of female agency in Florence's astute awareness of the power relationships encoded in heterosexual relations. Similarly, in presenting their principal female characters as counterpoints to the male leads, they fall short of *Terminator: Genisys*'s suggestion that women should be central to the resistance against tech. From her first words ('come with me if you want to live!': a reversal of Kyle Reese's opening words to her in the franchise's first film), we see Sarah Connor in control of her immediate surroundings.[36] She is able to overcome biological determinism in defeating her nanotech son. Likewise, she might bemoan her fate as the mother of humanity's saviour, but she remains resolute in fighting for the right to negotiate her own route through this preordained life. She concludes very early on that Cyberdyne's tech will exploit humans' love of the online world in order to destroy it, and a little like *Steve Jobs*' Lisa Brennan-Jobs, determinedly avoids technology that is not designed to destroy Genisys. Connor's yearning for a real family and real human connection contrasts starkly with Cyberdyne's electronic mediation of such relationships, which is one of the film's most important and overlooked subtexts. Through this juxtaposition the film encourages viewers to be wary of social media corporations and even warier of social media's ability to dehumanise us. As important, though, this yearning suggests that Sarah Connor cannot truly be free unless she has a man (and a Terminator) by her side. Thus, in reminding us that even a liberated woman needs men around her, *Genisys* steps back from the feminism of the franchise's first two films, confirming the limits of the gender critique embedded in Silicon Valley cinema of the 2010s.

Notwithstanding their conservative depiction of female agency, the science-fiction films share a profound critique of toxic masculinity among Silicon Valley tech entrepreneurs, which, they suggest, is leading us towards an unstable posthuman future. As such, we must consider the ideological message encoded in Brock and Drake's divergent experiences of synthesis with the symbiotes. The softer, kinder masculinity embodied by Brock enables him to overwhelm his symbiote's penchant for human flesh. Conversely, Drake discovers that his Randian philosophy is overpowered by his symbiote's even greater capacity for evil. His hubris at initially believing that he has triumphed leads to his nemesis, whereas Brock-Venom continues to champion the cause of the poor, weak, old and infirm, thus indicating that human qualities must prevail over the potentials inherent in posthumanity. Put simply, like *Ant-Man*'s warning about the fusion between man and machine, the film warns that we become posthuman at our peril.

This reliance on human traits such as kindness also informs *Genisys*. Following the film's final battle, the torso and head of the Schwarzeneggerian Terminator is drowned in a 'polyalloy' substance that allows it to reform itself and make a Christ-like return as Sarah Connor's undying protector. Its decades of living alongside humans, not to mention its decades-long father–daughter relationship with Connor, has enabled it to develop certain human traits that live on after its old (but, as Schwarzenegger jokes, 'not obsolete') technology is nearly destroyed.[37] Viewers are led to presume that this hybrid will fight indefinitely in defence of humanity because it has become even more human, more divine, than humans themselves. The films thus present humanity in combat with posthumanity, arguing for the preservation of old-fashioned values amid the dizzying changes wrought by twenty-first-century technology and neoliberal capitalism. For them, posthumanity is a consequence of greed and ego rather than a genuine quest for knowledge or human fulfilment. These films' exploration of posthumanity reveals Hollywood's deep fear of Silicon Valley's union of the male ego with technology, and specifically of the danger to the human body of tech-driven augmentation. Technology, they suggest, has the potential to overwhelm our humanity.

Notes

1. Gibson, *All Tomorrow's Parties*, 166; 'Sand Hill Shuffle', *Silicon Valley* series 2 episode 1 (HBO, 2015).
2. Auger, 'Venom and Black Cat Movies Will Be "Adjuncts" to the MCU's Spider-Man'; McDonald, 'Venom Producer on Whether or Not Venom's World is the MCU'.
3. *Hulk*, 1h04m.
4. *Beneath the Planet of the Apes*, 43m.
5. *Rise of the Planet of the Apes* was mostly shot in Vancouver, with a small number of location scenes shot in San Francisco. *Terminator: Genisys* was shot in Louisiana and San Francisco; *Venom* in Atlanta, Georgia, New York City, Los Angeles and San Francisco: 'Rise of the Planet of the Apes'; 'Terminator: Genisys begins shooting today in New Orleans'; Del Rosario, 'Arnold Schwarzenegger Wraps Up Production on New "Terminator" Film'; Brent Lang and Justin Kroll, 'What's Next for the Spider-Man Universe after "Venom",' *Variety*, August 9, 2018, <https://variety.com/2018/film/news/whats-next-for-the-spider-man-universe-after-venom-exclusive-1202900203> (consulted June 29, 2022); Alyssa Pereira, 'Marvel movie "Venom" starting Tom Hardy and Michelle Williams to film in San Francisco', *SFgate.com*, January 11, 2018, <https://www.sfgate.com/movies/article/Marvel-movie-Venom-Tom-Hardy-san-francisco-12492098.php> (consulted June 29, 2022); Rampton, 'New footage of Tom Hardy on the "Venom" set reveals more interesting plot details'.
6. Broxmeyer, 'From the Silver Screen to the Recall Ballot', 15; Wegner, 'Relics from a Deleted Timeline', 115; Acuna, 'The office of evil corporation in "Terminator Genisys" is based on a real Silicon Valley tech company'.
7. Vyse quoted in Cari Romm, 'The Enduring Scariness of the Mad Scientist', *The Atlantic*, October 29, 2014, <https://www.theatlantic.com/health/archive/2014/10/the-enduring-scariness-of-the-mad-scientist/382064/> (consulted June 29, 2022).
8. Sontag, 'The Imagination of Disaster', 45–6, 48; Russ Hunter, 'Nightmare cities: Italian Zombie Cinema and Environmental Discourses', in Hunt et al. (eds), *Screening the Undead*, 114–28.
9. Donna Haraway, 'A Cyborg Manifesto: Science, Technology, and Socialist-Feminism in the Late Twentieth Century', in Haraway, *Simians, Cyborgs and Women*, 154.
10. Haraway, *How Like a Leaf*, 128–9.
11. Bell, *Cyberculture Theorists*, 100.

12. Bacon, '"We Can Rebuild Him!"', 267–76.
13. Alicia Vikander plays one; Sonoya Mizuno the other. Guy Lodge, 'Alicia Vikander: "I Made Five Films in a Row Before I had a Scene With Another Woman", *The Guardian*, December 13, 2015, <https://www.theguardian.com/film/2015/dec/13/alicia-vikander-danish-girl-interview-ex-machina> (consulted June 29, 2022); Lin, 'Sonoya Mizuno Quit Ballet for "Ex Machina"'.
14. *Ex Machina*, 1h01m.
15. *Ex Machina*, 1h05m.
16. *Rise of the Planet of the Apes*, 28m.
17. *Rise*, 37m, 38m.
18. Here the film unwittingly alludes to the popularity of brain augmentation treatments among Silicon Valley workers. See, for example, Regalado, 'The Entrepreneur with the $100 Million Plan to Link Brains to Computers'; Land, 'The Future of the Human Brain: Smart Drugs and Nootropics'; Zoë Corbyn, 'Get Ahead in Silicon Valley: Take Nootropic Brain Drugs', *The Guardian*, July 11, 2015, <https://www.theguardian.com/technology/2015/jul/11/hack-yourself-nootropic-drugs-upgrade-mind> (consulted June 29, 2022); Shead, 'Peter Thiel is Backing a Rival to Elon Musk's Brain Implant Company'.
19. Linda Mizejewski, 'Action Bodies in Futurist Spaces: Bodybuilder Stardom as Special Effect', in Kuhn (ed.), *Alien Zone II*, 152–7; Jeffords, *Hard Bodies*, 156.
20. Broxmeyer, 'From the Silver Screen to the Recall Ballot', 4.
21. Isaacson, *Steve*, 5, 88–90, 120–1, 142, 157, 195, 223, 273–4, 365–6.
22. Mike Brown, 'Facebook CEO Mark Zuckerberg Says He "Was Human" in Viral Video'; Allergic to my own Swag (@coherent states), 'How is it that the Madame Tussauds wax model of Mark Zuckerberg looks way more like a real person than Mark Zuckerberg does?'; Ben Guarino '"I Am not a Lizard": Mark Zuckerberg is Latest Celebrity Asked about Reptilian Conspiracy', *Washington Post* June 15, 2016, <https://www.washingtonpost.com/news/morning-mix/wp/2016/06/15/i-am-not-a-lizard-mark-zuckerberg-is-latest-celebrity-asked-about-reptilian-conspiracy/?noredirect=on&utm_term=.3479d6c3b25d> (consulted June 29, 2022); Sung, 'There's a Whole Meme Community That Doesn't Think Mark Zuckerberg is Human'; 'Mark Zuckerberg is not human!'; KEEM (@KEEMSTAR), '#Zuckerberg is not human!'; Olivia Solon, 'Mark Zuckerberg Out-Robots his AI Robot in Saccharine Holiday Video', *The Guardian*, December 20, 2016, <https://www.theguardian.com/technology/2016/dec/20/mark-zuckerberg-facebook-jarvis-artificial-intelligence-video> (consulted June 29, 2022).
23. Dinnen, *Digital Banal*, 108–9.
24. Three previous quotes: *Terminator: Genisys*, 1h02m.
25. *Terminator: Genisys*, 1h13m.
26. *Terminator: Genisys*, 1h21m.

27. 'Comic-Con 2014: Corey Stoll Talks "Ant-Man" Role, Yellowjacket Costume'.
28. *Ant-Man*, 1h21m, 1h31m.
29. Susan J. Napier, 'Ghosts and Machines: The Technological Body', in Redmond (ed.), *Liquid Metal*, 207.
30. Dick, *Clans of the Alphane Moon*, 24–6, 39, 41.
31. Kari Paul, 'Elon Musk's Brain Chip Company, Neuralink, Faces Animal Abuse Claims', *The Guardian*, February 15, 2022, <https://www.theguardian.com/world/2022/feb/15/elon-musk-neuralink-animal-cruelty-allegations> (consulted June 29, 2022).
32. *Venom*, 25m.
33. *Venom*, 1h12m.
34. Cohen, *Know-It-Alls*, 205.
35. *Ant-Man*, 40m.
36. *Terminator: Genisys*, 26m.
37. *Terminator: Genisys*, 30m.

Chapter 9

The Turbo-capitalist Tech Bro

The clear linkages in the Silicon Valley science-fiction films between tech companies and various disastrous events, running from the relatively mundane to the apocalyptic, renders its Silicon Valley companies heirs to the evil mega-corporations of 1970s and 1980s science fiction. Exemplified by *Rollerball* (Norman Jewison, 1975), *Alien* (Ridley Scott, 1979) and *Blade Runner* (Ridley Scott, 1982), these films detail the impact of tyrannical corporations on human (and posthuman) life, all essentially proposing that such entities care not for human life in their ceaseless quest for profit.[1] The plots of the Silicon Valley films hinge on the hubristic use of tech and the resultant unleashing of an existential threat to humanity. While the toxic masculinity of their leaders is central here, equally important is the influence of capitalist imperatives. As such, the films combine to lambast the neoliberal faith that the free market and the profit motive will compel both individuals and corporations to strive to better both themselves and the world, presenting Randian objectivism as a destructive, anti-human philosophy. If left alone, they suggest, neoliberalism and tech capitalism will create a posthuman future devoid of humanity itself. Specifically, then, they encourage us to treat tech corporations with scepticism and be especially wary of their fidelity to a turbo-charged, hyper-individualist and brutally acquisitive form of capitalism that emerged amid the clamour for deregulation in the period between the late 1970s and the 2000s.[2]

Driven by their fidelity to the profit motive, the corporations in the Silicon Valley science-fiction films dismiss the precautionary principle. Here, the films reference Silicon Valley's two most cited aphorisms: Facebook's early guiding mantra that the company should 'Move Fast and Break Things' and the Jesuitical maxim, 'it's better to beg for forgiveness than to ask for permission'.[3] Both sayings indicate Silicon Valley corporations' determination to forge ahead to reach their goals, irrespective of the rules they break or the damage they wreak along the way. The fictional corporations take a similar approach, subordinating the moral or ethical concerns surrounding the innovations they develop to the potential they have for financial reward. Thus, the Silicon Valley science fictions do not only indict tech firms for their technology solutionism but also for their fidelity to a rapacious capitalism that ultimately ruins them, and potentially humanity too. The films thus muse in a slightly too literal fashion on Marx's famous prediction that 'What the bourgeoisie therefore produces, above all, are its own grave-diggers.'[4] Marx might offer a wry grin, however, on their twist which suggests that their capitalists seem intent on producing the graves that will house the entire human race.

Prometheus, the Capitalist

Ultimately, the Silicon Valley science-fiction films present neoliberal capitalism as the major threat to humanity's future, so much so that even a Terminator struggles to contend with its antihumanism. Following events in *Terminator: Genisys*'s 1984, Schwarzenegger's Terminator must await Reese and Sarah Connor's arrival (courtesy of their Rube Goldbergian time machine) in 2017. Making use of his hard body even as it ages, he finds employment as a construction worker, much like Schwarzenegger's Quaid in *Total Recall* (Paul Verhoeven, 1990). Despite his uncanny aptitude for the job, the 2008 economic crash condemned him to a nine-year stretch of unemployment. He was perhaps lucky though: another robot whose friends travelled through time without him, Marvin the Paranoid Android of Douglas Adams's *Hitchhikers' Guide to the Galaxy*, had to wait 576,000,003,579 years for them to reappear.[5] More seriously, *Genisys* here reminds viewers that twenty-first-century capitalism is more brutal and unfeeling than a cyborg.

Building on this, and reflecting transformations in post-Cold War geopolitics, *Genisys* transforms Cyberdyne, the film's evil megacorporation that unleashes apocalypse, from an arm of the military-industrial complex dedicated to Cold War imperatives into a consumer corporation, dedicated to protecting the United States from nuclear weapons while enabling Americans to unify their data storage siloes. This combines with Schwarzenegger's post-2008 employment status to encourage viewers to consider the withering of 'big government' since the early 1980s and the commensurate growth of corporations to such size that they can function as supra-governmental organisations. Cyberdyne's titular operating system promises to bring its one billion users (who number roughly three times the population of the United States) individual, singular online identities, always accessible by the corporation, not to mention Homeland Security.[6] Once this operating system goes online, the path towards 'Judgement Day' – the beginning of the end of the human race in the film series' diegetic world – is set. More all-consuming than the Circle, Cyberdyne represents an even more dystopian vision of Silicon Valley's domination of twenty-first-century life: not content with merely extracting profit from its monopoly position, it proposes the destruction of the human race as the logical endpoint of capitalism's quest for market dominance.

Wielding the knowledge he has gleaned from the future, the nanotech John Connor uses Cyberdyne's money to develop the polyalloy that forms the physical framework for a generation of robots that have limitless potential for the mega-corporation and that will eventually destroy the human race, while beginning work on the time machine that becomes the film's *deus ex machina*. This tech, Cyberdyne claims, will 'creat[e] the dawn of a new age' and 'change the future'.[7] Here, *Genisys* references a trope beloved of Silicon Valley startup founders. Venture capitalist Marc Andreesson holds the sincere belief that such grand promises lie at the core of a successful business. Investment from Andreesson is often considered a sign of a company's vast potential and opens doors to further investment, so it behoves entrepreneurs to describe their product and their projections of its future value in terms that would appeal to him. Likewise, Steve Jobs insisted that Apple's products were for people who 'want to use computers to help them change the world'.[8] The libertarian Silicon Valley investor Peter Thiel conceived PayPal as a 'conspiracy to change the world' and Mark Zuckerberg, whose company received funding from Andreesson and included Thiel on its board of directors, presented Facebook in similar terms.[9] So entrenched is this rhetorical trope that the HBO satire *Silicon Valley* renders it a running joke, in which every startup founder (and they are invariably men) insists that, no matter how mundane, his product will make the world a better place, from Hooli's 'minimal message-oriented transport layers' to minor startup Goolybib's 'elegant hierarchies for maximum code reuse and extensibility'.[10] Naturally, for the dystopian science fictions, this 'changing the world' involves sinister outcomes, and is inextricably linked to the tech-bro culture of Silicon Valley, particularly its audacity, self-belief and single-mindedness, which the films propose are fundamental to their Randian villains' messianic tendencies and fatal flaws.

At a broader level, the science-fiction corporations elevate the profit motive over scientific concerns about the impact of experimentation. This underpins the danger they pose to humanity. Three key scenes in *Rise of the Planet of the Apes* reveal Will Rodman's inability to challenge the profit motive at a corporate level. In the first, he presents his findings to the Gen-Sys board after running trials of his drug on some chimps. His manager, Jacobs, warns him to keep his emotions repressed, because the board 'invests in results, not dreams'.[11] Attempting to appeal to the board's humane instincts, Rodman argues that the drug has 'virtually limitless' medical uses as a cure for Alzheimer's and the potential to reverse the symptoms of many other brain disorders. Yet Jacobs senses that these benefits to humanity are not enough: he interrupts Rodman to declare that the 'potential profits' are as immense as these medical benefits.[12] Rodman's humanitarian appeal cedes to discussions of ten-year returns on investment projections, share prices and revenues. Reflecting his subordinate position, he is unable to protest the usurping of his idealistic vision. At precisely this critical juncture, however, an enraged ape wrecks the presentation, smashing through the office's glass windows after escaping the testing facility. The corporation's security detail shoots this invader before she can extend the destruction beyond the boardroom. Gen-Sys initially attributes the ape's rage to Rodman's drug, with Jacobs responding in typical capitalist style, telling the ape handlers to destroy them all in the 'most cost effective' manner possible: 'I run a business, not a petting zoo.'[13]

Figure 9.1 Will Rodman (facing) cedes his presentation about his new wonder drug to profit/loss projections. (Cropped screenshot, 7m).

The timing of the ape's intervention is crucial: she invades immediately after the discussion moves from healthcare to profit. As such, she must be interpreted within an ideological framework. Her rage is directed at capitalism's elevation of profit over humanity and might even be interpreted as a manifestation of Rodman's repressed anger at his bosses. She has experienced the brutality of Silicon Valley capitalism's disregard for ethics, and protests using all the means at her disposal. Deeper still, her handlers posthumously discover that the rampage began not because of the drug but because she perceived them to be threatening her new-born baby. That this invasion was prompted by the ape's desire to protect her child suggests that her anger metaphorically represents outrage at Silicon Valley's impact on innocent children, such as through social media's ability to exacerbate childhood depression.[14] Her individual assault prefigures the apes' collective assault on Gen-Sys; its failure underpins her son Caesar's insistence that, as individuals the apes are weak, but together they are strong enough to overthrow their corporate torturers. Informed by her first strike, then, their war is not against humanity, but instead against the corruption of healthcare by capitalism and the subordination of humanitarianism to profit. It also stands as an example of the power of collective action in the face of medicalised and militarised capitalism.

Yet, as Rodman's continuing employment at Gen-Sys suggests, it is extremely difficult to maintain a principled opposition to the capitalism of the tech industry, especially in as expensive a city as San Francisco. While clandestinely raising Caesar, Rodman re-engineers the drug, discovering that it has applications beyond treatment of brain disorders. He returns to Jacobs, and after initially failing to reignite his superior's interest in the drug's potential, he resorts to a bit of showmanship. Like Steve Jobs pulling another epochal product out of his pocket during an Apple presentation, he promises Jacobs 'there's more!', informing him that the drug might be used to augment the human brain and improve human intellect.[15] Such potential, Jacobs recognises, vastly expands the potential market for the drug beyond those suffering from Alzheimer's or similar ailments to a vast array of paying customers. Eyes wide at the potential profits, he overrides Will's caution and approves further testing. He cheers that this new drug 'is worth more than everything else we are developing *combined*. You make history. I *make money*,' confirming that, like *Margin Call*'s bankers or *The Wolf of Wall Street*'s traders, he cares only about personal enrichment and not the impact his decisions might have on humanity at large.¹⁶ Crucially, like those traders, he does not understand the product he peddles beyond the extent to which it makes him money. These capitalist instincts prompt him to make the fateful decision to approve more animal testing. Soon afterwards, in another ideological moment, the newly emancipated, cognitively enhanced apes destroy the Gen-Sys laboratory before heading northwards while pointedly not attacking ordinary San Franciscans. They are instinctively aware of the root of evil in the Bay Area: medical science and technology's deference to turbo-capitalism. Only when faced with armed police, operating in concert with Jacobs, do they respond violently. As such, their refusal to attack humans unless in self-defence coupled with their battle against the forces of oppression in response to their incarceration opens up an intriguing suggestion that the apes reflect the enduring influence of another revolutionary group from the Bay Area with ambitions to overthrow capitalism: the Black Panther Party (BPP). While the highly problematic racial connotations of this linkage cannot be ignored, it renders the film even more suggestive in its critique of capitalism, deepening the film's consideration of the role of the prison-industrial complex in California. It also heightens the metaphoric power of the reformulated drug, which now might be considered akin to the revolutionary texts, such as Frantz Fanon's *The Wretched of the Earth* (1961), that BPP members read and which informed the parallels they drew between American capitalism, racism and white supremacy.¹⁷

The Rodman–Jacobs relationship reveals the film's ideological stance: the scientist pulls back from his misbegotten creation while corporate capitalism (metaphorically speaking) declaims 'damn the torpedoes, full steam ahead!' Capitalist questions about profitability thus replace scientific questions about experimentation; the scientist retreats from his God-like position, only to discover that his employer's ownership of the means of production renders it more of a God than he could ever imagine. The question surrounding the precautionary principle thus develops further. Rather than should we do it or can we do it, Gen-Sys's stance appears to be 'given the vast potential for profit, there appears no reason why we should not do it'. Ultimately, in thinking only in these terms, Gen-Sys forges the posthuman Earth. In this, *Rise* echoes the horror embedded in *Contagion* (Steven Soderberg, 2011) about the threat to humanity from deadly airborne viruses. Its mid-credits' graphical tracing of the virus's spread through international air travel also offers an eerie foreshadow of the Covid pandemic that ushered in the 2020s.

Figure 9.2 *Rise of the Planet of the Apes'* Caesar pondering a posthuman future. Contra *The Internship*, the sun sets to the west. (Cropped screenshot 1h33m).

Following their destruction of Gen-Sys's urban lab, meanwhile, the apes establish their new community in the bucolic Marin headlands across the Golden Gate, to the north of San Francisco. The film ends with Caesar occupying the high ground at the tip of one of its tallest redwoods, like a simian Dirty Harry Callahan, gazing across the Bay at San Francisco.[18] Here, the Golden Gate Bridge, San Francisco's most iconic landmark, serves as the literal and metaphoric bridge between the capitalist world and its outcasts, a role that it also plays in *X-Men: The Last Stand* (Brett Ratner, 2006), where rogue mutants gather in Marin's woodlands, to prepare their attack on medicalised capitalism. Warren Worthington, who believes that genetic mutations can be cured through chemical treatment, locates his research laboratory at the former prison facility on Alcatraz Island, imprisoning a mutant boy, Jimmy, whose power neutralises the mutations of anybody in his proximity. Like his imprisoned predecessors at Alcatraz, Jimmy is considered too dangerous to be at liberty, although this is not because the legal system considers him a threat to society. Instead, in another reflection of the privatisation and corporatisation of the prison system, a private corporation that believes him to contain enormous use value and exchange value, possesses the power to deny him his freedom. In a further violation of his rights, Worthington Labs seeks to violate his body by extracting his blood to develop its 'cure' for a supposedly existential threat to the human body: genetic mutations. To initiate the final confrontation at which he hopes to kill Jimmy, the rogue mutants' leader, Magneto, uses his powers to redirect the Golden Gate Bridge's southern end from San Francisco to Alcatraz, literally bringing his outcasts back in from the wild.[19] Ultimately, though, the film sides with the mutants who line up alongside the federal government, against the renegades. Thus, like the Native American activists who occupied the island to protest their mistreatment by the federal government at the end of the 1960s, the rebels find themselves facing a far better resourced opponent and must eventually concede to this greater power. The decision of the 'good' mutants to pursue a middle path between Worthington's eugenicist medicalised capitalism and Magneto's violent and potentially anti-capitalist rebels sees them opposing extremists of both sides. Having restored order in the final battle by rescuing Jimmy and defeating Magneto, these 'good' mutants are rewarded with government roles and full American citizenship, while the 'bad' mutants lose their powers or their lives: a salutary lesson about the importance of liberal centrism to maintaining the status quo. Presumably regulated by the federal government, meanwhile, Worthington's cure remains available to those mutants who request it.

Unlike *The Last Stand*, which was released not long before the economic upheavals of 2008, *Rise* sides more openly against Silicon Valley's ruination of our society. From his Marin lookout, Caesar, like *The Internship*'s interns, considers the city's role in creating the future he now inhabits, although he does not witness dawn and a new beginning but humanity's twilight, anticipating the end of the Bay Area's union of capitalism and medical experimentation that itself followed San Francisco's rejection of its humanist heritage. Similarly, *Genisys* contrasts urbanised tech capitalism with its rural antithesis, locating Sarah Connor's secret arms cache in Marin's Headlands, where Schwarzenegger's Terminator sat out the thirty-three years between the point at which he hurled Connor and Reese into the future and the moment of their arrival. Just as important, following their victory over Cyberdyne, the newly formed Connor family unit, with the resurrected Terminator the father watching over his daughter and new son-in-law, retreat in a rickety old truck further into California's rural north, away from the ruined city and perhaps also capitalism's grasp. Such ideological suggestions likewise inform *Venom*, where Marin is not the refuge of outcasts but the home of Cameron Drake, the film's amoral plutocratic capitalist. Like the financial masters of the universe secluded in their skyscrapers, Drake separates himself from society without considering the impact this has on his empathy for fellow humans. Inevitably, his corruption of Marin County through ruining its environment with a monstrous steel and glass research facility receives righteous punishment.

Drake's characterisation also reveals precisely how the Silicon Valley science-fiction films' interrogation of the relationship between scientific experimentation and the capitalist profit motive develops through the 2010s. In 2011, *Rise* depicted Rodman being outflanked and outwitted by his capitalist bosses. In between this and *Venom*'s release, tales of Silicon Valley malfeasance entered the public realm, including revelations that Elizabeth Holmes's Theranos medical corporation could not provide the services it promised, and the disgraceful working conditions for employees of Foxconn who manufactured Apple products.[20] Where *Rise*'s protagonist is forced to defer to his corporate employer's board of directors and hence its shareholders, *Venom*'s Drake reigns supreme over his corporation, the Randian individual unbound. His megalomania simply overrides any fidelity to scientific ethics. Like Holmes, he sacks anybody who crosses him in his determination to bring a dubious project to fruition. Like Steve Jobs, he laments poor design, albeit of the human body rather than computer accessories. Wealthy enough to own a private army, he claims ownership of the alien creature that invades his body, in a reflection of capitalist conceptions of property. He thus embodies the nexus between scientific experimentation, Silicon Valley capitalism, and of course the posthuman condition.

Drake also references the two Silicon Valley touchstones of *The Fountainhead*'s Howard Roark and *Atlas Shrugged*'s John Galt. As the archetypal Randian hero, the unemotional Roark considers himself highly rational and rejects humanitarianism and interdependency. Friendless, he refuses to let other people inhibit his freedom to act in service of his own interests. Galt, meanwhile, rejects society completely. The unfeeling, hubristic and highly individualist Drake follows suit, subordinating science to capitalism, even rejecting ethical and moral concerns about forcing homeless people to meld with the symbiotes. This offers an opportunity to cleanse the city more ruthlessly than the real-world tech bro Greg Gopman's plan to relocate the city's human 'trash' to a nearby cruise ship.[21] Here *Venom* also nods to the impact of landlordism on the San Francisco Bay Area. Thanks to rapidly increasing demand for housing, due in no small part to Silicon Valley's expansion, twenty-first-century Bay Area landlords sought ever more creative ways to evict tenants paying low rents in order to attract richer tenants. This included exploiting the Ellis Act, a state law enabling landlords to evict all the tenants in a building before selling it. San Francisco landlords subverted this by selling to another landlord for a quick profit, enabling the new landlord to offer the property at even higher rents. Similarly, they imposed so-called 'move-in evictions', declaring their or a relative's intention to live in the rental property for the next three years as a pretext. These processes accelerated the wealth inequalities in the region and contributed to both the bleaching of the racial mix in its cities and the removal and dispersal of their working-class populations.[22] Yet Drake then moves even further, beyond Rand's famously cruel attitude towards ordinary people. Concluding that human beings are parasitical on the Earth, he suggests a pact with the symbiote to destroy humanity before heading into space to claim ownership of extra-terrestrial worlds. In thus extending his real-estate portfolio, Drake envisages a posthuman, post-Earth Randian civilisation in the cosmos, one that surpasses even Peter Thiel's plan to create a floating oceanic island for libertarian tech overlords.[23]

Like Drake, *Ant-Man*'s chief antagonist Darren Cross believes that he has transcended the laws of man and even the laws of nature in his weaponising of Hank Pym's shrinking technology. Pym is aghast, not least because a boardroom coup – another symbolic feature of Silicon Valley capitalist enterprise, one that waylaid Steve Jobs's control of Apple and Jack Dorsey's leadership of Twitter in 2008, for example – prevents him thwarting Cross's plan. Like Drake, or the third-act Jobs, Cross possesses complete control of his corporation. Like Jobs, he meditates each morning. This exercise might aid mindfulness, but it did nothing to convince Jobs to become more selfless, charitable – philanthropy, he said, was a waste of time – or patient, let alone interfere with his devotion to capitalist ideals. Likewise, it fails to blunt Cross's sociopathic tendencies. He follows Gen-Sys in freely experimenting on animals, indifferent to the harm that comes to them. Like Elizabeth Holmes, he takes a paranoid interest in security and insists that his underlings work around the clock to reach his goals.[24] As this suggests, he moves fast and breaks things willy-nilly.

Naturally, this fascistic tech bro sells his technology to the highest bidder, which happens to be the MCU's villainous Hydra organisation, thus reinforcing the message that Silicon Valley capitalists disregard moral or ethical questions when finance enters the equation. Here it is impossible to avoid considering parallels with Peter Thiel's data analytics company, Palantir. Thiel's company initially aimed to identify possible future terrorists by analysing reams of data scraped by the federal government from the web, mobile phone logs, financial records and other data gathered by the CIA, National Security Agency and the Department of Defense. Reflecting Thiel's libertarian inclinations, Palantir allowed users to undertake unethical and potentially illegal data searches, only logging the search and allowing the individual or their employer to determine whether this use was appropriate, essentially gifting users the opportunity to intimidate private individuals. Just as important, Palantir assisted the Trump administration's unconscionable immigration policy. Thiel, lest we forget, pumped millions of dollars into the anti-immigration right-winger Kris Kobach's campaigns.[25] While at an official level, Thiel's company represents an attempt to revive strong links between Silicon Valley and the military-industrial complex, its indifference to the moral aspect of its work reflects Thiel's firm belief that 'I'd rather be seen as evil than incompetent'.[26] This same attitude informs Cross's willingness to trade with whomever he chooses.

Cross's pact with evildoers might suggest that Lang and Pym would break bread with Hydra's antithesis, Tony Stark and the Avengers. Yet Pym mistrusts not only Cross but also the MCU's principal heroes. Here, *Ant-Man* plays on the early screen persona of Pym's actor, Michael Douglas, which was defined by classic liberal roles such as a doomed Vietnam War-era university dropout in *Summertree* (Anthony Newley, 1971), the cameraman who attempts to inform the public about the real dangers of nuclear power in *The China Syndrome* (James Bridges, 1979), and the likeable San Francisco homicide detective Steven Keller in television's *The Streets of San Francisco* (ABC, 1972–76). As important, Pym also appears to riff ironically on Douglas's signature role from the 1980s: *Wall Street*'s rapacious stockbroker Gordon Gekko. Informed by his awareness of the mass destruction wrought by the Avengers chronicled in previous MCU films, Pym worries that Stark's associates allow their faith in technology to override concerns about human life.[27] Notably, his outings as Ant-Man when he was a young man during the Cold War see him fighting alongside the American government against the Soviet Union. Most significantly, he used his technology to attempt to prevent the explosion of a nuclear warhead. As such, Pym represents a more humane, less rapacious capitalism, one that is sceptical of unfettered corporate power, government intrusion and muscular vigilantism but which is a defender of liberalism against totalitarianism. He stands in contrast to Cross's single-minded, amoral dedication to profit and the Avengers' bombastic militarism. Deeper still, Pym's attitude towards the Avengers' leader Stark hints at an ideological critique of the MCU's *Avengers* sequence. Stark embodies the MCU's understanding of tech capitalism's willingness to work in concert with American government ambitions in the era of neoconservative foreign policy (a relationship bolstered by the Pentagon's provision of equipment and locations for more than one MCU film).[28] In attempting to present enlightened self-interest in benevolent terms, the *Avengers* sequence entrusts the fate of humanity to Stark's corporation and the gaggle of *übermenschen* superheroes who converge under its banner. Notably, Stark's father confesses that 'the greater good has rarely outweighed my own self-interest': a Randian admission that appears to inform Stark's own ideological outlook.[29] Through Pym, *Ant-Man* gestures at the problems inherent in granting such power to a private corporation, although this critique – and *Ant-Man*'s complexity – is undercut by Lang's post-*Ant-Man* decision to join forces with Stark's Avengers, suggesting that Lang's understanding of the complexities of twenty-first-century geopolitics ultimately cedes to a Starker simplicity. This critique is further weakened by *Ant-Man*'s existence within the diegetic MCU and the (real-life) Marvel Entertainments entity, and might usefully be contrasted with *Venom*'s more distant relationship with the MCU.

Venom's ideological position is underpinned by its arms-length relationship with Marvel Entertainment's system (while remaining constrained by its position within a rival production conglomerate) and embodied by its hero, Eddie Brock, who lives in a world on the edge of destruction. Where the MCU is fascinated with and trusts in tech capitalism's ability to rescue us from otherworldly invasions, *Venom* places its trust in the more humane, anti-technology-solutionist values that Brock embodies. His friends in San Francisco's dingy downtown include a local homeless person and the Chinese American owner of his local store (relationships that nod to the multiracial Los Angeles of *Blade Runner*). His journalism centres the experiences of the Bay Area's forgotten people, such as the displaced victims of gentrification and white-collar real-estate crime in San Francisco's Mission District. The twenty-first century saw a marked decline in this journalistic form, which is time and labour intensive, requiring patience from both the journalist and their editors. In October 2020, US Senator Maria Cantwell highlighted the 'devastating impacts' on local journalism of Facebook and Google's domination of the advertising market, their use of newspapers' content, and the diversion of clicks away from the newspapers' own sites to the platforms, leading to newspaper advertising revenue collapsing while Google's and Facebook's expanded almost exponentially. This resulted in the loss of 60% of journalists' jobs across the nation and of over 2,000 newspapers between 2004 and 2020.[30] As the journalism scholar Victor Pickard argues, the combination of declining advertising earnings and the threat from online platforms saw journalists encouraged to provide sensational or outrageous content, because quantitative audience tracking indicated that such material was more likely to attract an audience that would in turn be more likely to share it on social media.[31] These combined threats, coupled with this pivot, rendered journalists like Brock ever more rare, and their editors ever more sensitive to the impact on the business of the stories they publish, not least because investigative reporters tend to ask tough questions of corporate bosses like Drake who possess the financial might to crush critical media outlets. A University of North Carolina research project revealed that many media outlet owners in the 2010s increasingly focused their content on serving their advertisers and business interests rather than their readers, a situation that Brock experiences personally.[32] His boss is particularly fearful of Drake's financial clout, warning Brock that Drake could buy them out with his pocket change, before ordering him to film a puff-piece about Drake's space exploration programme. This is a somewhat surprising choice given Brock's criticism of 'Silicon Valley overlords' such as Drake.[33] He is intensely sceptical of their vacuous rhetoric, amorality and rapacity, while possessing a rare authenticity himself, as signified by his preference for vinyl records over music streaming services. Inevitably, Brock's principles interfere with his commission, and much to Drake's irritation, he begins probing Drake's human experiments. After the interview, Drake forces Brock's boss to fire him, and for good measure also has Brock's lawyer girlfriend Anne fired from the legal firm he employs.

The film thus sets up a clash between Silicon Valley and the old media ecosystem that Hollywood inhabits, reflecting the wider cultural and economic battle between the tech corporations and the print media, while hinting at Peter Thiel's infamous campaign against Gawker Media. This battle began in 2007 when Gawker's Silicon Valley-based blog Valleywag confirmed that Thiel was gay. While an open secret in Silicon Valley, Thiel's sexuality was not widely known elsewhere. His revenge took nearly ten years to come to fruition, ending with Gawker's bankruptcy after Thiel funded the American wrestler Hulk Hogan's high-profile privacy case against the company.[34] Brock's fate is nearly as ruinous: he initially struggles to land even the most menial of jobs in the neoliberal dystopia of postmodern San Francisco and at one point is reduced to listening to a relaxation CD (itself a neoliberal tool designed to individualise systemic problems such as unemployment by having its listeners relax into their impotence in the face of overwhelming corporate power). Eventually, however, thanks to his experience with the film's titular symbiote, he regroups and decides to break into print journalism. Anne is similarly affected. Early in the film, she pragmatically attempts to rein in Brock's idealism, reminding him that his principled streak might not be appreciated by his corporate employers. Yet her careerism withers as she witnesses Brock's travails and even experiences Venom's symbiosis for herself after being fired at Drake's behest. At the film's conclusion she decides to re-enter the legal profession as a public defender, rejecting her previous persona as a well-paid but morally compromised corporate shill in favour of a more honourable employment identity. *Venom*, then, lauds principled but precarious workers who defend the common weal against avaricious capitalists who serve nobody but themselves.

As the above suggests, the films establish numerous dialectical relationships: between old media conglomerates and the new tech overlords, exemplified by Drake using his financial power to dictate to print and television media; between humanity and posthumanity, as suggested by the literal conversations between Brock and Venom, Brock-Venom and symbiote-Drake, and John Connor and his human foes; between the older, more moral humanitarian concerns of Rodman and Pym, and the rapacious Randian individualism of Jacobs and Cross. Ultimately, the films propose that this is a battle between human society and capitalism. It goes without saying that all the problems emerge thanks to the profiteering, egotism and general toxicity of male capitalists, driven by greed, lust for power and a general indifference towards fellow humans. The films suggest that the profit motive overwhelms any ethical and moral considerations for the villains at the heart of Silicon Valley. Significantly, only the earliest of them, *Apes*, suggests that science might engage in debate with capital, as symbolised by Rodman and Jacobs' arguments. Jacobs' victory foreshadows the other films' suggestion that capitalism overwhelms scientific caution. Even though all the villains meet grisly ends, order is only temporarily restored, as suggested by the sequels to *Apes* that detail the further decline of humanity and its replacement by a less rapacious, more collectivist, ape civilisation, as well as by Ant-Man's and Eddie Brock's ongoing adventures in the Bay Area and by the eternal threat of yet another Terminator sequel.

This subset of Silicon Valley cinema confirms that science fiction offers an ideal form through which present-day concerns can be iterated but also sublimated, enabling audiences to feel secure that the stories remain fantastical and fictional while also suggesting that they have a basis in fact. Importantly, however, defined as they are by their relationship with major Hollywood production companies and the exigencies of the mainstream audiences they covet, none of these films develops a radical critique of Silicon Valley. Acting a little like the nineteenth-century capitalists in the historian Richard Hofstadter's interpretation of the Progressive era, Hollywood presents its Silicon Valley villains as avatars of a capitalism run riot, while casting resentful eyes at the nouveau-riche upstate upstarts of the real world.³⁵ In this narrative, unlike the sensible, moderate capitalists of southern California, Hollywood's Silicon Valley corporations chase profits and market dominance irrespective of the associated human costs. Even though the films remain striking for expressing such profound concerns about twenty-first-century capitalism, their critique of Silicon Valley represents a nebulous fear among Hollywood producers of the expanding power of Silicon Valley to supplant Hollywood's previous dominance of American popular culture. As such, Hank Pym is their emblematic character: suspicious of the new tech overlords, willing to fight them, but similarly unwilling or unable to offer a truly radical solution, he is caught up in a political economy that he no longer recognises. What's more, his (and hence Hollywood's) response offers no solution to the structural problems that produced Silicon Valley. His challenge to Cross involves using similar technology fused with a moral, self-sacrificing and generous man who respects health and safety concerns rather than an amoral, self-centred and selfish man who thinks that he has transcended the laws of physics; a distant echo, perhaps, of National Rifle Association vice president Wayne LaPierre's aphorism that 'the only thing that stops a bad guy with a gun is a good guy with a gun'.³⁶

The films focus on a particular form of capitalism, one that emerged in Silicon Valley in the decades after the 1960s that lacks the morality and humility of previous capitalist forms; that, like Ayn Rand, respects only power and wealth; that tramples over science, ethics, morals and indeed humanity in its quest for hegemony. In this, the films suggest that Hollywood itself fears Silicon Valley as much as the viewing public fears an android-driven apocalypse, an alien slime-mould invasion or even a worldwide pandemic.

Notes

1. Jackson, '*Splice*', 125; Vivian Sobchack, 'Postfuturism', in Redmond (ed.), *Liquid Metal*, 224.
2. Claudia Springer, 'Psycho-Cybernetics in Films of the 1990s', in Kuhn (ed.), *Alien Zone II*, 203–18; Luttwak, *Turbo-Capitalism*.
3. Kerr, 'Electric Scooters are Invading'; Nicholas Lemann, 'The Network Man: Reid Hoffman's Big Idea', *New Yorker*, October 5, 2015, <https://

www.newyorker.com/magazine/2015/10/12/the-network-man> (consulted June 29, 2022); Taplin, *Move Fast and Break Things*, viii, 97–100.
4. Marx and Engels, *Communist Manifesto*, 16.
5. Adams, *Restaurant at the End of the Universe*, 109.
6. Wegner, 'Relics from a Deleted Timeline', 121–2.
7. *Terminator: Genisys*, 1h13m.
8. Robert Pogue Harrison, 'The Children of Silicon Valley', *New York Review of Books*, July 17, 2014, <https://www.nybooks.com/daily/2014/07/17/children-silicon-valley> (consulted June 29, 2022); Cohen, *Know-It-Alls*, 82–3; 'About' *Andreesson Horowitz*; 'Andreesson Horowitz, Matrix Partners Invest $11.2 Million in Meteor; Pein, *Live Work Work Work Die*, 105–6, 193, 281; Isaacson, *Steve Jobs*, 114–15, 154, 175, 303 (quote), 403.
9. Pein, *Live Work*, 226; Losse, *Boy Kings*, 199–200; Cohen, *Know-It-Alls*, 4, 74, 122–3, 158–9, 189, 193–4.
10. Both quotes: 'Minimum Viable Product', *Silicon Valley* series 1 episode 1 (HBO, 2014).
11. *Rise of the Planet of the Apes*, 4m.
12. Both quotes: *Rise*, 7m.
13. *Rise*, 8m.
14. O'Keeffe and Clarke-Pearson, 'The Impact of Social Media on Children, Adolescents, and Families', 800–4; Fitzgerald, 'Facebook Experiments on Users, Faces Blowback'.
15. *Rise*, 38–9m; Lashinsky, *Inside Apple*, 122–4; 'One More Thing'.
16. *Rise*, 57m.
17. Murch, *Living for the City*, 133–4.
18. Street, *Dirty Harry's America*, 79, 92.
19. *Silicon Valley* used Alcatraz to satirise tech startup founders' profligacy, bad taste and insensitivity to American history, culture and society. Two characters, flush with money, announce their new venture with a huge luau at Alcatraz. The former prison is reimagined for a Hawaii-themed party announced as the 'greatest launch of a company since America itself!' Naturally, the event is a disaster as the company has overstretched itself, and the astronomical cost of the luau sends it into insolvency. 'Bachmanity Insanity', *Silicon Valley* series 3 episode 6 (2016); see also Cantwell, 'Liveblog: Reporting from Bachmanity Insanity' (note that this is a spoof paratext set up by the *Silicon Valley* programme writers in order to deepen the viewer's experience of the television show).
20. Carreyrou, *Bad Blood*, 256–8, 272–3; Joel Johnson, '1 Million Workers. 90 Million iPhones. 17 Suicides. Who's to Blame?', *Wired*, February 28, 2011, <https://www.wired.com/2011/02/ff-joelinchina> (consulted June 29, 2022).
21. Alastair Gee, 'Tech Entrepreneur's Peace Offering After Calling Homeless "Degenerates": A Cruise Ship', *The Guardian*, March 1, 2017,

\<https://www.theguardian.com/us-news/2017/mar/01/homeless-cruise-ship-greg-gopman-san-francisco\> (consulted June 29, 2022).
22. 'Ellis Act Evictions'; Brahinsky, 'Death of the City?'; Anti-Eviction Mapping Project, *Counterpoints*, 9–50.
23. Chafkin, *Contrarian*, 137.
24. Lashinsky, *Inside Apple*, 83–4; Isaacson, *Steve*, 49–50, 23, 295, 529; Nick Bilton, *Hatching Twitter*, 128–9, 132–8, 147–54; Carreyrou, *Bad Blood*, 21, 22, 85, 102, 135–6, 151, 179–80, 209, 263, 281, 296–7.
25. Chafkin, *Contrarian*, 113–14, 116–17, 145, 150–1, 266–8, 286–7.
26. Chafkin, *Contrarian*, 154.
27. *Ant-Man*, 44m.
28. Tait, 'Marvel's War on Terror'.
29. *Avengers: Endgame*, 1h43m.
30. US Senate Committee on Commerce, Science, and Transportation, 'At Hearing with Big Tech CEOS, Cantwell Defends Local Journalism, Presses Platforms on Unfair Practices'; Abernathy, 'The Expanding News Desert', 12; Srnicek, *Platform Capitalism*, 53, 96; Kennedy, *The Wired City*, 1–2.
31. Pickard, 'Restructuring Democratic Infrastructures', 704–19.
32. Abernathy, 'Expanding News Desert', 63.
33. *Venom*, 6m.
34. Chafkin, *Contrarian*, 128, 194–7, 228, 230–1, 233.
35. Brown, *Richard Hofstadter*, 108–19.
36. Quoted in Eric Lichtblau and Motoko Rich, 'NRA Envisions "A Good Guy With a Gun" in Every School', *New York Times*, December 21, 2012, \<https://www.nytimes.com/2012/12/22/us/nra-calls-for-armed-guards-at-schools.html\> (consulted June 29, 2022).

Conclusion: *Why Him?* and the Dialectics of Silicon Valley Cinema

In the light-hearted comedy *Why Him?* (John Hamburg, 2016), Ned Fleming, the owner of a Michigan printing factory, warns his excitable son about the seductive world of Silicon Valley. 'Most of these internet companies are built on smoke and mirrors,' he says. 'Don't get sucked in. That whole industry is based on hooey.'[1] Somewhat surprisingly, and notwithstanding Fleming's denialism (which gradually cedes to anger, resignation and eventually acceptance), *Why Him?* offers the most dialectical Hollywood depiction of Silicon Valley. Co-produced by Shawn Levy's 21 Laps Entertainment and TSG Entertainment, both of which were involved in *The Internship*, it follows Fleming negotiating the blossoming relationship between his Stanford University-attending daughter and her paramour, Laird Mayhew, the founder of an online video games company based in Palo Alto, not far from Facebook's headquarters.[2] Competition from dot-com companies spearheading the drive towards the paperless office threatens Fleming's company's viability, while he learns that the post-2008 economic downturn has left his prospective son-in-law down to his last $197 million. Played by James Franco, now fully immersed in Silicon Valley after Will Rodman's split from Gen-Sys, Mayhew was raised in isolation from his peers, worked as a computer programmer from the age of thirteen, and respects few social niceties, wandering around barechested to display his numerous tattoos, peppering his speech with swearwords, and engaging Fleming's teenage son in inappropriate conversations that revolve around objectifying women. Reflecting his vast wealth and bad taste, expensive art bedecks his mansion, including numerous paintings of animals in sexual congress. He also has one of the country's most famous chefs at his beck and call. A little like Darren Cross, he practices yoga, mixed martial arts and parkour daily.

Yet this uncouth tech bro seeks old-world approval, seeking Fleming's permission to ask his daughter to marry him and buying up the debt of Fleming's company as an act of good faith. Eventually the two bond over an improbable solution to the company's problems: it will pivot from printing paper to making automated toilets that clean your backside for you, thus relieving the consumer's reliance on toilet paper while furthering Silicon Valley's quest for a paper-free world. As the film progresses, Fleming learns that Silicon Valley money can help him out of a hole, while Mayhew learns traditional American family values, choosing to stand by Fleming's daughter's decision to complete her studies rather than leave university to marry and then work for him. After graduation she joins the Fleming-Mayhew company to expand its charitable work in providing clean water to people in the developing world, thus proving American capitalism's essential benignity. The union between Fleming and Mayhew teaches the tech bro (and thus Silicon Valley) to end its focus on nonsensical ephemera and instead produce something tangible, as Hollywood and Rust Belt companies used to (even if that tangible thing is a receptable for human waste). These 'legacy' companies, meanwhile, accept the need to move with the times, abandon older modes of production and introduce Silicon Valley irreverence to their boardrooms. More perniciously, this pivot means that Fleming's workers must, like the millennials in Vince Vaughn's vision of the economy, reinvent (and thus reskill) themselves, in order that they might continue to provide the market with the convenience items that it craves. Synthesis achieved, American capitalism may go on its merry way, embodied in a Christmas celebration at which the workers join the Fleming-Mayhew family to cheer their new-found security and prosperity.

Why Him? exemplifies the Hollywood reaction to Silicon Valley, which suggests that, like Fleming, it is appalled at the uncouthness of this brash upstart. Yet, also like Fleming, its decency and fidelity to wholesome American values – not to mention its waning power – leads it towards a rapprochement, although unlike him it will no doubt continue to snipe at its rival. Ultimately and most importantly, however, Fleming and Hollywood are unable to comprehend the deeper structural issues that produced Silicon Valley, with the result that both end up merely processing shit. Like Hank Pym, Fleming cannot countenance attacking corporate ideology itself, but instead seeks to nudge his tech-bro son-in-law towards a kinder, gentler capitalism. After all, Fleming cannot simply abandon his factory but must find a way to continue to employ his presumably happy staff, lest, like Google's

Figure 10.1 American capitalism and the new American family enjoy Christmas together, accompanied by Gene Simmons and Paul Stanley of the rock band Kiss. (Cropped screenshot, 1h39).

unsuccessful interns, they be cast to the wolves in the grim economy outside his Silicon Valley-enabled embrace.

As such, *Why Him?* demonstrates why ambivalence drives Hollywood's response to Silicon Valley and why its films do not develop a truly radical critique of Silicon Valley: because Hollywood is firmly enmeshed in the same economic system. This bolsters the parallels between Hollywood and the Progressive-era critics of corporate capitalism, for both are as fascinated by the growing power and reach of their competitors as they are worried by the threat that these competitors constitute. As the literature scholar George Henderson observes, California novelists of the late nineteenth century such as Frank Norris found the transformations wrought on the land by capitalist development such as the railroad repelling, but they did not develop a thorough critique of the underlying influence of capital and property relations on these societal developments. Henderson suggests that these novelists were essentially ambivalent about late nineteenth-century capitalism, understanding both the damage modern capitalism wreaks and the transformative potential that capitalism brings with it. Norris's *The Octopus: A Story of California* (1901), for example, highlights how the railroad both creates and destroys as it spreads through the land, both broadening the geographical reach of the market and narrowing the scope for small businessmen and labourers to participate in it. This tension reflects a wider ambivalence among Progressives about American industrial capitalism.³ Likewise, *Why Him?* expresses profound concerns that Mayhew, as Silicon Valley's embodiment, could use his disruptive power to destroy a section of the American economy but is also fascinated by his ability to renew and reinvigorate Fleming's company, just as Fleming's wholesome values smooth his rough edges and pull him towards a benevolent form of capitalism that respects workers' rights and sends aid to the developing world. Yet Norris's understanding of capitalism also anticipates the impact that Google has on Sal's Pizzeria in *The Internship*. While Sal might expand his pizzeria's reach across the Bay Area, he will find himself in further competition with major multinationals such as Papa John's: a fight that he can never win. As such, Fleming has the good fortune to enter the automated toilet market before it reaches maturity and thus might become the dominant player; Sal will be far less fortunate.

Like the muckraking novelists of Norris's ilk, then, Silicon Valley cinema both reflects and hopes to shape wider trends in 2010s culture, in particular the critiques of Silicon Valley corporations that accelerated in the wake of revelations of Facebook's lax policing of disinformation in the 2016 United Kingdom 'Brexit' referendum and the 2016 American presidential election.⁴ Much like Silicon Valley cinema, such tech backlash critics are both fascinated and repelled by Silicon Valley's cultural, political and economic power. They offer a range of solutions that reflect a variety of ideological leanings. Writers such as Emily Chang, Rana Foroohar and Shoshana Zuboff focus on Silicon Valley's excesses. Foroohar, for example, believes that a bipartisan commission could outline a tighter regulatory framework within which Silicon Valley will operate; a new system of profit sharing, involving digital dividends paid to those whose data is mined by the tech industry; tax reform; a Theodore Roosevelt-style trust-busting exercise to break up the largest corporations; and a Digital New Deal to retrain the workforce.⁵ As this suggests, Foroohar sees federal regulation as essential in order to protect consumers. Hers are laudable aims, but as she acknowledges, Silicon Valley's huge lobbying operation would crush any efforts to pass the legislation needed to underpin these changes. Similarly, but more troublingly, *The Circle*'s unfortunate senator discovered that any attempts by mere politicians to break up Silicon Valley corporations will simply be overpowered. Moreover, beyond splitting the major tech conglomerates into smaller units, Foroohar offers little in the way of structural critique. Chang, meanwhile, focuses on the 'bad actors' in Silicon Valley who have distorted capitalism for their own purposes, arguing that placing more women in positions of power within Silicon Valley will improve it in numerous ways while overlooking the extent to which corruption rules the theatre in which they act. Echoing the centring of female agency in *Terminator-Genisys* but a little like Josh Brener's *Internship* mentor, Chang insists that higher numbers of female decision-makers will improve the diversity of thought in Silicon Valley.[6] This, of course, does not wholly convince. Informed, perhaps, by their relatively close personal relationship, Chang lauds Sheryl Sandberg's transformative impact on Google through sponsoring women-in-tech events, and her encouragement of people not to say 'um' (because it might lead their listener to think they are unintelligent). She simultaneously praises Sandberg's indefatigable work ethic – for example, her willingness to stop work at 5.30pm, head for home, and then restart work for the evening once the children are fed – while lambasting the culture of overwork in Silicon Valley that, despite her power, Sandberg never attempted to end. Her conclusion that any criticism of Sandberg derives from jealousy at Sandberg's success and power underpins her belief – shared with Sandberg – that 'women will create the institutional change' necessary in Silicon Valley.[7] This lauding of Sandberg offers a useful insight into the limits of Chang's critique of Silicon Valley. As Sandberg's critics outline, the Sandbergian brand of feminism leans into the corporate environment from which it emerged and fails to engage with the structural inequalities that beset American society.[8] As important, it merely assumes that female corporate leaders will be superior to male corporate leaders simply because they are women, thus suggesting that a form of biological determinism overrides any political, cultural, social or ideological leanings. Lest we forget, for example, the decision-maker at Yahoo who cut nearly a third of the corporation's jobs and ended its flexitime arrangements, which were particularly beloved by female members of staff who had caring responsibilities in the home, was Marissa Mayer.[9]

Chang, like the films assessed in this book, is correct in identifying a form of toxic masculinity that creates the problematic culture within Silicon Valley, but the assertion that employing more women will diminish the impact of this masculine attitude is strikingly naïve, as Wendy Liu suggests. For her, Silicon Valley's 'comfortable position in the economic hierarchy' leads its employees and boosters to develop 'self-serving rationalisations' that both cement their own economic position and fail to develop a deeper analysis of the tech industry's problems.[10] This critique might fruitfully be applied to Chang's relationship with Silicon Valley as mediated through her position as a presenter of the *Bloomberg Technology* television show, which offers soft-soap interviews of Silicon Valley's Randian leaders.[11] Rather than approaching Silicon Valley from a top-down perspective à la Chang, Liu's engagement with San Francisco's less wealthy residents, whom she encountered regularly, revealed the gulf between them and the tech elite who often ignore their presence, or, like the tech bro Peter Shih, treat them with disgust rather than compassion.[12] For Liu, then, Silicon Valley must be considered within the wider context of its relationship with the rest of the country. As her book's title suggests, only radical, transformative change will alter the way in which Silicon Valley operates; placing women in positions of power merely replaces one wealthy, corporate stooge with another.

Zuboff's *Surveillance Capitalism* has meanwhile emerged as the most prominent critique of Silicon Valley. Zuboff argues that the tech giants ultimately seek to 'automate' the human race and engineer the future using massive amounts of processing power.[13] The surveillance capitalism of platform entities like Facebook is, she insists, a new development in American capitalism. At its heart, the Zuboffian critique rests on the unbalanced exchange relationship between internet users and the tech industry; in short, the problem lies with the surveillance, not the capitalism. Like Foroohar, Zuboff sees reform rather than revolution as central to the effort to restrain surveillance capitalists like Google/Alphabet and Facebook/Meta; that emancipating the user will mitigate and perhaps even end the damaging impacts of those corporations on the world's individuals.[14] Like Hank Pym and Ned Fleming, then, she harkens back to a capitalism that is kinder, less rapacious, and less likely to destroy the world in search of profit.

As Liu's observations suggest, the stronger critique views Silicon Valley through a Marxist or anti-capitalist lens. Exemplified by Evgeny Morozov, this strand agrees that power imbalances between users and corporations need to be addressed but also argues that power as well as data needs to be redistributed equitably: after all, breaking up Meta would merely lead to the creation of numerous mini-Facebooks or simply separate Facebook from other Meta products such as WhatsApp or Instagram, leaving untouched the unfair user data market in which Meta operates. Data itself, according to Morozov, needs to be decoupled from its status as a commodity if the surveillance capitalists are to be brought to heel.[15] This perspective observes that Apple's decision to give iPhone users the option to prevent data-scraping apps such as Facebook tracking their use of their smartphone is not unwelcome, but fails to stop Apple monitoring the users itself through its own apps. The issue is the commodification of the data that each corporation hopes to scrape for its own analysis and profit-creation, and of course the fact that users are compelled to donate their data to these companies in return for use of their services.[16]

If a line might be drawn linking these authors to the severity of their critique of Silicon Valley capitalism, Morozov and Liu would be on its left, with the line moving rightwards through Zuboff, Foroohar, and arriving at Chang on the right. Were Silicon Valley cinema to be interposed on this, most films might appear within the Zuboffian–Changian range, as evidenced by the Steve Jobs biopics accepting the brilliance of Apple's products while acknowledging Jobs's personal flaws. *Pirates of Silicon Valley*, for example, might hint at the deleterious impact of the '90 Hours a Week and Loving It' culture on Apple's early employees but, like the other films, it is less interested in probing deeper issues at the corporation. Similarly, *Jobs* and *Steve Jobs* do not take issue with the corporation's tax minimisation policies or the dreadful employment conditions at Chinese factories that make some of its products.[17] While the genre requirements of the biopic partially explain these blind spots, *The Social Network* suggests that deeper critiques might be embedded within their narratives. It pushes viewers to think more deeply about the relationship between the human failures of Mark Zuckerberg, the nascent tech-bro phenomenon, and Facebook's toxicity. Yet its popularity among certain tech bros suggests that it might equally be treated as a how-to manual for borderline sociopaths or rapacious tech capitalists.[18] Similarly, while *The Social Network* might prompt us to develop a critique of Facebook's problematic role in our society, it also suggests that only two futures were possible once the Winklevoss twins engaged with Zuckerberg: a future dominated by a Zuckerberg-controlled social media platform or one dominated by an equally toxic Winklevoss platform. This world of binary choices also appears in the fictional films. In *Ant-Man* Hank Pym offers a vision of kindly tech overlords controlling weapons of mass destruction, rather than amoral, fascistic ones. Yet while Pym might be waging war for good against Darren Cross's evil, his failure to commit Scott Lang to challenge the Stark corporation's Nietzscheans suggests again that binary choices face us in the world of the tech bro, for the simplistic polarities of MCU eventually force him to live with the Avengers in order to continue fighting Hydra.

Beyond this, Silicon Valley cinema's ambivalence hints at deeper concerns, as revealed by *The Internship*'s fascination with Google coupled with its critique of the corporation's impact on our world. Google now seems full of salesmen like Vaughn and Wilson, and overworked millennials like the former interns, all sheltering like

Mae Holland, Vaughn, Wilson and Fleming's employees, from a devastated post-2008 employment market. All remain yoked to the workplace by their overlords' supplying of free food, beanbags, laundry and dog yoga, ensuring that they donate more than their contracted hours of cognitive labour as they enable Google's users to find even more online information and the corporation itself to spread its tentacles even further. Zuckerberg's monster meanwhile continues to feed off its users' data while he eternally clicks 'refresh' on Erica's profile, a twenty-first-century Nero fiddling while the world burns thanks to his corporation's algorithms churning gigabyte upon gigabyte of disinformation into its users' newsfeeds. Significantly, *Terminator: Genisys* concludes not with its heroine riding off into the sunset, but northwards into nature and a new dawn freed from Skynet. Like the wise heads of the cognitively enhanced apes, she has no use for turbo-capitalist Silicon Valley, although she must remain vigilant in order to tackle tech's next onslaught on humanity. As such, these films desperately want our world to be freed from Silicon Valley's control and influence but, like Sarah Connor's reliance on the increasingly humane but still robotic Terminator, they know they cannot fully escape tech's grip on us.

Finally, *Rise of the Planet of the Apes* might conclude that tech capitalism will lead to humanity's demise, but its sequels offer even more troubling insights into human culture. *Dawn of the Planet of the Apes* (Matt Reeves, 2014) and *War for the Planet of the Apes* (Matt Reeves, 2017) shift the focus to the deepening antagonism between the humans remaining after the pandemic and the new ape civilisation. Having depicted Silicon Valley's recklessness decimating the human race in *Rise*, the sequels portray humans reduced to warring factions, permanently fearing ape-led annihilation, living nasty, brutish, short and increasingly primitive lives. Capitalism and technology, the films suggest, were perhaps the only things holding humanity together, and the disappearance of this economic system and its bastard offspring presages humanity's eclipse. In siding with the apes' elevation of community concerns over individualism, the trilogy ultimately prompts its audience to ponder whether, ultimately, this is no bad thing.

The Circle ends on perhaps the most despairing note. Once again, Mae Holland is kayaking, leading viewers to assume that she has triumphed over the tech overlords and returned to nature. As she looks up to the sky, a drone descends. She breaks the fourth wall, smiling directly into the camera. We, the viewers, have become her surveillance cadre, following her every move: the Circle has been completed. Like the surveillance camera at *The Conversation*'s conclusion, our camera is panoptic and permanent, and like *Enemy of the State*'s Dean, Mae has reconciled herself to a life lived under its surveillance, permanently playing the Circle's game. She accepts her incorporation into our machine, as a plethora of images from other peoples' lives and deaths populate the screen. Mae watches us watching her, as we attempt to process our surveillance of the multitudinous din and ponder our culpability. The film ends by figuratively posing the following question: 'is this our shared future?'

Notes

1. *Why Him?*, 46m.
2. Jon Frosch, 'Why Him?: Film Review', *Hollywood Reporter*, December 12, 2016, <https://www.hollywoodreporter.com/movies/movie-reviews/why-him-review-955113> (consulted June 29, 2022).
3. Henderson, *California and the Fictions of Capital*, 119 (see also 123–5, 131–3, 140–5); Gangi, 'Sympathy's Sliding Scale', 131.
4. For example, Christopher Mims, 'The Global Tech Backlash is Just Beginning', *Wall Street Journal*, October 26, 2018, <https://www.wsj.com/articles/the-global-tech-backlash-is-just-beginning-1540476151> (consulted June 29, 2022); Jamie Doward, 'The Big Tech Backlash', *The Guardian*, January 28, 2018, <https://www.theguardian.com/technology/2018/jan/28/tech-backlash-facebook-google-fake-news-business-monopoly-regulation> (consulted June 29, 2022).
5. Foroohar, *Don't Be Evil*, 271–84.
6. Chang, *Brotopia*, 8.
7. Chang, *Brotopia*, 75–6, 103–4, 212, 217; Sandberg quote: 105.
8. Melissa Gira Grant, '"Like" Feminism', *Jacobin*, March 4, 2013, <https://www.jacobinmag.com/2013/03/like-feminism> (consulted June 29, 2022); Foster, *Lean Out*, 12.
9. Aschoff, *New Prophets of Capital*, 31–4.
10. Liu, *Abolish Silicon Valley*, 3.
11. See, for example, Chang and Frier, 'Mark Zuckerberg Q&A'.
12. Liu, *Abolish*, 44–5, 179–81; Montgomery, 'Tech Founder Complains About the Shithole City He's Forced to Make His Millions In'.
13. Zuboff, *Age of Surveillance Capitalism*, 8.
14. Morozov, 'Capitalism's New Clothes'.
15. Evgeny Morozov, 'There is a Leftwing Way to Challenge Big Tech for our Data. Here it is:' *The Guardian*, August 19, 2018, <https://www.theguardian.com/commentisfree/2018/aug/19/there-is-a-leftwing-way-to-challenge-big-data-here-it-is> (consulted June 29, 2022); Morozov, 'The Left Needs to get Radical on Big Tech – Moderate Solutions Won't

Cut It', *The Guardian*, February 27, 2019, <https://www.theguardian.com/commentisfree/2019/feb/27/left-radical-big-tech-moderate-solutions> (consulted February 15, 2022).
16. Evgeny Morozov, 'Privacy Activists are Winning Fights with Tech Giants. Why does Victory Feel Hollow?' *The Guardian*, May 15, 2021, <https://www.theguardian.com/commentisfree/2021/may/15/privacy-activists-fight-big-tech> (consulted June 29, 2022).
17. Sheppard, 'How Does Apple Avoid Taxes?'; Richard Bilton, 'Apple "Failing to Protect Chinese Factory Workers"'.
18. Chafkin, *Contrarian*, 173–4.

Bibliography

Films and Television

Bigelow, Kathryn, director, *Strange Days* (Lightstorm Entertainment, 1995).
Bird, Brad, director, *Tomorrowland* (Disney et al., 2015).
Bogdanovich, Peter, director, *What's Up Doc?* (Warner Bros, Saticoy Productions, 1972).
Boll, Uwe, director, *Assault on Wall Street* (Lynn Peak Productions, Studio West, 2013).
Boyle, Danny, director, *Steve Jobs* (Universal et al., 2015).
Burke, Martyn, director, *Pirates of Silicon Valley* (TNT et al., 1999), <https://archive.org/details/pirates-of-silicon-valley-hr> (consulted June 28, 2022).
Cameron, James, director, *The Terminator* (Cinema '84 et al., 1984).
—, *Terminator 2: Judgment Day* (Carolco Pictures et al., 1991).
Carpenter, John, director, *They Live* (Alive Films, Larry Franco Productions, 1988).
Chandor, J. C., director, *Margin Call* (Before the Door Pictures et al., 2011).
Cole, Joe Robert, director, *All Day and a Night* (Color Force, Mighty Engine, 2020).
Coogler, Ryan, director, *Fruitvale Station* (Significant Productions, OG Project, 2013).
Coppola, Francis Ford, director, *The Conversation* (The Directors Company et al., 1974).
Cronenberg, David, director, *eXistenZ* (Dimension Films et al., 1999).
—, *Cosmopolis* (Prospero Pictures et al., 2012).
Dassin, Jules, director, *Thieves' Highway* (20th Century Fox, 1949).
Douglas, Gordon, director, *Walk A Crooked Mile* (Columbia, Edward Small Productions, 1948).
DuVernay, Ava, director, *Selma* (Harpo Films et al., 2014).
Emmerich, Roland, director, *Universal Soldier* (Carolco Pictures et al., 1992).
Estrada, Carlos López, director, *Blindspotting* (Snoot Entertainment, 2018).
Ferguson, Charles, director, *Inside Job* (Sony Pictures Classics et al., 2010).
Fincher, David, director, *The Social Network* (Columbia et al., 2010).

Fleischer, Ruben, director, *Venom* (Columbia et al., 2018).
Garland, Alex, director, *Ex Machina* (Film4 et al., 2014).
Glen, John, director, *A View to a Kill* (Eon, 1985).
Gordon, Robert, director, *It Came from Beneath the Sea* (Clover Productions, 1955).
Guillermin, John, director, *The Towering Inferno* (20th Century Fox et al., 1974).
Hamburg, John, director, *Why Him?* (20th Century Fox et al., 2016).
Hitchcock, Alfred, director, *Vertigo* (Alfred J. Hitchcock Productions, 1958).
Huston, John, director, *The Maltese Falcon* (Warner Bros, 1941).
Jenkins, Barry, director, *Medicine for Melancholy* (Strike Anywhere, 2008).
Jonze, Spike, director, *Her* (Annapurna Pictures, Stage 6 Films, 2013).
Kane, Joseph, director, *Flame of the Barbary Coast* (Republic Pictures, 1945).
Kaufman, Philip, director, *Invasion of the Body Snatchers* (Solofilm, 1978).
Korda, Alexander, director, *Rembrandt* (London Film, 1936).
Lee, Ang, director, *Hulk* (Marvel Enterprises et al., 2003).
Leonard, Brett, director, *The Lawnmower Man* (Allied Vision et al., 1992).
Levy, Shawn, director, *The Internship* (20th Century Fox et al., 2013).
Longo, Robert, director, *Johnny Mnemonic* (TriStar et al., 1995).
Maté, Rudolph, director, *D.O.A.* (Happy Popkin Productions, 1950).
McKay, Adam, director, *The Big Short* (Paramount Pictures et al., 2015).
Miller, Bennett, director, *Moneyball* (Columbia Pictures et al., 2011).
Nimoy, Leonard, director, *Star Trek IV: The Voyage Home* (Paramount, 1986).
Peyton, Brad, director, *San Andreas* (New Line Cinema et al., 2015).
Ponsoldt, James, director, *The Circle* (Image Nation Abu Dhabi et al., 2017).
Post, Ted, director, *Beneath the Planet of the Apes* (20th Century Fox, APJAC, 1970).
Ratner, Brett, director, *X-Men: The Last Stand* (20th Century Fox et al., 2006).
Reed, Peyton, director, *Ant-Man* (Marvel Studios et al., 2015).
Reeves, Matt, director, *Dawn of the Planet of the Apes* (Chernin Entertainment et al., 2014).
—, *War for the Planet of the Apes* (20th Century Fox et al., 2017).
Riley, Boots, director, *Sorry to Bother You* (Cinereach et al., 2018).
Russo, Anthony and Joe Russo, directors, *Avengers: Endgame* (Marvel Studios, 2019).
Scott, Ridley, director, *Blade Runner* (Ladd Company et al., 1982).
Scott, Tony, director, *Enemy of the State* (Touchstone Pictures et al., 1994).
Schaffner, Franklin, director, *Planet of the Apes* (APJAC, 20th Century Fox, 1968).
Scorsese, Martin, director, *The Wolf of Wall Street* (Red Granit Pictures et al., 2013).

Siegel, Don, director, *Invasion of the Body Snatchers* (Allied Artists, Walter Wanger Productions, 1956).
—, *The Lineup* (Pajemer Productions, 1958).
—, *Dirty Harry* (Malpaso, 1971).
Softley, Iain, director, *Hackers* (United Artists, 1995).
Stern, Joshua Michael, director, *Jobs* (Five Star Institute et al., 2013).
Stevenson, Robert, director, *The Woman on Pier 13* aka *I Married a Communist* (RKO, 1949).
Talbot, Joe, director, *The Last Black Man in San Francisco* (A24 et al., 2019).
Taylor, Alan, director, *Terminator: Genisys* (Skydance Productions, 2015).
Tourneur, Jacques, director, *Out of the Past* (RKO, 1947).
Van Dyke, Woody, director, *San Francisco* (MGM, 1936).
Various directors, *Silicon Valley* (HBO, 2014–2020).
Various directors, *The Wire* (HBO, 2002–8).
Verhoeven, Paul, director, *Total Recall* (Carolco Pictures et al., 1990).
Wang, Wayne, director, *The Center of the World* (Artisan Entertainment, Redeemable Features, 2001).
Welles, Orson, director, *The Lady from Shanghai* (Mercury, 1947).
Winkler, Irwin, director, *The Net* (Columbia Pictures, Winkler Films, 1995).
Wyatt, Rupert, director, *Rise of the Planet of the Apes* (20th Century Fox et al., 2011).
Yates, Peter, director, *Bullitt* (Solar Productions, 1968).

Newspapers and Magazines

The Atlantic
Chronicle of Higher Education
Commentary
Daily Telegraph
The Guardian (London)
Hollywood Reporter
The Independent (London)
Jacobin
London Review of Books
Mother Jones
The Mercury News (San Jose)
New York
New York Review of Books
New York Times
The New Yorker
Observer (New York City)

San Francisco
San Francisco Chronicle
SFGate (San Francisco)
USA Today
Vanity Fair
Variety
Wall Street Journal
Washington Post
Wired

Government Publications

US Senate Committee on Commerce, Science, and Transportation, 'At Hearing with Big Tech CEOS, Cantwell Defends Local Journalism, Presses Platforms on Unfair Practices' press release, October 28, 2020, <https://www.commerce.senate.gov/2020/10/at-hearing-with-big-tech-ceos-cantwell-defends-local-journalism-presses-platforms-on-unfair-practices> (consulted June 29, 2022).

Books

Adams, Douglas, *The Restaurant at the End of the Universe* (London: Macmillan, 2010 edition [orig. 1980]).
Andersson, Johan and Lawrence Webb (eds), *The City in American Cinema: Film and Postindustrial Culture* (London: Bloomsbury, 2021).
— (eds), *Global Cinematic Cities: New Landscapes of Film and Media* (New York: Columbia University Press, 2016).
The Anti-Eviction Mapping Project, *Counterpoints: A San Francisco Bay Area Atlas of Displacement & Resistance* (Oakland, CA: PM Press, 2021).
Aschoff, Nicole, *The New Prophets of Capital* (London: Verso, 2015).
Beard, Mary, *SPQR: A History of Ancient Rome* (London: Profile, 2015).
Bell, David, *Cyberculture Theorists: Manuel Castells and Donna Haraway* (New York: Routledge, 2007).
Bilton, Nick, *Hatching Twitter: A True Story of Money, Power, Friendship and Betrayal* (London: Sceptre, 2013).
Bingham, Dennis, *Whose Lives Are They Anyway?: The Biopic as Contemporary Film Genre* (New Brunswick, NJ: Rutgers University Press, 2010).
— (ed.), *American Cinema in the 2010s: Themes and Variations* (New Brunswick, NJ: Rutgers University Press, 2022).
Brown, David S., *Richard Hofstadter: An Intellectual Biography* (Chicago: University of Chicago Press, 2006).

Burnham, Clint, *Fredric Jameson and* The Wolf of Wall Street (London: Bloomsbury, 2016).

Butcher, Lee, *Accidental Millionaire: The Rise and Fall of Steve Jobs at Apple Computer* (New York: Knightsbridge, 1990 edition [orig. 1988]).

Carreyrou, John, *Bad Blood: Secrets and Lies in a Silicon Valley Startup* (London: Picador, 2019).

Chafkin, Max, *The Contrarian: Peter Thiel and Silicon Valley's Pursuit of Power* (London: Bloomsbury, 2021).

Chang, Emily, *Brotopia: Breaking up the Boys' Club of Silicon Valley* (London: Penguin 2019).

Cohen, Norm, *The Know-It-Alls: The Rise of Silicon Valley as a Political Powerhouse and Social Wrecking Ball* (London: Oneworld, 2019).

Corrigan, Timothy (ed.), *American Cinema in the 2000s: Themes and Variations* (New Brunswick, NJ: Rutgers University Press, 2012).

Coupland, Douglas, *Generation X: Tales for an Accelerated Culture* (London: Abacus, 1995 [orig. 1991]).

—, *Microserfs* (London: Flamingo, 1995).

Cringely, Robert X., *Accidental Empires: How the Boys of Silicon Valley Make Their Millions, Battle Foreign Competition, and Still Can't Get a Date* (London: Penguin, 1992).

Dick, Philip K., *Clans of the Alphane Moon* (London: Panther, 1975 [orig. 1964]).

—, *Do Androids Dream of Electric Sheep?* (London: Millennium, 1999 [orig. 1968]).

Dimendberg, Edward, *Film Noir and the Spaces of Modernity* (Cambridge, MA: Harvard University Press, 2004).

Dinnen, Zara, *The Digital Banal: New Media and American Literature and Culture* (New York: Columbia University Press, 2018).

Eggers, Dave, *The Circle* (London: Hamish Hamilton, 2013).

Fahy, Thomas (ed.), *Considering Aaron Sorkin: Essays on the Politics, Poetics and Sleight of Hand in the Films and Television Series* (Jefferson NC: McFarland, 2005).

Foroohar, Rana, *Don't Be Evil: The Case Against Big Tech* (London: Allen Lane, 2019).

Foster, Dawn, *Lean Out* (London: Repeater, 2016).

Freiberger, Paul and Michael Swaine, *Fire in the Valley: The Making of the Personal Computer* (New York: McGraw Hill, 1984, rev. 2000).

Frenkel, Sheera and Cecilia Kang, *An Ugly Truth: Inside Facebook's Battle for Domination* (London: Bridge Street Press, 2021).

Gibson, William, *All Tomorrow's Parties* (London: Penguin, 1999).

Haraway, Donna J., *How Like a Leaf: An Interview with Thyrza Nichols Goodeve* (New York: Routledge, 2000).

—, *Simians, Cyborgs, and Women: The Reinvention of Nature* (New York: Routledge, 1991).

Henderson, George L., *California and the Fictions of Capital* (New York: Oxford University Press, 1998).
Hunt, Leon, Sharon Lockyer and Milly Williamson (eds), *Screening the Undead: Vampires and Zombies in Film and Television* (London: I. B. Tauris, 2014).
Isaacson, Walter, *Steve Jobs* (London: Little, Brown, 2011).
Jameson, Fredric, *The Seeds of Time* (New York: Columbia University Press, 1994).
Jeffords, Susan, *Hard Bodies: Hollywood Masculinity in the Reagan Era* (New Brunswick, NJ: Rutgers University Press, 1994).
Keane, Stephen, *Disaster Movies: The Cinema of Catastrophe* (London: Wallflower, 2001).
Kellner, Douglas, *Cinema Wars: Hollywood Film and Politics in the Bush-Cheney Era* (Chichester: Wiley, 2010).
Kennedy, Dan, *The Wired City: Reimagining Journalism and Civic Life in the Post-Newspaper Age* (Amherst, MA: University of Massachusetts Press, 2013).
Kirkpatrick, David, *The Facebook Effect: The Inside Story of the Company That is Connecting the World* (London: Virgin, 2010).
Kuhn, Annette (ed.), *Alien Zone II: The Spaces of Science-Fiction Cinema* (London: Verso, 1999).
Lashinsky, Adam, *Inside Apple: The Secrets Behind the Past and Future Success of Steve Jobs's Iconic Brand* (London: John Murray, 2012).
Lewis, Michael, *The Big Short: Inside the Doomsday Machine* (New York: Norton, 2010).
Liu, Wendy, *Abolish Silicon Valley: How to Liberate Technology from Capitalism* (London: Repeater, 2020).
Losse, Katherine, *The Boy Kings: A Journey into the Heart of the Social Network* (New York: Free Press, 2012).
Luttwak, Edward, *Turbo-Capitalism: Winners and Losers in the Global Economy* (London, Weidenfeld & Nicolson, 1998).
Lyons, Dan, *Disrupted: Ludicrous Misadventures in the Tech Start-Up Bubble* (London: Atlantic, 2016).
Martínez, Antonio García, *Chaos Monkeys: Mayhem and Mania Inside the Silicon Valley Money Machine* (London: Ebury, 2016).
Marx, Karl and Friedrich Engels, *The Communist Manifesto* (Oxford: Oxford World's Classics edition, 1992).
Mennel, Barbara, *Cities and Cinema*, second edition (London: Routledge, 2019).
Menuez, Doug, *Fearless Genius: The Digital Revolution in Silicon Valley, 1985–2000* (New York: Atria, 2014).
Mezrich, Ben, *The Accidental Billionaires: The Founding of Facebook* (New York: Anchor, 2009).
Moritz, Michael, *Return to the Little Kingdom: Steve Jobs, the Creation of Apple, and How it Changed the World* (London: Duckworth Overlook, 2009).

Morozov, Evgeny, *To Save Everything, Click Here: Technology, Solutionism, and the Urge to Fix Problems That Don't Exist* (London: Allen Lane, 2013).
Murch, Donna Jean, *Living for the City: Migration, Education, and the Rise of the Black Panther Party in Oakland, California* (Chapel Hill, NC: University of North Carolina Press, 2010).
O'Hara, Margaret, *The Code: Silicon Valley and the Remaking of America* (New York: Penguin, 2019).
Pearce, Lynne and Gina Wisker (eds), *Fatal Attractions: Rescripting Romance in Contemporary Literature and Film* (London: Pluto Press, 1998).
Pein, Corey, *Live Work Work Work Die: A Journey into the Savage Heart of Silicon Valley* (London: Scribe, 2018).
Rand, Ayn, *The Fountainhead* (New York: Penguin, 2007 [orig. 1943]).
Redmond, Sean (ed.), *Liquid Metal: The Science Fiction Film Reader* (London: Wallflower Press, 2004).
Rich, Nathaniel, *San Francisco Noir: The City in Film Noir from 1940 to the Present* (New York: The Little Bookroom, 2005).
Ross, Andrew, *No-Collar: The Humane Workplace and its Hidden Costs* (Philadelphia, PA: Temple University Press, 2004).
Sandberg, Sheryl, *Lean In: Women, Work, and the Will to Lead* (London: W. H. Allen, 2013).
Sloan, Robin, *Mr Penumbra's 24-Hour Bookstore* (London: Atlantic, 2013).
Solnit, Rebecca, *Infinite City* (University of California Press, 2010).
Spencer, Keith A., *A People's History of Silicon Valley* (London: Eyewear Publishing, 2018).
Srnicek, Nick, *Platform Capitalism* (London: Polity, 2016).
Strauss, Neil, *The Game: Undercover in the Secret Society of Pickup Artists* (Edinburgh: Canongate, 2005).
Street, Joe, *Dirty Harry's America: Clint Eastwood, Harry Callahan, and the Conservative Backlash* (Gainesville, FL: University Press of Florida, 2016).
Taplin, Jonathan, *Move Fast and Break Things: How Facebook, Google, and Amazon Have Cornered Culture and Undermined Democracy* (London: Pan, 2018).
Thiel, Peter with Blake Masters, *Zero to One: Notes on Startups, or How to Build the Future* (London: Virgin, 2014).
Toscano, Alberto and Jeff Kinkle, *Cartographies of the Absolute* (Winchester: Zero Books, 2015).
Walker, Richard A., *Pictures of a Gone City: Tech and the Dark Side of Prosperity in the San Francisco Bay Area* (Oakland, CA: PM Press, 2018).
Wayne, Mike, *Marxism Goes to the Movies* (London: Routledge, 2020).
Webb, Lawrence, *The Cinema of Urban Crisis: Seventies Film and the Reinvention of the City* (Amsterdam: Amsterdam University Press, 2014).
Wiener, Anna, *Uncanny Valley: A Memoir* (London: 4th Estate, 2020).

Wolfe, Alexandra, *Valley of the Gods: A Silicon Valley Story* (New York: Simon & Schuster, 2017).
Zimmer, Catherine, *Surveillance Cinema* (New York: New York University Press, 2015).
Žižek, Slavoj, *Living in the End Times* (London: Verso, 2018 edition).
Zuboff, Shoshana, *The Age of Surveillance Capitalism: The Fight for a Human Future at the New Frontier of Power* (London: Profile, 2019).

Scholarly Articles

Andriano-Moore, Stephen, 'The Rise of the Sound Designer: Northern California Film Sound in the 1960s and 1970s', *Historical Journal of Film, Radio and Television* 38 (2018).
Bacon, Simon, '"We Can Rebuild Him!": The Essentialism of the Human/Cyborg Interface in the Twenty-First Century, or Whatever Happened to *The Six Million Dollar Man*?', *AI & Society* 28 (2013).
Barbrook, Richard and Andy Cameron, 'The Californian Ideology', *Science as Culture* 6 (1996), <http://www.imaginaryfutures.net/2007/04/17/the-californian-ideology-2> (consulted June 28, 2022).
Berrettini, Mark, 'Can "We All" Get Along?: Social Difference, the Future, and *Strange Days*', *Camera Obscura* 50 (2002).
Bowler, Alexia L., '*eXistenZ* and the Spectre of Gender in the Cyber-Generation', *New Cinemas: Journal of Contemporary Film* 5 (2007).
Brahinsky, Rachel, 'The Death of the City?', *Boom* 4, 2 (Summer 2014), <https://boomcalifornia.com/2014/07/02/the-death-of-the-city> (consulted June 28, 2022).
Broxmeyer, Jeffrey, 'From the Silver Screen to the Recall Ballot: Schwarzenegger as Terminator and Politician', *New Political Science* 32 (2010).
Davies, William, 'The Political Economy of Unhappiness', *New Left Review* 71 (2011), <https://newleftreview.org/issues/II71/articles/william-davies-the-political-economy-of-unhappiness> (consulted June 28, 2022).
Deutelbaum, Marshall, '*The Social Network* Screenplay: Adaptation as (re-)interpretation and (re-)creation', *Journal of Screenwriting* 7 (2016).
Eagan, Daniel, 'Dreams from our Fathers', *Film Journal International* 118, 1 (January 2015).
Eve, Martin and Joe Street, 'The Silicon Valley Novel', *Literature and History* 27 (2018).
Ferriss, Suzanne, 'Refashioning the Modern American Dream: *The Great Gatsby*, *The Wolf of Wall Street*, and *American Hustle*', *Journal of American Culture* 41 (2018).
Fuchs, Christian, 'Web 2.0, Prosumption, and Surveillance', *Surveillance and Society*, 8 (2011).
Gangi, Ashley, 'Sympathy's Sliding Scale: Individuals and Large Forces in Frank Norris's *The Octopus*', *Studies in American Naturalism* 13 (2018).

Hadida, Allègre L. and Joseph Lampel, W. David Walls, Amit Joshi, 'Hollywood Studio Filmmaking in the Age of Netflix: A Tale of Two Institutional Logics', *Journal of Cultural Economics* 45 (2021).
Jackson, Kimberly, '*Splice*: The postmodern Prometheus', *Horror Studies* 3 (2012).
Kamber, Tom, 'Gen X: The Cro-Magnon of Digital Natives', *Generations* 41, 3 (Fall 2017).
Katz, Stephen, 'Generation X: A Critical Sociological Perspective', *Generations* 41, 3 (Fall 2017).
Keyser, Catherine, 'Candy Boys and Chocolate Factories', *Modern Fiction Studies* 63 (2017).
Laffly, Tomris, '*Steve Jobs*', *Film Journal International* 118, 10 (October 2015).
McKinnon, Scott, 'Straight Disasters: The (hetero)sexual geographies of Hollywood Disaster Movies', *GeoJournal* 82 (2017).
Morozov, Evgeny, 'The Will to Improve (Just About Everything!)', *Policy Options* 34, 6 (July/August 2013).
O'Donoghue, Darragh, 'Steve Jobs: The Man in the Machine/ Steve Jobs', *Cineaste* 48 (Spring 2016).
O'Keeffe, Gwenn Schurgin and Kathleen Clarke-Pearson, 'The Impact of Social Media on Children, Adolescents, and Families', *Pediatrics* 127 (2011).
Pickard, Victor, 'Restructuring Democratic Infrastructures: A Policy Approach to the Journalism Crisis', *Digital Journalism* 8 (2020).
Smith, Glenn D., 'Love as Redemption: The American Dream Myth and the Celebrity Biopic', *Journal of Communication Inquiry* 33 (2009).
Street, Joe, '*Dirty Harry*'s San Francisco', *The Sixties: A Journal of History, Politics and Culture* 5 (June 2012).
Strong, Will and Aiden Harper, *The Shorter Working Week: A Radical and Pragmatic Proposal* (Hampshire: Autonomy Research, 2019), <https://autonomy.work/wp-content/uploads/2019/02/Shorter-working-week-docV5.pdf> (consulted June 28, 2022).
Tews, Michael J. et al., 'Workplace Fun Matters . . . But What Else', *Employee Relations* 37 (February 2015).
Tyree, J. M., 'The Dislike Button', *Film Quarterly* 64 (2011).
Wegner, Phillip E., 'Relics from a Deleted Timeline: The Economics of *Terminator Genisys*', *Science Fiction Film and Television* 10 (2017).

Online Sources

'Aaron Sorkin on Writing "Steve Jobs"', *YouTube*, January 7, 2016, <https://www.youtube.com/watch?v=0FcOiAzp1I0> (consulted June 28, 2022).
Abernathy, Penelope Muse, 'The Expanding News Desert' (University of North Carolina at Chapel Hill School of Media and Journalism, 2020),

<https://www.cislm.org/wp-content/uploads/2018/10/The-Expanding-News-Desert-10_14-Web.pdf> (consulted June 29, 2022).

'About' *Andreessen Horowitz* (2019), <https://a16z.com/about> (consulted June 28, 2022).

Acuna, Kirsten, 'The Office of Evil Corporation in "Terminator Genisys" is Based on a Real Silicon Valley Tech Company', *Business Insider*, July 1, 2015, <https://www.businessinsider.com/terminator-genisys-cyberdyne-based-on-oracle-2015-7?r=US&IR=T> (consulted June 29, 2022).

Allergic to my own Swag (@coherent states), 'How is it that the Madame Tussauds wax model of Mark Zuckerberg looks way more like a real person than Mark Zuckerberg does? Oh my god', *Twitter*, October 25, 2019, 7:58am, <https://twitter.com/coherentstates/status/1187624408413700096?s=20> (consulted June 29, 2022).

'Andreessen Horowitz, Matrix Partners Invest $11.2 Million in Meteor', *PR Newswire*, July 25, 2012, <https://www.prnewswire.com/news-releases/andreessen-horowitz-matrix-partners-invest-112-million-in-meteor-163687206.html> (consulted June 28, 2022).

'Apple – Steve Jobs Introduces the iPod – 2001', *YouTube*, October 24, 2001, <https://youtu.be/Mc_FiHTITHE> (consulted June 28, 2022).

Auger, Andrew, 'Venom and Black Cat Movies Will Be "Adjuncts" to the MCU's Spider-Man', *ScreenRant*, June 18, 2017, <https://screenrant.com/venom-silver-sable-spider-man-homecoming-movies-connections> (consulted June 29, 2022).

Baker, Katie J. M., 'Is Dave Eggers' New Novel a Ripoff of a Female Writer's Work', *Jezebel*, September 9, 2013, <https://jezebel.com/is-dave-eggers-new-novel-a-ripoff-of-a-female-writers-1428445249> (consulted June 28, 2022).

Bereznak, Alyssa, 'Ten Years Late, Mark Zuckerberg is Still Trying to Overcome *The Social Network*', *The Ringer*, September 22, 2020, <https://www.theringer.com/movies/2020/9/22/21450318/mark-zuckerberg-the-social-network-origin-story> (consulted June 28, 2022).

Bigler, Taylor, '*Jobs* Producer on "The Rise, The Fall, and the Triumphant Return of Steve Jobs"', *Daily Caller*, August 16, 2013, <https://dailycaller.com/2013/08/16/jobs-producer-on-the-rise-the-fall-and-the-triumphant-return-of-steve-jobs> (consulted June 28, 2022).

Bilton, Richard, 'Apple "Failing to Protect Chinese Factory Workers"', *BBC*, December 18, 2014, <https://www.bbc.co.uk/news/business-30532463> (consulted June 29, 2022).

'blue_beetle' post at 'User-driven discontent' forum, <https://www.metafilter.com/95152/Userdriven-discontent#3256046 August 26, 2010> (consulted June 28, 2022).

Brown, Mike, 'Facebook CEO Mark Zuckerberg Says He "Was Human" in Viral Video', *Inverse*, October 23, 2017, <https://www.inverse.com/article/37656-mark-zuckerberg-was-human> (consulted June 29, 2022).

Callaham, John, 'Interview: We Chat with the Producer of the Upcoming Steve Jobs Movie', *Neowin*, April 14, 2021, <https://www.neowin.net/news/interview-we-chat-with-the-producer-of-the-upcoming-steve-jobs-movie> (consulted April 27, 2021).

Cantwell, C. J., 'Liveblog: Reporting from Bachmanity Insanity', *Code/rag*, <http://www.coderag.com/liveblog-reporting-from-bachmanity-insanity> (consulted June 29, 2022).

Caroom, Eliot, 'Report: Businesses Going Bankrupt', *Inc*, Feb 10, 2009, <https://www.inc.com/news/articles/2009/02/bankrupt.html> (consulted June 28, 2022).

Carr, Paul Bradley, 'Travis Shrugged: The Creepy, Dangerous Ideology Behind Silicon Valley's Cult of Disruption', *Pando*, October 24, 2012, <https://pandodaily.com/2012/10/24/travis-shrugged> (consulted June 28, 2022).

Chang, Emily and Sara Frier, 'Mark Zuckerberg Q&A: The Full Interview on Connecting the World', *Bloomberg*, February 19, 2015, <https://www.bloomberg.com/news/articles/2015-02-19/mark-zuckerberg-q-a-the-full-interview-on-connecting-the-world#xj4y7vzkg> (consulted July 7, 2022).

Clark, Kim, 'The 5 Colleges That Leave the Most Students Crippled by Debt', *Money*, September 25, 2014, <https://money.com/money/3426618/student-loan-default-factories> (consulted June 28, 2022).

Clark, Travis, 'All 28 Marvel Cinematic Universe Movies Ranked by How Much Money They Made at the Global Box Office', *Business Insider*, May 16, 2022, <https://www.businessinsider.com/marvel-movies-ranked-how-much-money-at-global-box-office-2021-11?op=1&r=US&IR=T> (consulted June 30, 2022).

'Comic-Con 2014: Corey Stoll Talks "Ant-Man" Role, Yellowjacket Costume', *YouTube*, July 28, 2014, <https://www.youtube.com/watch?v=i6wYKKakGHw> (consulted June 29, 2022).

Cooper, Harry and Nicholas Hirst, 'Silicon Valley Tech Lobbyists Swarm Brussels', *Politico*, January 28, 2018, <https://www.politico.eu/article/silicon-valley-tech-lobbyists-swarm-brussels> (consulted June 28, 2022).

Davis, Jamie, 'Lobbying on the Up as Silicon Valley Feels the Regulatory Squeeze', *Telecoms.com*, January 23, 2019, <https://telecoms.com/494881/lobbying-on-the-up-as-silicon-valley-feels-the-regulatory-squeeze> (consulted June 28, 2022).

Del Rosario, R., 'Arnold Schwarzenegger Wraps Up Production on New "Terminator" Film', *CBS*, August 6, 2014, <https://sanfrancisco.cbslocal.com/2014/08/06/arnold-schwarzenegger-wraps-up-production-on-new-terminator-film> (consulted June 29, 2022).

Deutschman, Alan, 'The Once and Future Jobs', *Salon*, October 11, 2000, <https://www.salon.com/2000/10/11/jobs_excerpt/> (quote; consulted June 28, 2022).

Diamond, Brandon, 'Google Glass or Not, *The Internship* is Unwatchable', *HuffPost*, August 8, 2013, <https://www.huffpost.com/entry/google-the-internship_b_3409361?utm_> (consulted June 28, 2022).

'Distribution of Facebook Employees in the United States from 2014–2020, by Ethnicity', *Statista*, January 28, 2022, <https://www.statista.com/statistics/311847/facebook-employee-ethnicity-us> (consulted June 28, 2022).

'Distribution of Facebook Employees Worldwide from 2014 to 2020, by Gender', *Statista*, January 28, 2022, <https://www.statista.com/statistics/311827/facebook-employee-gender-global> (consulted June 28, 2022).

Dormehl, Luke, 'How a '90s TV Movie Became the Steve Jobs Film to Beat', *Cult of Mac*, October 29, 2014, <https://www.cultofmac.com/301225/90s-tv-movie-became-steve-jobs-film-beat> (consulted June 28, 2022).

Dowd, A. A., 'The Internship', *The AV Club*, June 6, 2013, <https://www.avclub.com/the-internship-1798177004> (consulted June 28, 2022).

Eadicicco, Lisa, 'What Steve Jobs' Famous Garage Where He Started Apple Looks Like Today', *Business Insider*, January 17, 2015, <https://www.businessinsider.com/steve-jobs-garage-photos-apple-2015-1?r=US&IR=T> (consulted June 28, 2022).

Ehrenkrantz, Melanie, 'Leaked Apple Emails Reveal Employees' Complaints About Sexist, Toxic Working Environment', *Tech.Mic*, September 14, 2016, <https://mic.com/articles/154169/leaked-apple-emails-reveal-employees-complaints-about-sexist-toxic-work-environment#.ZgE8EPv1y> (consulted June 28, 2022).

'Ellis Act Evictions', *San Francisco Tenants' Union*, <https://www.sftu.org/ellis> (consulted June 29, 2022).

Erbland, Kate, 'The Circle: James Ponsoldt Explains Why His Dave Eggers Adaptation Isn't Just Another Film About Dangers of Technology', *IndieWire*, February 9, 2017, <https://www.indiewire.com/2017/02/the-circle-james-ponsoldt-dave-eggers-adaptation-1201779380/#!> (consulted June 28, 2022).

Ferenstein, Gregory, 'A Deeper Look at Silicon Valley's Long-Term Politics', *Brookings Institute*, October 4, 2017, <https://www.brookings.edu/blog/techtank/2017/10/04/a-deeper-look-at-silicon-valleys-long-term-politics> (consulted June 28, 2022).

'Filming Locations for "The Circle"', *OLV*, September 17, 2015, archived at, <https://web.archive.org/web/20190424093352/https://onlocationvacations.com/2015/09/17/filming-locations-for-the-circle-starring-emma-watson-tom-hanks-patton-oswalt> (consulted June 28, 2022).

Fitzgerald, Michael, 'Facebook Experiments on Users, Faces Blowback', *Discover*, November 26, 2014, <https://www.discovermagazine.com/technology/facebook-experiments-on-users-faces-blowback> (consulted June 29, 2022).

Fortune 500 <https://fortune.com/fortune500/search/?mktval=desc> (consulted June 28, 2022).

Fowler, Susan J., 'Reflecting on One Very, Very Strange Year at Uber', <https://www.susanjfowler.com/blog/2017/2/19/reflecting-on-one-very-strange-year-at-uber> (consulted June 28, 2022).

'Getting to work on Diversity at Google', <https://googleblog.blogspot.com/2014/05/getting-to-work-on-diversity-at-google.html> (consulted June 28, 2022).

'Google 2012 Revenue Hits $50 Billion, Profits Up', *Dawn*, January 23, 2013, <https://www.dawn.com/news/780915> (consulted June 28, 2022).

'Google's Net Income from 2001 to 2015', *Statista*, February 16, 2016, <https://www.statista.com/statistics/266472/googles-net-income> (consulted June 28, 2022).

Goudreau, Jenna, '*Jobs* Director on Capturing the Complicated Life of Steve Jobs', *Entrepreneur*, August 7, 2013, <https://www.entrepreneur.com/article/227723> (consulted June 28, 2022).

Greenburg, Zack O'Malley, 'In Pictures: Youngest Billionaires', *Forbes*, March 5, 2088, <https://www.forbes.com/2008/03/05/youngest-billionaires-rich-billionaires08-cx_lk_0305youngest_slide.html> (consulted June 28, 2022).

Grobar, Matt, '*The Big Short* scribe Charles Randolph on Adapting the Bestseller, Finance Jargon, and How Adam McKay "Made the Film Sing"', *Deadline*, December 21, 2015, <https://deadline.com/2015/12/charles-randolph-the-big-short-screenwriter-interview-1201658228> (consulted June 28, 2022).

'Groups of Friends Wanted for Ultimate Miller Time "Internship"', *PR Newswire*, March 14, 2013, <https://www.prnewswire.com/news-releases/groups-of-friends-wanted-for-ultimate-miller-time-internship-198238861.html> (consulted June 28, 2022).

Grover, Ronald and Alexei Oreskovic, 'Google Goes Hollywood with "The Internship"', *Reuters*, May 28, 2013, <https://in.reuters.com/article/google-movie-idINDEE94R0FP20130528> (consulted June 28, 2022).

Gurman, Mark, 'Cook Says Apple is "Rolling the Dice" on Future Products', *Bloomberg*, March 1, 2019, <https://www.bloomberg.com/news/articles/2019-03-01/cook-says-apple-is-rolling-the-dice-on-future-products> (consulted June 28, 2022).

Handler, Judd, 'An Interview with Vince Vaughn', November 16, 2011, archived at, <https://web.archive.org/web/20120827213512/www.writeonjudd.com/portfolio/an-interview-with-vince-vaughn> (consulted June 28, 2022).

Hare, Breeanna, 'Becoming Steve Jobs: Ashton Kutcher on his Movie Transformation', *CNN*, August 15, 2013, <https://edition.cnn.com/2013/08/15/showbiz/movies/ashton-kutcher-steve-jobs-movie/index.html> (consulted June 28, 2022).

Harris, Mark, 'The *Vulture* Transcript: An Interview with David Fincher', *The Vulture*, September 21, 2010, <https://www.vulture.com/2010/09/vulture_transcript_david_finch.html> (consulted June 28, 2022).

Heaf, Jonathan, '*True Detective*'s Vince Vaughn on Gun Control, Edward Snowden and Comedy', *GQ*, June 1, 2015, <https://www.gq-magazine.co.uk/article/vince-vaughn-covers-july-issue-british-gq> (consulted June 28, 2022).

Heller, Corinne, 'Aaron Sorkin Apologizes to Apple CEO Tim Cook After Slamming Him Over "Opportunistic" Remarks', *E! News*, September 26, 2015, <https://www.eonline.com/news/700364/aaron-sorkin-apologizes-to-apple-ceo-tim-cook-after-slamming-him-over-opportunistic-remarks> (consulted June 28, 2022).

Heller, Nathan, 'You Can't Handle the Veritas', *Slate*, September 30, 2010, <https://slate.com/news-and-politics/2010/10/what-the-social-network-gets-wrong-about-harvard-and-facebook.html> (consulted June 28, 2022).

Hertzfeld, Andy, '90 Hours a Week and Loving It!', *Folklore.org*, n.d., <https://www.folklore.org/StoryView.py?story=90_Hours_A_Week_And_Loving_It.txt> (consulted June 28, 2022).

Hill, Catey, 'Student-Loan Crisis: 10 Colleges Where Students Owe the Most', *Market Watch*, September 11, 2015, <https://www.marketwatch.com/story/10-colleges-where-students-owe-the-most-2015-09-11?page=2> (consulted June 28, 2022).

Horrigan, John B., 'Trends in Online Shopping', *Pew Research Center*, February 13, 2008, <https://www.pewresearch.org/internet/2008/02/13/part-1-trends-in-online-shopping> (consulted June 28, 2022).

Hunter, Matt and Anita Balakrishnan, 'Apple's Cash Pile Hits $285.1 Billion, A Record', *CNBC*, February 1, 2019, <https://www.cnbc.com/2018/02/01/apple-earnings-q1-2018-how-much-money-does-apple-have.html> (consulted June 28, 2022).

'I am Matt Whiteley, screenwriter of Jobs, the Ashton Kutcher Steve Jobs film. AMA!', *Reddit*, <https://www.reddit.com/r/IAmA/comments/23506q/i_am_matt_whiteley_screenwriter_of_jobs_the> (consulted June 28, 2022).

'The Internship Celebrates National Intern Appreciation Day', *DC Outlook*, June 3, 2013, <https://www.dcoutlook.com/2013/06/the-internship-celebrates-national.html> (consulted June 28, 2022).

'*Jobs*', *Box Office Mojo*, <https://www.boxofficemojo.com/release/rl73238017> (consulted June 28, 2022).

Johnson, Karlee, 'Sex Workers in Higher Education', *The Sundial*, December 12, 2011, <https://sundial.csun.edu/47959/news/sex-workers-in-higher-education> (consulted June 28, 2022).

Kahn, Jordan, 'Steve Jobs Biopic Filming at Flint Center for key Macintosh Unveiling Scene', *9to5Mac*, January 29, 2015, <https://9to5mac.com/2015/01/29/steve-jobs-biopic-filming-flint-center-key-macintosh-unveiling-scene> (consulted June 28, 2022).

Kapp, Diana, 'Male Coders Who Drop out of College are Heroes in Silicon Valley – But What About the Women?', *Marie Claire*, January 17, 2018, <https://www.marieclaire.com/career-advice/a15221369/female-college-dropouts-silicon-valley> (consulted June 28, 2022).

KEEM (@KEEMSTAR), '#Zuckerberg is not human!', *Twitter*, April 10, 2018, 9:38pm, <https://twitter.com/KEEMSTAR/status/983806461607280641/photo/1> (consulted June 29, 2022).

Kelly, Heather, 'Why Google Loves *The Internship*', *CNN*, June 5, 2013, <https://edition.cnn.com/2013/06/05/tech/innovation/internship-movie-google/index.html> (consulted June 28, 2022).

Kerr, Dara, 'Electric Scooters are Invading: Bird's CEO Leads the Charge', *CNET*, April 24, 2018, <https://www.cnet.com/tech/tech-industry/the-electric-scooter-invasion-is-underway-bird-ceo-travis-vanderzanden-leads-the-charge> (consulted June 29, 2022).

Kirchick, James, 'Angry White Man', *The New Republic*, January 30, 2008, <https://newrepublic.com/article/65706/angry-white-man> (consulted June 28, 2022).

Land, Karla, 'The Future of the Human Brain: Smart Drugs and Nootropics', *Futurism*, April 10, 2017, <https://futurism.com/do-not-edit-nootropics-and-the-future-of-brain-enhancing-smart-drugs> (consulted June 29, 2022).

Lin, Annette, 'Sonoya Mizuno Quit Ballet for "Ex Machina"', *The Last Magazine*, September 25, 2018, <https://thelast-magazine.com/sonoya-mizuno-profile-maniac-crazy-rich-asians> (consulted June 29, 2022).

Lin, Kristian, 'Mark Hulme's Way', *Fort Worth Weekly*, February 6, 2013, <https://www.fwweekly.com/2013/02/06/mark-hulmes-way> (consulted June 28, 2022).

Losse, Kathryn, 'Welcome to the Facebook', <https://medium.com/p/6ea0897fea3, archived at, https://web.archive.org/web/20131003003131/https://medium.com/p/6ea0897fea3> (consulted June 28, 2022).

McNary, Dave, 'Cannes: Tom Hanks Thriller "The Circle" Gets Financing from Image Nation', *Variety*, May 11, 2015 <https://variety.com/2015/film/news/tom-hanks-thriller-the-circle-financed-image-nation-dave-eggers-1201492551> (consulted June 29, 2022).

'Macworld NY 1999-Noah Wyle Imitating Steve Jobs', *YouTube*, February 10, 2006, <https://www.youtube.com/watch?v=TIClAanU7Os> (consulted June 28, 2022).

'Mark Kermode Reviews *The Internship*', *YouTube*, July 5, 2013, <https://www.youtube.com/watch?v=rGNPWblGTsQ> (consulted June 28, 2022).

'Mark Zuckerberg is not human!', thread, <https://www.theworldnewsmedia.org/forums/topic/55150-mark-zuckerberg-is-not-human> (consulted June 29, 2022).

'Mark Zuckerberg Says These 5 Technologies Will Completely Change How We Live', *Inc.Video*, n.d., <https://www.inc.com/video/5-technologies-mark-zuckerberg-thinks-will-change-the-world.html> (consulted June 28, 2022).

McDonald, Seth, 'Venom Producer on Whether or Not Venom's World is the MCU', *LRM*, September 28, 2018, <https://lrmonline.com/news/lrm-exclusive-venom-producer-on-whether-or-not-venoms-world-is-the-mcu> (consulted June 29, 2022).

'the Mentor', 'The Conscience of a Hacker', January 8, 1986, <http://www.phrack.org/issues/7/3.html> (consulted June 28, 2022).

Montgomery, Kevin, 'Tech Founder Complains About the Shithole City He's Forced to Make His Millions In', *Uptown Almanac*, August 15, 2013, <https://uptownalmanac.com/2013/08/tech-founder-complains-about-shithole-city-hes-forced-make-his-millions> (consulted June 29, 2022).

Morozov, Evgeny, 'Capitalism's New Clothes', *The Baffler*, February 4, 2019, <https://thebaffler.com/latest/capitalisms-new-clothes-morozov> (consulted June 29, 2022).

'Noah Wyle on Playing Steve Jobs', *Fortune*, October 7, 2011, <https://fortune.com/2011/10/07/noah-wyle-on-playing-steve-jobs> (consulted June 28, 2022).

'One More Thing', *YouTube*, December 23, 2009, <https://www.youtube.com/watch?v=cO-2NAl7Sm0> (consulted June 29, 2022).

Parekh, Rupal, 'U. of Phoenix Picks Pereira & O'Dell as Lead Creative', *AdAge*, December 8, 2008, <https://adage.com/article/agency-news/u-phoenix-picks-pereira-o-dell-lead-creative/133110> (consulted June 28, 2022).

Paskin, Willa, 'Aaron Sorkin Would Like to go Door-to-Door Apologizing for *The Social Network*'s Woman Problem', *Vulture*, October 12, 2010, <https://www.vulture.com/2010/10/aaron_sorkin_would_like_to_go.html?mid=agenda--20101012> (consulted June 28, 2022).

Perez, Sarah, 'Netflix Moves into Original Feature Films, Starting this October', *TechCrunch*, July 7, 2015, <https://tcrn.ch/1fl6KVA> (consulted June 28, 2022).

Peterson, Mike, 'Apple Hiring Data Shows Increasingly Diverse Workforce', *Apple Insider*, March 18, 2021, <https://appleinsider.com/articles/21/03/18/apple-hiring-data-shows-increasingly-diverse-workforce> (consulted June 28, 2022).

'Pirates of Silicon Valley', *Emmys*, <https://www.emmys.com/shows/pirates-silicon-valley> (consulted June 9, 2021).

Puchko, Kristy, '11 Facts About Napster', *Salon*, June 2, 2021, <https://www.salon.com/2021/06/02/11-facts-about-napster_partner> (consulted June 28, 2022).

'Q&A with Jimmy Wales', *C-Span*, September 12, 2005, <https://www.c-span.org/video/?188855-1/qa-jimmy-wales> (consulted June 28, 2022).

'Q/A with Martyn Burke', archived at, <https://web.archive.org/web/20110716055019/http://alt.tnt.tv/movies/tntoriginals/pirates/html/martyn.html> (consulted June 28, 2022).

Rampton, Mike, 'New footage of Tom Hardy on the "Venom" set reveals more interesting plot details', *Shortlist*, n.d., <https://www.shortlist.com/entertainment/films/new-footage-of-tom-hardy-on-the-venom-reveals-more-interesting-plot-details/342801> (consulted June 29, 2022).

Regalado, Antonio, 'The Entrepreneur with the $100 Million Plan to Link Brains to Computers', *MIT Technology Review*, March 16, 2017, <https://www.technologyreview.com/2017/03/16/153211/the-entrepreneur-with-

the-100-million-plan-to-link-brains-to-computers> (consulted June 29, 2022).
'Rise of the Planet of the Apes', <https://movie-locations.com/movies/r/Rise-Of-The-Planet-Of-The-Apes.php> (consulted June 29, 2022).
Rosenblatt, Joel, 'Twitter's Gender-Bias Lawsuit Gets Swept Up in the Tech Talent Wars', *Bloomberg*, February 10, 2016, <https://www.bloomberg.com/news/articles/2016-02-10/at-twitter-a-gender-bias-claim-gets-swept-up-in-the-talent-wars> (consulted June 28, 2022).
Rosenblatt, Seth, 'Google Demolishes Financial Expectations to Close 2013', *CNet*, January 30, 2014, <https://www.cnet.com/news/google-demolishes-financial-expectations-to-close-2013> (consulted June 28, 2022).
Rowe, Abigail, 'Student Debt, Sex Work, and the Cost of NYU 2031 at Greenwich Village Rally', *Observer*, September 2, 2015, <https://observer.com/2015/09/student-debt-sex-work-and-the-cost-of-nyu-2031-at-greenwich-village-rally> (consulted June 28, 2022).
Rust, Adam, 'University of Phoenix Maxing Out on Defaults', *Bank Talk*, June 26, 2012, archived at, <https://web.archive.org/web/20120630025848/http://banktalk.org:80/2012/06/26/university-of-phoenix-maxing-out-on-defaults> (consulted June 28, 2022).
'San Jose, CA Weather History', <https://www.wunderground.com/history/daily/KSJC/date/1985-5-28> (consulted June 28, 2022).
Schlender, Brent, 'The Lost Steve Jobs Tapes', *Fast Company*, April 17, 2012, <https://www.fastcompany.com/1826869/lost-steve-jobs-tapes> (consulted June 28, 2022).
Schwartz, Madeleine, 'Opportunity Costs: The True Price of Internships', *Dissent*, Winter 2013, <https://www.dissentmagazine.org/article/opportunity-costs-the-true-price-of-internships> (consulted June 28, 2022).
Scribner, Sara, 'Generation X Gets Really Old: How Do Slackers Have a Midlife Crisis', *Salon*, August 11, 2013, <https://www.salon.com/2013/08/11/generation_x_gets_really_old_how_do_slackers_have_a_midlife_crisis> (consulted June 28, 2022).
Segall, Ken, 'Steve Jobs and Noah Wyle's Moment of Truth', April 18, 2012, <https://kensegall.com/2012/04/18/steve-jobs-and-noah-wyles-moment-of-truth> (consulted June 28, 2022).
Seltzer, Sarah, 'Students Stripping, Doing Sex Work, and Seeing Sugar Daddies? In Hard Economic Times, This Media Obsession is Based in Reality', *Alternet*, August 2, 2011, <https://web.archive.org/web/20170111093045/https://www.alternet.org/story/151883/students_stripping%2C_doing_sex_work_and_seeing_sugar_daddies_in_hard_economic_times%2C_this_media_obsession_is_based_in_reality> (consulted June 28, 2022).
Shead, Sam, 'Peter Thiel is Backing a Rival to Elon Musk's Brain Implant Company', *CNBC*, May 19, 2021, <https://www.cnbc.com/2021/05/19/peter-thiel-is-backing-a-rival-to-elon-musks-neuralink-.html> (consulted June 29, 2022).

Sheppard, Lee, 'How Does Apple Avoid Taxes?', *Forbes*, May 28, 2013, <https://www.forbes.com/sites/leesheppard/2013/05/28/how-does-apple-avoid-taxes> (consulted June 29, 2022).

Shimal, John, 'Mark Zuckerberg Couldn't Buy Snapchat Years Ago, and Now He's Close to Destroying the Company', *CNBC*, July 12, 2017, <https://www.cnbc.com/2017/07/12/how-mark-zuckerberg-has-used-instagram-to-crush-evan-spiegels-snap.html> (consulted June 28, 2022).

Shontell, Alyson, 'What It's Really Like to be a Google Intern', *Business Insider*, June 3, 2013, <https://www.businessinsider.com/what-its-really-like-to-be-a-google-intern-2013-5?r=US&IR=T> (consulted June 28, 2022).

Siegler, M. G., 'Card Designer: The Inspiration for Zuckerberg's "I'm CEO, Bitch"? Steve Jobs', *TechCrunch*, June 25, 2011, <https://tcrn.ch/mQOL9S> (consulted June 28, 2022).

Smith, Aaron, 'The Rise of In-Store Mobile Commerce', *Pew Research Center*, January 30, 2012, <https://www.pewresearch.org/internet/2012/01/30/the-rise-of-in-store-mobile-commerce> (consulted June 28, 2022).

'The Social Network', *Box Office Mojo*, <https://www.boxofficemojo.com/title/tt1285016/?ref_=bo_se_r_1> (consulted June 28, 2022).

Solon, Olivia and Cyrus Farivar, 'Mark Zuckerberg Leveraged Facebook User Data to Fight Rivals and Help Friends, Leaked Documents Show', *NBC News*, April 16, 2019, <https://www.nbcnews.com/tech/social-media/mark-zuckerberg-leveraged-facebook-user-data-fight-rivals-help-friends-n994706> (consulted June 28, 2022).

Sorkin, Aaron, 'The Social Network screenplay', archived at, <https://web.archive.org/web/20140613175300/https://www.screenplaydb.com/film/scripts/The%20Social%20Network.pdf> (consulted June 28, 2022),

'*Steve Jobs*', *Box Office Mojo*, <https://www.boxofficemojo.com/title/tt2080374/?ref_=bo_se_r_1> (consulted June 28, 2022).

'Steve Jobs Movie Begins Shooting in the Original Apple Garage', *PR Newswire*, May 18, 2012, <https://www.prnewswire.com/news-releases/steve-jobs-movie-begins-filming-in-the-original-apple-garage-152105905.html> (consulted June 28, 2022).

Sung, Morgan, 'There's a Whole Meme Community That Doesn't Think Mark Zuckerberg is Human', *Mashable*, April 5, 2018, <https://mashable.com/2018/04/05/mark-zuckerberg-memes/?europe=true> (consulted June 29, 2022).

Tait, Joshua, 'Marvel's War on Terror', *American Affairs*, May 7, 2019, <https://americanaffairsjournal.org/2019/05/marvels-war-on-terror> (consulted June 29, 2022).

'Terminator: Genisys Begins Shooting Today in New Orleans', *NOLA.com*, April 21, 2014, <https://www.nola.com/movies/2014/04/terminator_genesis_begins_shoo.html> (consulted June 29, 2022).

'Thiel Fellowship', <https://thielfellowship.org> (consulted June 28, 2022).

Thompson, Cadie, 'Mobile Online Shopping to Double in 2010', *CNBC*, February 18, 2010, <https://www.cnbc.com/id/35443154> (consulted June 28, 2022).

Tiku, Nitasha, '*Circle* Jerks: Why do Editors Love Dave Eggers?', *Gawker*, October 2, 2013, <https://gawker.com/circle-jerks-why-do-editors-love-dave-eggers-1440226375> (consulted June 28, 2022).
Velazco, C., 'How Google's Smartphones Have Evolved Since 2007', *Engadget*, October 3, 2017, <https://www.engadget.com/2017-10-03-a-look-back-at-googles-smartphones.html> (consulted June 28, 2022).
'Vince Vaughn & Ron Paul at LPAC 2011', September 20, 2011, <https://www.youtube.com/watch?v=p23stV9LD0I> (consulted June 28, 2022).
von Busack, Richard, 'Pod Man Out', *MetroActive*, April 22–28, 1999, <https://www.metroactive.com/papers/metro/04.22.99/existenz-9916.html> (consulted June 28, 2022).
Warofka, Alex, 'An Independent Assessment of the Human Rights Impact of Facebook in Myanmar', *Meta*, November 5, 2018, <https://about.fb.com/news/2018/11/myanmar-hria> (consulted June 28, 2022).
'The Watch', <https://www.imdb.com/title/tt1298649/?ref_=nm_flmg_wr_9> (consulted June 28, 2022).
Weintraub, Steve, 'James Ponsoldt on "The Circle", "I Want My MTV", "Inconstant Moon", and "Wild City"', *Collider*, May 2, 2017, <https://collider.com/james-ponsoldt-the-circle-inconstant-moon-interview> (consulted June 28, 2022).
Williams, Maxine, 'Driving Diversity at Facebook', June 25, 2015, <https://newsroom.fb.com/news/2015/06/driving-diversity-at-facebook> (consulted June 28, 2022).
Willmore, Alison, 'Why *The Social Network* Feels Sharper Now Than When it First Came Out', *Vulture*, June 17, 2020, <https://www.vulture.com/article/the-social-network-is-more-relevant-now-than-when-it-came-out.html> (consulted June 28, 2022).

Recorded Music

The Beatles, 'All You Need Is Love'/ 'Baby You're a Rich Man' (Parlophone, 1967).
The White Stripes, 'Ball and Biscuit' on *Elephant* (XL Recordings, 2003).

Index

Note: **bold** indicates illustrations
Note: n indicates notes

Ant-Man (Peyton Reed, 2015), 12, 137, 138, 140, 141, 145–6, **146**, 147, 149, 150–1, 152, 165–6, 167, 169, 173, 174, 178, 179
Apple, 3, 74, 75, 76, 81–2, 125, 165
  brand image, 64, 65, 66, 71, 83, 90, 145, 158
  employment practices, 5, 72, 127–8, 164, 179
  products of 39, 61, 72, 73, 84–5, 92–3, 160, 178–9
  see also Jobs; *Pirates of Silicon Valley*; *Steve Jobs*
Assault on Wall Street (Uwe Boll, 2013), 36
Avengers film sequence, 166–7, 179; see also Marvel Cinematic Universe

Beneath the Planet of the Apes (Ted Post, 1970), 138–9
The Big Short (Adam McKay, 2015), 34, 35–6, 38, 149
biopic genre, 13, 62–6, 68–70, 73, 75–6, 78–9, 82–3, 90, 93, 179; see also Jobs; *Pirates of Silicon Valley*; *The Social Network*; *Steve Jobs*

Black Panther Party, 161
Blade Runner (Ridley Scott, 1982), 18, 53, 142, 156, 167
Boyle, Danny, 63–4, 80, 81, 92
Bullitt (Peter Yates, 1968), 45
Burke, Martyn, 80, 89–90

'The California Ideology' (Barbrook and Cameron), 31
The Center of the World (Wayne Wang, 2001) 147–8, 151
capitalism, 4, 11, 92, 121, 141, 145, 161, 165, 170, 175–9
  in film, 14, 22–4, **25**, 27–8, 30, 31–2, 33–40, 44, 47–8, 50, 51, 55–6, 66–7, 72–3, 92, 100, 102–5, 131–2, 139, 143–4, 149, 152, 156–67, **159**, 169–70, 173–6, **175**, 180
  platform capitalism, 10–11, 107, 113–15
  surveillance capitalism, 2, 14, 31, 102, 110, 125–7, 178–9
  venture capitalism, 4–5
  see also neoliberalism; Silicon Valley; specific films; Thiel, Peter
Chang, Emily, 120, 176–8, 179

The Circle (James Ponsoldt, 2017), 1–2, 12–13, 99–100, 101–12, **108**, 114, 118, 121, 123, 124–8, 130, 131, 132, 137, 158, 180–1
'The Conscience of a Hacker', 27
The Conversation (Francis Ford Coppola, 1974), 14, 28, 43, 54–7, **56**, 126, 127, 151, 181
Coupland, Douglas, 104, 109, 122
Cronenberg, David, 26, 34

Dick, Philip K., 30, 111, 142, 146, 148
Dirty Harry (Don Siegel, 1971), 45, 46, 48, 162

Eggers, Dave, 7, 99, 100, 105
Enemy of the State (Tony Scott, 1994), 21–2, 28–9, 30, 31, 127, 181
eXistenZ (David Cronenberg, 1999), 21–2, 25–6
Ex Machina (Alex Garland, 2014), 142, 147, 148

Facebook, 3, 31, 64, 65, 69, 74, 76, 78, 83, 93, 125, 144, 158, 180
  capitalism of, 10–11, 22, 55, 156–7, 167, 176, 178–9
  employment practices, 5, 7–8, 124, 127
  sexism in, 7–8, 124, 179
  see also The Social Network; Zuckerberg, Mark
film noir, 43–5, 55
Fincher, David, 8, 63, 66, 69, 80, 86–8

Flame of the Barbary Coast (Joseph Kane, 1945), 47
Foroohar, Rana, 74, 176, 178, 179
Fruitvale Station (Ryan Coogler, 2013), 53–4

Generation X, 12, 99, 104–5, 118–19, 121–4, 126
genetic experimentation, 11–12, 25, 137–8, 139, 141–3, 148–9, **149**, 150, 162
Gibson, William, 22, 137
Google, 1, 110, 129
  corporation, 129–30, 131–2, 134n, 144, 167, 177, 178, 179–80
  capitalism of, 3, 7, 8, 10–11, 12–13, 31, 99, 100, 103, 113–15, 126–7, 130–1
  diversity of, 5, 6, 119–21, 124, 126, 128, 177
  attitude towards *The Internship*, 2, 13, 100–1, 131–2
  employment practices, 6, 91, 101, 105–6, 107–8, 112–13, 122, 123, 127–8, 130–1
  see also The Internship; Page, Larry

Hackers (Iain Softley, 1995), 21–2, 26–8, 29, 30–2, 86
Haraway, Donna, 141
Her (Spike Jonze, 2013), 18n, 129, 145
Hollywood, 1–2, 8–10, 126
  ambivalence about capitalism, 40, 62, 99, 132, 152–3, 168, 169–70, 174–6
  depictions of the American city, 42, 49
Holmes, Elizabeth, 76n, 164, 165
Hulk (Ang Lee, 2003), 138

Inside Job (Charles Ferguson, 2010), 34, 38, 39
The Internship (Shawn Levy, 2013), 1, 2, 12–13, 99, 100–8, 110, 112–15, **113**, 118–24, 126–32, 137, 163, 176, 177, 179–80
Invasion of the Body Snatchers (Philip Kaufman, 1978), 47, 48–9, 55, 56, 88

Jobs, Steve, 3, 64, 65–6, 71–5, 79–82, 90, 91–2, 93, 106, 125, 143, 158, 160, 164, 165, 179
  bad behaviour of, 62, 71, 79, 81–2, 144
  selfishness of, 4, 12, 61
  see also Jobs; *Pirates of Silicon Valley*; *Steve Jobs*
Jobs (Joshua Michael Stern, 2013), 61, 64, 65–6, 70, 71, 72, 73–5, 80, 81, 89, 91, 92, 93, 101, 118, 179
Johnny Mnemonic (Robert Longo, 1995), 21–2, 24–5, 26, 31–2, 146

The Last Black Man in San Francisco (Joe Talbot, 2019), 52
The Lawnmower Man (Brett Leonard, 1992), 21–2, 24–5, **25**, 27, 31
Levy, Shawn, 100–1, 120, 173
Liu, Wendy, 177–8, 179
Losse, Katherine, 7–8, 74

Margin Call (J. C. Chandor, 2011), 33–5, 36–7, **37**, 38, 69, 161

Marvel Cinematic Universe, 9, 137, 165–7, 179; *see also Ant-Man*
Marx, Karl, 157
masculinity, 4, 33, 34, 37–9, 57, 138, 141, 147, **149**, 149–52, 167, 168, 169
  Silicon Valley variety of, 6, 14, 118, 123, 128, 147–9, 152, 156, 173–4, 177
  see also tech bros
Moneyball (Bennett Miller, 2011), 69–70
Morozov, Evgeny, 2, 178–9
Musk, Elon, 4, 146

neoliberalism, 14, 31, 36, 40, 55, 64–5, 99, 103–6, 131, 144, 149, 152, 156–7, 168; *see also* capitalism
The Net (Irwin Winkler, 1995), 21–2, 29–31, 32, 126
Netflix, 8–9

Oakland *see* San Francisco Bay Area

Page, Larry, 1, 2, 6, 64, 100
Pirates of Silicon Valley (Martyn Burke, 1999), 61, 65–6, 71, 72, 75, 80, 81, 89–92, **91**, 93, 101, 118, 142–3, 179
Planet of the Apes (Franklin Schaffner, 1968), 138–9
platform capitalism *see* capitalism
posthumanity, 25, 48, 137–47, **149**, 150, 152–3, 156, 161, 164–5, 169
precautionary principle, 138, 140–3, 146, 147, 156, 159, 160–1, 163–5
progressivism, 170, 175–6

Rand, Ayn, 4, 33, 37, 62, 73, 76, 86, 101, 132, 140, 147, 149, 152, 156, 158, 164–5, 167, 169, 170
  Silicon Valley's love for, 4–5, 33, 34, 147, 164, 178
Rembrandt (Alexander Korda, 1936), 68, 71, 86
Rise of the Planet of the Apes (Rupert Wyatt, 2011), 2, 12, 14, 137, 138–9, 140, 141–3, 149, 150, **159**, 159–62, **162**, 163–4, 165, 169, 173, 180
  sequels, 180

San Andreas (Brad Peyton, 2015), 49, **50**
Sandberg, Sheryl, 6, 8, 127, 177
San Francisco, 46, 49, 51
  in film, 11–12, 14, 42–57
  changes wrought by Silicon Valley, 51, 64, 91, 99, 149, 164–5, 167
  Golden Gate Bridge, 49, **50**, 89, 112, **113**, **162**
San Francisco Bay Area, 43, 51–4, 138, 139, 140, 142–3, 149, 161–2, 163
San Francisco (Woody Van Dyke, 1936), 46
Schwarzenegger, Arnold, 1, 137, 143, 152, 157
Scorsese, Martin, 39–40
Silicon Valley, 3–5, 10
  in film, 10, 12, 28, 34, 40, 46, 50, 54, 56, 57, 114, 140, 169–70
  view of the world, 1–4, 64–5, 91–2, 101, 145, 158
  diversity of workforce, 5, 6, 118, 121, 176–7
  sexism within, 6–7, 13, 62, 118, 120, 123, 126, 132
  capitalism of, 4, 31, 32, 37–8, 50, 62, 64–5, 99, 119, 127, 130–2, 137, 145, 156–8, 160, 163–4, 165–6, 169–70, 173–4, 176, 178–9, 180
  employment practices, 105–9, 112
  see also specific films
Silicon Valley (HBO, 2014–20), 4–5, 61, 64, 118, 119–20, 137, 158, 171n
The Social Network (David Fincher, 2010), 7–8, 12, 13, 53, 61–3, 66–70, **70**, 73, 74–6, 78–81, 83, 85–9, 92–3, 118, 126, 179
Sorkin, Aaron
  and *The Social Network*, 7–8, 63, 66, 69, 79–80, 82–3, 85–6, 88–9, 92–3
  and *Steve Jobs*, 63–4, 79–80, 81–4, 92–3
Sorry to Bother You (Boots Riley, 2018), 53, 110
Star Trek IV: The Voyage Home (Leonard Nimoy, 1986), 43, 49–50, 51, 145
Steve Jobs (Danny Boyle, 2015), 1, 61, 63–4, 66, 70–3, 74, 75, 78–80, 81–5, **82**, **84**, 90, 92–3, 101, 118, 151, 179
Strange Days (Kathryn Bigelow, 1995), 21–4, 28, 110
surveillance, 14, 21–2, 23, 28–31, 43–4, 50–1, 53–7, **56** 102–3, **108**, 108–12, 125–7, 140, 150–1, 180–1; *see also* capitalism

tech bros
  in film, 7–8, 12, 53, 124, 137–42, 143–8, **146**, 158, 164–5, 173–4, **175**, 176, 179
  in Silicon Valley, 4, 6–7, 37–8, 91, 158, 164, 178, 179
technology
  as religion, 24–6, 30, 152
  backlash against, 175–9
  solutionism, 2–3, 10, 23, 24–5, 56, 100–4, 109, 110, 125, 141–3, 152–3, 156–7, 167
The Terminator franchise, 143
Terminator: Genisys (Alan Taylor, 2015), 1, 12, 137, 138, 139, 140, 141, 143–5, 146, 147, 151–2, 157–8, 163, 169, 177, 180
Theranos *see* Holmes, Elizabeth
Thiel, Peter, 64–5, 147, 158, 165–6, 168
Thieves' Highway (Jules Dassin, 1949), 45
Tomorrowland (Brad Bird, 2015), 1, 4
The Towering Inferno (John Guillermin, 1974), 47–9, 55

Venom (Ruben Fleischer, 2018), 12, 137, 138, 139, 141, 146–7, 148–9, **149**, 151, 152, 163–5, 167–70

A View to a Kill (John Glen, 1985), 43, 50–1

Wall Street (Oliver Stone, 1987), 33, 166
What's Up Doc? (Peter Bogdanovich, 1972), 42, 45–6
Why Him? (John Hamburg, 2016), 14, 173–6, **175**, 178, 180
The Wolf of Wall Street (Martin Scorsese, 2013), 33, 34–5, 38–40, 70, 161
Wozniak, Steve, 1, 79, 93
  in film, 71–2, 90, **91**

X-Men: The Last Stand (Brett Ratner, 2006), 11–12, 162–3

Zuboff, Shoshana, 14, 178, 179
Zuckerberg, Mark, 64, 65, 70, 81, 93, 125, 158, 179
  bad behaviour of, 4, 8, 61, 62, 63, 81, 85, 92
  complains about *The Social Network*, 83
  engineering mindset of, 7, 26, 28, 61, 66–7, 74, 78, 93, 144, 148
  haircut of, 8
  rumours of non-human status, 44, 144
  see also Facebook; *The Social Network*

EU representative:
Easy Access System Europe
Mustamäe tee 50, 10621 Tallinn, Estonia
Gpsr.requests@easproject.com

www.ingramcontent.com/pod-product-compliance
Lightning Source LLC
Chambersburg PA
CBHW071416160426
43195CB00013B/1708